THE MEANING OF LIFE

with Gay Byrne

Conversations on Love, Beliefs, Morality, Grief and Everything In Between

Gill & Macmillan

Gill & Macmillan
Hume Avenue, Park West, Dublin 12
with associated companies throughout the world
www.gillmacmillanbooks.ie

© RTÉ 2013
978 07171 5851 5

Typography design by Make Communication
Print origination by Carole Lynch
Printed and bound by CPI Group (UK) Ltd, CR0 4YY

This book is typeset in Linotype Minion and
Neue Helvetica.

The paper used in this book comes from the
wood pulp of managed forests. For every
tree felled, at least one tree is planted,
thereby renewing natural resources.

A CIP catalogue record for this book
is available from the British Library.

5 4 3 2 1

CONTENTS

INTRODUCTION

"What's it all about? Why are we here? Is there a God? What happens when we die?"

Search me. I'm just the fella who asks the questions. Don't expect me to be able to answer them.

The Meaning of Life dropped into my lap like Newton's apple, in 2008. Would I be interested, the would-be series producer, Roger Childs, asked me, in applying my mind and some of the interviewing skills picked up over fifty-odd years to a celebrity interview series based on the things people do and the stuff they believe to give life meaning?

Tread carefully, I thought.

The series was to come out of RTÉ's Religious Programmes stable, which I took to be a pretty cast-iron guarantee that it would be under-resourced and tucked away in some overlooked "God slot." I wasn't far wrong.

That said, when I agreed to give it a whirl, I found that there can be a strange liberation with a late Sunday-evening slot. Interviews that would have been limited to eight to ten bullet-point questions in the peak-time glare of a *Late Late Show* can be given space to breathe in that twilight zone.

I discovered that there are also benefits to recording, although it took some getting used to after five decades of live, one-take broadcasting. If guests are generous enough to give you an hour and a half of their time—sometimes even more—you can simply let the cameras roll. If there is a pause in the conversation, I feel less under pressure to jump in and fill it, which means that, very often, guests will themselves fill the space with what might otherwise have remained unuttered, even private, thoughts. Never mind that the finished programme will still, generally speaking, be only half an hour long. Winnowing a long interview to create a short programme is the producer's and editor's problem, not mine. My job is simply to ensure that the guests feel comfortable enough to answer questions that, for a talk show, are unusually searching and personal.

When I say that *The Meaning of Life* is a celebrity interview series, I am being a little disingenuous. Celebrity is simply the Trojan horse we use to smuggle, I hope, thoughtful content into the mainstream television schedules. The public figures we interview are not, by and large, there to discuss fame or fortune, except inasmuch as those things impinge on their search for meaning. I have found they seldom do. Our guests also understand that they are not being invited on to promote their latest book, play, album or movie. They are there to discuss questions with which we *all* have cause to wrestle, on occasion— questions about the way the experiences of a lifetime shape, and are shaped by, our beliefs, opinions and values.

You might think that, with no commercial "plugging" value and certainly no big fat fee, big names would run a mile from a series like this. Not so. Implicit in our invitation to take part is the compliment that we think they might have something interesting to say. You would be surprised how seldom big stars are given credit for having any depth, substance or intelligence. When it happens, they appreciate it.

Occasionally, I regret that we are not a bit braver about interviewing people *without* a high public profile, who might, nonetheless, have interesting insights to share about faith, morality and the search for meaning. Perhaps that is another day's work. In the meantime, we must content ourselves with a guest list that has so far included two former Presidents, a former Taoiseach, three Nobel Peace Prize nominees, a lord and former First Minister of Northern Ireland, five knights of the realm, two Oscar winners, two Golden Globe winners, three Grammy winners, a Eurovision Song Contest winner, a football World Cup finalist, an All-Ireland winner, IFTA winners, BAFTA winners, a Perrier winner, a Costa winner, a European Literature Prize winner and Lord only knows what other sorts of luminary.

We have deliberately cast the net wide to include public figures from the worlds of music, comedy, sport, business, literature, politics, movies, entertainment and, yes, even religion.

That said, it seems to me that the main reason the series continues to attract strong audience interest and positive critical attention is not the profile of its guests so much as the fact that viewers can imagine *themselves* in the hot seat. "How would I answer that one . . . ? What do I think . . . ?"

I am told that, after our interview with Mary McAleese aired, in the autumn of 2012, the term #meaningoflife trended for two days on Twitter (whatever that means)—not, I suspect, because of the content of that programme, but because people started to exchange views about the things that give their own lives meaning.

I am often struck by the sort of feedback the series generates. There is, of course, the expected influx of letters taking issue with the beliefs of our guests and offering kind advice for the salvation of our souls. But there is also another kind of passionately enthusiastic response, usually from people who hear their own views and beliefs articulated by a famous guest. "What oft was thought, but ne'er so well expressed," as Alexander Pope once put it. Mary McAleese's eloquent description of her personal credo was one such example. A whole swathe of committed, but troubled, Christians had found their champion and simply loved her interview. But then, Bob Geldof's strident atheism struck a similar, if opposite, chord with a different constituency.

What about my own favourites? I am often asked. I try not to answer, in the same way that any sensible parent will ignore the question "Which of your children do you love the most?"

Brenda Fricker, Colin Farrell and Gabriel Byrne stunned people with their candour, especially in discussing moments of vulnerability. Norah Casey, Brendan O'Carroll, Bob Geldof and Andrea Corr moved people with their reflections on grief and loss.

Terry Wogan and Maeve Binchy astonished some people by "outing" themselves as non-believers, while Martin Sheen, Mary Byrne and Niall Quinn surprised others with the depth of their religious convictions.

I am often asked about my own role in the programmes. What distinguishes a good interview from a bad one? What's the secret of getting people to talk? The great secret is that there is no great secret. It's obvious: if you want someone to talk, listen. And keep listening.

Meaning of Life interviews are not confrontational, not argumentative, not meant to point out to someone the error of their ways. They are simply intended to find out how people think and feel about things. After that, it's their own business.

It has been suggested, many times, that someone should turn the tables on me and ask about the things that give *my* life meaning. That misses an important point about interviewing: the referee wears black. As soon as I articulate an opinion or belief, I colour the way people answer my questions. Our subject is our guests' beliefs and opinions, not mine. Certainly, no-one should look to me for right answers on this subject area. Not only could I not give one, but probably I would not *know* one even if I heard it. But I will keep listening.

After seven series, and counting, I could not include *all* the views of *all* our guests in this book. Instead, I have tried to distil a selection. I am hugely grateful to all forty-two of the people who have accepted our invitation to sit in the chair opposite to date. That trust is something I do not treat lightly. Their interviews may not have made me any wiser, but they have certainly given me enough food for thought for several banquets.

Tuck in.

GAY BYRNE, MAY 2013

MARTIN SHEEN

In the Name of the Son . . .

A glance at a news-stand on my way to the Merrion Hotel, Dublin, on a Saturday afternoon in February 2011 was enough to convince me that Martin Sheen wouldn't show. On practically every front page were lurid details of his son Charlie's dismissal by a Hollywood TV studio after an anti-Semitic rant and his unrepentant flit to a luxury resort with his ex-wife and a porn-star girlfriend. Why on earth would Martin Sheen honour his commitment to a personal interview, with all this going on in his family and so much prurient interest from the world's media?

He did show. In fact he arrived early in our designated interview room, greeting every member of the crew with a warm smile and handshake, before sitting down in the make-up chair.

We fully expected him to ask that Charlie's situation be treated as off-limits during our interview. Instead, when my producer sat down beside him to brief him quietly about the series and to thank him for sparing us time for an interview amidst such a media circus, Martin simply opened one eye and said, "He's surrounded by such scoundrels! And none of them cares one bit about him. They'll all evaporate when the money's gone."

Suddenly, instead of being a celebrity in the spotlight, he was simply a father, worried sick about his addict son. He told us that he and Charlie's brother Emilio Estevez—in Europe to promote their terrific father-son movie *The Way*—were having to curtail their trip in order to go home to be with Martin's wife, Janet, and to see what contact they could make with Charlie.

In the meantime, Martin was ours for forty-five minutes, although we had been warned by his movie's publicist that he had an unmissable appointment afterwards and that there would be no possibility of an overrun.

We had met before, in 1984, when I interviewed Martin on *The Late Late Show*. As you will see, he remembered that previous encounter, which enabled us to get quickly past the formalities as the interview began.

❧

GB: Could I start by asking you what is your present state of mind?

MS: Well, it could be better. It's been a rough week . . . There are some personal family problems that we're having to deal with, and it's always more difficult when you're away.

GB: Okay. We'll come back to that later.

MS: All right.

GB: You see, you made a comment at the premiere the other night of *The Way*, that you fell in love with acting in your teens, and now, in your seventieth year, you love it just as much as ever you did.

MS: Oh, yes, yeah.

GB: So, I get this picture, on the one hand, of a successful, happy, contented man, and then the list of citations and arrests for riot and civil commotion . . . and troublemaking and all of that. How do you square those two things?

MS: Well, they came out of an urgency, a commitment to peace and social justice, you know, my moral outrage . . . with peace and nuclear issues, with homelessness, with women's rights, gay rights, children's rights—all of these issues are in play when I step forward and commit myself publicly in an act of civil disobedience and public demonstration . . . And done with a great sense of joy as well, because if you believe in an issue and you're willing to sacrifice yourself for it, and you're willing to accept the consequences, there's nothing better than that. If you believe in something, it's got to cost you something. And if it doesn't cost you something, you're really left to question its value.

GB: A lot of people, though, would say, "Well, we're all committed and we're all Catholic, but you don't have to take it so seriously."

MS: [Laughs.]

GB: Why bring all this trouble on yourself?

MS: Well, you have to think of all the people in our faith who are celebrated as exemplary, including, you know, the Master, the founder of our faith, who was killed for speaking the truth, the whole truth and nothing but the truth, all the time. So, when the Church first started, it was very radical. It was about peace and service and community.

GB: So, what is a radical Catholic?

MS: [Laughs.] Mother Teresa was a very radical Catholic, I would say. Dorothy Day comes to mind in America. She was one of my heroes.

She founded the *Catholic Worker* during the Depression, over in New York. She was a converted Catholic and was a pacifist and went to prison for opposing nuclearism and violence and really changed the face of the American Catholic Church.

GB: Has your activism cost you?

MS: I hope so! [Laughs.] I say that with a bit of irony, but I'm sure it has, yeah. And I'm also sure that it's helped me. I'd like to think that someone picks up the phone and says, "You ought to hire that guy. He's got a good conscience."

GB: Okay. When you had your heart attack, on the set of *Apocalypse* [*Now*], this was after a fair interlude of wild living.

MS: It was, yes.

GB: Okay, so, ultimately that brought you back to the practice of your faith.

MS: Well, it began the journey. I was very near the end, and obviously those around me saw that and got a priest in the Philippines to me, and I had the last rites. And I became instantly devout and terrified that if I died that I was going straight to Hell. So I came back to the faith like a bolt of lightning, because of a near-tragedy. However, I was not comfortable with what I had done, because I rejoined the faith out of fear, and no sense of purpose or love. So, I went on a continual journey for another four years.

GB: A journey of what?

MS: A journey of self-examination. You know, Who am I? And why am I here? . . . And it culminated in Paris, when I was doing a little film there in May of 1981, and I ran into an old and very dear friend, Terrence Malick. He's a very devout man, a brilliant scholar . . . and he kind of guided me. He would give me literature to read, and, finally, the last work he gave me was *The Brothers Karamazov,* and I could not stop reading it. . . . And it so inspired me, and it made me realise that this was a defining moment. That book, for me, and that message, was a template in my life. And if I was going to move, I had to move now, and quickly. And I did.

So, on May 1st, I went banging on the church door like Martin Luther. I said, "Father, I would like to go to Confession and to spend a very long time!" And it was one of the great moments of my life . . . And there was no longer any fear. There was a sense of belonging, of course, but that my brokenness was okay. I could get healed here. I had a lot of work to do, a lot of service to give and a lot of love to experience. I only learned later this phrase that Teilhard de Chardin said about love. He said, "When we discover that we are loved, we have discovered fire for the second time." That's the kind of Catholic I wanted to be. I wanted to be on fire.

GB: And can you have that feeling without being spiritual or even without being Christian, or even without being Catholic?

MS: Oh, yes, of course. It belongs to every member of the human race as long as you're human. We, as Christians, believe that God transcended and became human. That's the whole foundation of our faith, isn't it? And yet, when you think about it, the genius of God—to choose to hide where we would least likely look: within ourselves. And when we come to that realisation, through no fault or worth of our own, but just by the fact that we're human, that we are loved and that God would choose to dwell there, then we start looking at all the other people in the world, and we are inclined to see that presence in everyone.

GB: In 1987, I think it was, on *The Late Late Show*, you were very honest about not only being able to square the staying in a luxury suite in India and seeing all this poverty beside you, but as well, squaring that with the life you lead, which is a very nice life as an actor in Hollywood. You have a nice home, a lovely family, you have a nice swimming pool. And how do you square that . . . ?

MS: I'm not attached to it. It's not that important to me. I didn't always have a nice home and a swimming pool, you know. The older I get, the less I need. For example, *The West Wing*—I never had more success or more financial advantage. And we ended up giving most of it away.

GB: Go back to your parents. Was it a very religious household? Your mam, Mary Anne from Borrisokane, and your dad from Galicia.

MS: They were very Catholic. My dad was a scrupulously honest man, and there was no virtue that he was more impressed with than honesty, and he expected it from all of us. He was very frugal, of course . . . And yet he was very generous.

And my mother, of course, was a very devout Catholic, and I remember a family Rosary. And it was something that you felt very comfortable doing, you know. It wasn't something we tried to get out of. And

I'm glad that I had those sessions with her, because there weren't many. You know, she died when I was almost eleven, so there are memories, and they're very precious.

GB: While I think of it, tell me what you think of Janet Templeton.
MS: [Laughs.] The world!

GB: How long is it now?
MS: We met in December 1960, and we were married in December 1961, so we've been together over fifty years.

GB: What are you doing married to the same woman, in Hollywood, for fifty years?
MS: I haven't a clue! Honestly? She told you the truth, the whole truth and nothing but the truth, all the time. So, she made me very uncomfortable! . . . The idea is to love me enough to risk my wrath by telling me the truth so that I know myself, and then we'll have a happy marriage, then we'll have an honest relationship. I once asked her, "Would you marry me again today?" just a few years ago. She said, "Are you kidding?"

GB: [Laughs.]
MS: I adore her . . . I can't imagine my life without her. I really can't.

GB: You're here now for the premiere of *The Way.*
MS: Yeah. A most unusual subject to take for a movie: the Camino de Santiago . . .

GB: And your son Emilio directed it, and the movie is dedicated to your father, his grandfather. So, it was obvious at the premiere that this is more than just a movie for you and the family . . .
MS: Yeah, it's a deeply personal journey. Not just because of my heritage with Spain, and particularly Galicia, where my father is from, which is where Santiago is.

GB: It seems to me it's about a father who never actually knew his son. . .
MS: Yes.

GB: Until it was too late, right?
MS: Yes, exactly, yeah.

GB: You mentioned Charlie earlier on. So, now that the father-son has come up, on the day that it has been announced that his series is cancelled because of his recent outburst, which was intemperate, to say the least, about his colleagues and his bosses, I don't suppose any parent gives up hope on a child, no matter how old or what they're doing. Do you pray for Charlie?

MS: Yeah, yeah, every day. And I've been doing so for quite a while.

GB: And what do you think will be the outcome?

MS: I dread to think. I don't know. I'm just getting this now, in just the last twenty-four hours, so it's devastating. We're going to cut short our journey to Malta because of it. My wife is just back against the wall.

GB: I can imagine.

MS: So, I've been asked to come home, and we're going to cut our journey short.

GB: Okay, okay. Is that enough about that?

MS: Yeah. Thanks.

GB: You talked about praying . . .

MS: Uh-huh . . .

GB: In what way do you pray, and what is the God you pray to?

MS: That's a good question. I pray . . . I love the Rosary, because it's so meditative, and I put names on each bead, you know—people I'm lifting up or intentions I want to lift up, or I send the prayer for healing somewhere. Most of it is that. So, I love formal prayer. But in fact I'm just trying to learn to do the meditative prayer, where I just remain still and welcome God in. But there's still a lot of obstacles. You know, like St Teresa talked about "the reptiles" and "the people in the dungeons of our hearts" and so forth, and I haven't cleaned out my jail cells or gotten rid of my reptiles yet. So, there's a great fear about coming in touch with God. You really have to surrender.

GB: Is there an image in your mind of God when you pray?

MS: A presence. I hear a presence, I feel a presence. No question. The Mass, the Communion, is very, very important to me. When I get in line, I say a little prayer to myself. You know, I say, "I am Ramon, called Martin, your brother, and you're welcome here." I just try to open the door to myself, and then, when I go back to the pew, I just sort of try and be quiet and allow that presence and give thanks and praise. If I had to say, the majority of my prayer, whether it's formal or informal, it's thanksgiving. "Uphold me, O Lord, as you have promised, and I shall live. And do not disappoint me in my hope." That's my prayer now.

GB: Do you believe in the Real Presence?

MS: The transubstantiation?

GB: Yes.

MS: I do, yes. I couldn't, I wouldn't bother, if it wasn't that. I mean, you know, the only miracle that is not witnessed in the Gospel is the Resurrection. That's the really only important one, because if somebody had seen it and was an eyewitness, you know, you wouldn't have to believe. It would be a fact. And that's not what faith is about. Faith is a choice, you know. It's got to cost you something. It's got to cost you your non-belief. [Laughs.]

But we don't know what God is. We don't have a clue. And all the images we have of God only prove what God is not. It is such a deeply personal commitment that God has to be something personal. If your God is not personal, it's impersonal. If it's impersonal, who cares? You know, it has no meaning. And if it doesn't motivate your life, you know, if the thirst for the Divine does not take you within yourself to go outside yourself to others, and if it's not done with joy, then our image of God then is very small and limited.

Very often on *The Meaning of Life* we will record as much as three to four times the amount of material that we can possibly include in our slots. However, after our first tape change I realised we were in trouble. Interesting though it was to hear about Martin's experiences as a teenage caddy among the racist country-club snobs of Ohio, or to discover his encyclopaedic knowledge of Sinatra lyrics, I knew we had not really got to the meat of our intended interview as the time at which we had agreed to wrap things up approached.

"We promised you we would let you go in the next five minutes or so," I said. "That's a pity. I feel we're only really getting to the important stuff. I suppose there's no possibility of a little more time? I know you've got another appointment to keep."

"Do you know what it is?" he said. "Whenever I'm in Dublin, I like to go to the six o'clock vigil Mass at Clarendon Street. It's my favourite Mass here. I love the Carmelites . . . But I'm enjoying this. And I can catch another Mass. What's next?"

He likes to use the catch-phrase of his most famous television character, *The West Wing*'s President Josiah Bartlet. So, we got going again.

GB: Fine. Okay. I don't want to talk about roles defining you, but I want to talk about President Bartlet . . .

MS: Okay.

GB: Why is President Bartlet so important to people?

MS: Well, Aaron [Sorkin] took from his lifetime the three most import-ant presidents: John Kennedy, of course, Jimmy Carter and Bill Clinton, who was in office when we started. And he took the very best part of their character and their characterisation, and he created Jed Bartlet . . . And the only thing I asked him for, after we were rolling for a few episodes, I said, "Wouldn't it be interesting if this guy were a Catholic?"

"Oh," he said, "why?"

I said, "Because then he would have to do everything in a moral frame of reference. Wouldn't that be interesting?"

And he said, "Yeah, you're right."

So, he not only made me a Catholic, but he made me a graduate of the University of Notre Dame, which made me happy as Larry. [Laughs.]

GB: Okay. You see the liberal causes that you espouse are readily identified with people in the movie business, but your anti-abortion stance is very strong indeed.

MS: Uh-huh.

GB: And tell me what you told me on *The Late Late Show* in 1987 as to why that is.

MS: Well, we had, you know, pregnancies . . . with our grandsons, three specifically. And, you know, we welcomed these children and encour-aged the mothers to have the children and gave them support. And people would say, "These are your grandchildren? Where are the parents?" And I said, "Well, we don't have any in-laws: we have outlaws!"

GB: But it goes back to Janet, does it not . . . ?

MS: Well, she . . . we had our children very . . . young. I was twenty-one, twenty-two when Emilio was born. But when we got to the fourth one, I wasn't making a lot of dough, and we weren't living high off the hog, and we were doing a lot of parenting. And suddenly she's pregnant again. And she didn't quite know what to do. And she went to a therapist, and the therapist said, "Well, you have children. You have three very healthy children. How do you feel about them?"

"Oh, I love them to bits," she said.

"Well, then, that's your choice, isn't it? You know what you're giving up."

And that was all she needed. She knew. And she had the child. And that child is now Renée, another light in our lives, our youngest daughter.

GB: Go back to Janet. Was she not born because of a rape?
MS: Yeah. She got furious when I said that . . . I said that on . . . was it your show?

GB: I think it was on my show, yes.
MS: She—her mother was raped, yeah.

GB: And so, you reckon, if there had been an abortion, she would not exist?
MS: Wouldn't have known . . . and she even found out later that her mother really thought about dumping her in the Ohio River after she was born. And decided to take her back to Kentucky and leave her with two old aunts, and, as a result, Janet grew up—for six years of her life she never knew her mother . . . Her mother came to collect her with this new husband and took her to Cleveland, Ohio . . . Then I met her in New York.

GB: At seventy-one, there must be intimations of mortality.
MS: Yeah, sure.

GB: What do you think is going to happen to you when you die?
MS: I haven't a clue.

GB: You must have a clue. You must have a hope.
MS: No, I have an imagination, but I haven't a clue. But I'm sure that it has something to do with happiness. [Laughs.]

GB: But is it completely out of the question that the light-switch goes off and that's the end of it? Is that out of the question?
MS: Yeah.

GB: Yeah? There is no way you will entertain that thought?
MS: I will not tolerate that. [Laughs.] The Indians—from India—I'm given to understand, they say that we wake up in death. We get to the door of death and we look back, and we say, "Oh, I was Gay Byrne." "Oh, I was Martin Sheen." "Oh, I know who I am now. All right, fine, yeah."

I got close once, you know. It was an interesting experience. And the only word I can describe the whole thing in a nutshell was the word "familiar". Everything was familiar, and there was no fear. I was only afraid later, when I realised how close I came in the actual event. I got out of it and came back and decided to live. I actually decided to live.

GB: Okay. Just a few quick ones. Who was Jesus, as far as you're concerned?

MS: I personally believe, I accept, that he was the Messiah. He was. He embodied God. He was the Son of God. Now, how did he evolve to that? When did he know that he was the Son of God? That's the great mystery . . . I mean, did it happen at his Bar Mitzvah? Did it happen at his first miracle or when he was on Mount Tabor, when he was transformed? Did it happen in the Garden? Did it happen when he was murdered? Did it happen when he was resurrected or ascended? When did he know that he was eternal, that he was the Son of God?

But the question *we* have to answer is: when did you realise that *you* were divine? You know, I think Jesus awakens in us our potential in our brokenness. If we are humble enough to admit that we are powerless, we have no power, then we begin to understand what real power is. And that's the presence.

GB: Do you believe that you will be reunited with your mum and dad at some stage, or do you believe actually that they are watching over you?

MS: They're always with me.

GB: Do you pray to them, talk to them?

MS: Of course, yeah. They're in the Communion of Saints.

GB: The Communion of Saints—very comforting theology.

MS: Oh, yes, I love that. Let me put it this way: I don't believe we go to Heaven. I believe we become Heaven. And that's something we choose consciously while we're still in the flesh. And conversely I think we choose Hell.

GB: Suppose it's all true, and suppose you get to meet Him . . .

MS: Yeah . . .

GB: . . . at the pearly gates, you meet God. What will you say to Him?

MS: *Deo gratias.* Thanks be to God.

GB: Say no more. That's a perfect ending.

MS: I won't!

GB: Thank you. [Laughter.]

The interview finished, and Martin obliged with the usual formalities of signatures and photos, before heading for the door. On the way out, though, he stopped and turned back to us. "Hey, say one for Charlie, will you, everyone?"

Looking around the faces of the crew, I could see that at least one or two of them would.

BOB GELDOF

Prophet and Loss

I first met Bob Geldof on *The Late Late Show* in the late 1970s. It was my first taste of the verbal grenade-throwing that has since become globally familiar. It didn't endear him, that night, to the audience, many of whom took exception to his scathingly irreverent and irreligious attack on the people who were then running what he called the "Banana Republic" of Ireland. Thirty years before Murphy, Moriarty and Mahon laid bare the failings of our bishops, banks and builders, Bob nailed them in a phrase about "the purple and the pinstripe". It may not have been what Ireland wanted to hear at the time, but it was probably exactly what it needed.

That talent and moral energy are the two main reasons I was wrong that night to predict that he would be forgotten within a year. It is a bit of soothsaying about which he has enjoyed teasing me from time to time ever since. Forgiven, but not forgotten. That said, we are very fond of one another, and he gave a most generous speech at the 2007 IFTA ceremony, where I received my lifetime achievement gong.

But, honestly, who would have guessed that that snarling *enfant terrible* would turn into the moral colossus behind Live Aid and Live 8?

The Nobel Peace Prize nominee and honorary knight of the realm was once asked what fuelled his moral indignation. He answered simply, "Rage." That fits for this latter-day Old Testament prophet, berating hypocrites in the market square. But rage against what or whom? And why?

Actually, I think mere rage on its own is too simple an explanation. Bob has also been shaped and motivated by the particular tragic circumstances of his upbringing. It would be facile to talk about a "mum-shaped hole", but I do think that his mother's death, when he was just nine, instilled a profound sense of the injustice of life, which remains with him still. I am sure that it returned with a vengeance when his beloved Paula died. He entered a very dark place then.

I am therefore delighted to report that, when we met for this interview, in October 2011, Bob Geldof was, probably for the first time in all the years I've known him, at peace with the world. He had just turned sixty—the *enfant terrible* is neither an *enfant* nor *terrible* these days. He had also recently suffered the loss of both his father and his sister in the previous few months. Nevertheless, he was displaying something suspiciously close to happiness. If it lasts, it will be the ruin of him.

BG: . . . It's a day-by-day thing, Gay.

GB: And what has wrought this change?

BG: In my case, the realisation that stuff was okay came one night in Turkey on a boat, as I slipped into bed after another great evening with friends and my missus and the kids down one end and their kids. And I just thought, "What's wrong with you? It doesn't get better: friends, your lover, your children, great food, great wine, great music. God, it's good." And I knocked off a little song called *Here's to You*, and there's a line in it: "I'm in love with you tonight"—the "you" being life.

GB: That's nice. I like that. Take me back, then. Whence came all this anger and disgruntlement and rage?

BG: I assume it was a way of, in the beginning, understanding the conditions of my life, around the age of eleven, when my mum died and Dad had no cash, and his job at the time was leaving the house on Monday to travel around the country and sell his stuff. So, there was no-one around, really, in the house, and I was floundering really badly. You know, sexuality is dawning—that's very confusing. I think that's possibly where the antsy-ness began.

GB: Earlier, you lost Dad and you lost your sister. Did you learn anything from those two events?

BG: No, not really. My dad I was glad to see go, finally. Great man. Full of curiosity, which is the great human quality, I think.

GB: Was he glad to go himself?

BG: Yeah, I think so. I got back, luckily, in time. My sisters were there with him. And he became aware that we were all in the room. He said, "You're all here." So, I said to him, "Dad, it's fine. Off you go when you want to. I mean, you did great. Nothing to worry about. We've all got cash, the kids are fine. Well done, you. When you're ready, go." And he did.

GB: Wonderful . . .

BG: But my sister was a shock . . . And four or five weeks after we buried my dad at Glasthule Church, there we were again, and I'm pressed into, on these occasions, the peroration. I started by saying, "Welcome to the Geldof Monthly Mortality Club . . ." But she comes to me at all moments. Yeah, there's a palpable loss.

GB: I told you, I think, once before, that I read in your book an image which stayed absolutely with me of you coming home from school to this big house. And you put the key in the door and you knew that all the other fellas were gone home to their mum.

BG: Yeah.

GB: And you knew putting the key in the door that there was no mum . . .

BG: Yeah.

GB: . . . and there would never be a mum. And I thought that was a wretchedly sad image.

BG: It was a hopelessness. For every child, the parents are the central pillar of their universe. I mean, they are the parameters within which they can move, and they are, of course, authority. That's all they know, that authority is there. If authority abandons you, if it dies, of course it's not the person's fault; but, for the child, authority has abandoned you. How can you trust any lesser emblem of authority? And so priests, teachers, police—they're not to be respected. They will abandon you. You can't trust anyone . . . So, I move from this, on the one hand, fairly free life, in that, uniquely, probably, I go home, chuck my books down, turn on Radio Luxembourg and pick up a book and do absolutely nothing. And if the next day an authority says, "You will do what I say." "Really? Fuck you!" And this was fun, of course, but I was a pain.

GB: Defiance all the way along the line . . .

BG: Disruptive, and that's kind of stayed with me, unfortunately. And it is childish. It really is. I mean, I remember, Bono and I went to see the Pope, and it was JP2. And of course I understood the great privilege, and I actually admired the guy: I admired the goalie, the poet, the erudite individual, the intellectual. But the Pope, you know . . . For a start-off, it's huge authority, so immediately I'm going [mimes simmering rage] . . . and Bono's muttering . . .

GB: [Laughs.] Just be nice . . . !

BG: Yeah, just once! I remember he said once, "The trouble with Geldof is he has Tourette's of the soul . . ."

GB: [Laughs.]

BG: There's the row, all in their purple outfits, the cardinals and this crippled man, who shrugs off the aides and makes this superhuman effort to walk by himself to his throne. The word "throne" starts sticking in my throat, you know. And absolute respect, at that point, for the man . . . And I think Diarmuid Martin had read out for the Pope this incredible piece of rhetoric about debt forgiveness, and that was wonderful. And I said, "Did you notice his shoes?" You know, Polish Prada. And Bono said, "For fuck's sake . . . !" He said, "Actually, now you mention it, I did . . ." And I was just going, "What is wrong with you? You just met this key historic figure. Regardless of what you think of him as a person, he is, you know, the spiritual help of these vast numbers of people. Who the hell are you . . . ?"

GB: But why do you ask yourself that question? You know the answer to it . . .

BG: And I know where it stems from . . .

GB: Yes.

BG: It stems from all this . . .

GB: When it comes to the religion, we were all brainwashed, let's face it. Did you chuck that on a moment or was it a slowly dawning realisation that you were being sold a pup?

BG: I don't think I ever bought it . . . I mean, of course, culturally, we went to Mass . . . I tried to understand it. You know, this sounds very smart-ass, but I was reading—I read very early—I just devoured books, because there was nothing at home. But the fundamental moment where I thought, "This is not a bad thing," was in the Boy Scouts. And there were three flights out of Ireland at the time, on the old Viscounts: Manchester, London and Lourdes. And my dad saved up to get me with the seventy-seventh, I think it was, group to Lourdes. And I still have the little carton of salt and pepper and the serviette that Aer Lingus served, because I thought, I'll never be on a plane again. And I went to Lourdes, and we were dumped in all that filthy water—just your undies on. And I went to the grotto, and what struck me forcefully, and to this day, was not the people who were ill but the people who took care of them. And I go, "What's that? What's going on there? How could you lose your life for another who has no life at all?" And presumably they were finding the life from that. That struck me as not being Catholic, not being anything but essentially and beautifully human. But I didn't get that from Catholicism. I didn't get beauty. I didn't get humanity from it.

GB: But you found, then, something of what you were looking for in the Simon Community, and you went and worked with them . . .

BG: Don't know how I heard about them, but I pitched up at this house on the quays at around fifteen or sixteen, and the first night I was there—bare room, pretty scabby, these two girls around a wooden table, pinched, whey-faced, cheap . . . "Have you got any Mi-Wadi?" And we gave them Mi-Wadi orange squash, at which point there's this shouting at the bottom of the stairs and there's this pounding on the door and this guy screaming at these girls to get out and back on the street now. And we'd better open the door now, right now, or we were all going to get it. So, the guy in charge that night opens the door, he's pushed aside, and this squat little fella in a leatherette black coat comes in with a stick and starts beating up these two girls, because they came to this house for Mi-Wadi. And, pathetically, I did nothing. Scared stiff. And this was this crowd, the Simon Community.

And we used to get free vegetables from the grocers when they closed at night. If they hadn't sold it, they'd give it to us, because it would go off. And around two, when the bakeries kicked in, we'd go and collect free bread. We'd make a fire in Smithfield market or some place like that—an open space—and the hopeless and the lost and the put-upon and the trampled and the beaten-down that I'd read about so romantically in these books . . .

GB: Here they were . . .

BG: . . . And these lost men who'd lost their families and taken to drink, and these pinched girls—not the glamorous hookers of Hollywood but these sad people—and the schizophrenics, the bag-ladies, the bag-men—and I found a companionship. And they were far more interesting as people than anything the priest could ever possibly tell me. So, all those things were, I think, important to me. Certainly, I'd go to school exhausted—a little boy who doesn't go to the launderette, he doesn't iron his shirts, he doesn't get his hair cut. So, I was just trouble.

GB: Do you never feel absolutely vindicated? The things that you claimed that you were going to do, you succeeded in doing, so, do you never get a sense of, well, "I was right all along" and "I did that . . ."?

BG: The only time that works is when we do *Banana Republic* . . .

GB: That's exactly what I have in mind, because *Banana Republic*, talking about "the purple and the pin-stripe" and what was going on . . .

BG: And the silence.

GB: . . . And the silence! Yes, we were on to it on the radio programme at that stage: the little girl in Granard who was found in the grotto. But you were already on the case at that stage . . .
BG: Yeah.

GB: . . . before the Mahon Tribunal, before the Murphy Report, before the Ryan Report—all of that.
BG: But that was what we did. You've got to understand that the punk thing came out of a moment, like the best pop music comes out of a necessity. Say, Dylan's great anthems, which are genius, encapsulated a time.

GB: Going back to *Banana Republic* and all of that, do you think you outgrew Ireland? I think you did.
BG: I don't think I outgrew it. I was always uncomfortable there, because, I think, the circumstances. My panic manifested itself literally in breathlessness: I developed asthma at eleven, so it's psychosomatic.

GB: Okay. Live Aid, all of that. No, we're not going to go through all of that again . . .
BG: Good.

GB: As Jesus said, the poor are always with us. You're still working very hard on this: Bono and you are talking to leaders, and you're going around the world trying to do something about it. Do you ever think you're wasting your breath?
BG: No.

GB: Why?
BG: Because it worked.

GB: Poverty is still there. The hungry are still with us.
BG: Well, far more limited. The success and the progress of Africa is precisely there in the Horn of Africa. Kenya and Ethiopia are suffering the same endemic drought. We now know it's climate change. Now, Somalia is where the famine is. There's hunger in Kenya, there's hunger in Ethiopia, but they're able to deal with it. And not only that: they're able to deal with a mass influx of people of another religion and culture coming into their country and able to deal with the infrastructure of dealing with that. I mean, forget it, twenty-five years ago those people would just be wiped out.

Of the twelve fastest-growing economies in the world, six are African, and Kenya is one of them. Not only that: ten per cent of their GDP goes through the mobile phone, uniquely in the planet. Africa has adapted modern technologies to the post-model. So, between medievalism and the middle of the twenty-first century they made that jump, exactly as Ireland did, from agriculture to the modern age, bypassing industrialism. A measure of their success is the fact that Ethiopia has doubled its population and can easily contain that. I think in twenty-five years it'll be 114 million. When we were dealing with it, it was 32 million. They can support that many people because of fundamental changes in the economy and in the harvest growths. What they can't do is deal with climate change.

So, this is the story of the two Africas. People think I'm mad, but they thought I was mad when I said these things twenty-five years ago, of 2140, when, without a shadow of a doubt, Africa will be one of the polar economic centres of the world. Mark my words. Last year Africa spent more on consumer goods than Brazil. Their economies are at the point now of lift-off that China had at their point of take-off. Far more impediments in the way of that progress, but, I'm telling you, why invest in China when the Chinese are investing in Africa? That's where we have to be.

GB: Since I briefly mentioned Jesus there, who do you think he was?
BG: I think he was a pain in the ass. I think that he was this annoying failed carpenter who really got fed up with the authorities, and they just did him. And obviously, clearly, a hugely charismatic person. Paul came along and turned him into this iconic central figure for this other idea, which we've emblemised into this bearded guy—a man very dissatisfied with the society that had grown up in these occupied territories and said, "There are other values way greater than this nonsense," and challenged them—good ideas that have served the test of time and become embodied in the idea of this individual.

You know, I believe absolutely the story of the Passion. I mean, you can clearly see the dilemma the authorities were in and that these other guys wanted rid of this guy, because he was a pain, a very public pain, and this was bad for business. So, a good man and one that you could hang your hat on and say, "No, that's cool. I'll go by this sort of stuff."

GB: Was he divine?
BG: No.

GB: Was he the Son of God?

BG: No.

GB: Is there a God?

BG: No.

GB: Nothing.

BG: No.

GB: So, at the end of things, then, it's pull the plug, lights out, gone, finished.

BG: Gone. Thank God.

GB: Oh, don't say that. You've had such a fantastic, amazing, brilliant life.

BG: I've had a weird life, and exhausting.

GB: Yes.

BG: But, as I say, "blessed oblivion"—you know, thanks very much, good night. And nothing. And I truly understand that the greatest intellects in the world—past, present and in the future—will believe otherwise, but it just makes no sense to me. I mean, I spent an afternoon with the Dalai Lama, in a monastery in Budapest, and I was challenging him on some of his ideas. And, you know, who am I to challenge the Dalai Lama? Anyway, just curious, I was being provocative and asking him unseemly questions—you know, "*Why* should I come back?" I mean, it's such a limited human idea. You just keep going round until you get good enough to go to Nirvana. And he said, "Well, that's too bad, Bob."

GB: [Laughs.]

BG: And I said, "But I don't want Nirvana. I don't want it. You know, happiness is a human condition. I can't think of anything more boring than bliss. Where is the challenge?" And he said, "Well, we might make an exception in your case!"

GB: [Laughs.]

BG: I said, "Thank you very much." But it just seems so odd; the rhetoric of religion seems odd to me: "the Supreme Being". Think about it: "the Supreme Being". Aaaargh! What is it? Are we living in *Star Wars*? "Oh Lord, Lord . . ." What is it? *Lord of the Rings*? "Lord!" You know, fuck off. Lord! I mean, what is that? The language is so weird.

GB: Well, what takes the place of that in terms of a moral grounding in your life?

BG: Humans are, by definition, moral creatures, for a very logical reason: we cannot exist unto ourselves. We need the help of others. Kill someone and it hurts you because there's less support. So, by definition, you're hard-wired into understanding that damaging another human being so that they're not at full, operable capacity damages you. And I guess from that stems an idea of morality. Now, then, what's the purpose of life? Life itself. Real simple. I don't see why it's a conundrum. Wow!

GB: Was Paula a believer?

BG: Yes, in a weird way . . . in God. We have an old priory—we live in Kent—and at the end of the cloister corridor is the old door into the church. 1150 it was built. It's been a functioning church for a thousand years. Every Sunday we wake up to the worst choir in history. And she'd go and sit in there by herself.

GB: I'm not gonna go through all that again, but after the horribleness of all of that, just very briefly, what brought you out of that?

BG: Love.

GB: Love.

BG: Corny, I know . . .

GB: Jeanne?

BG: In the shape of a woman called Jeanne, yes. I wasn't looking for it. I didn't believe I'd ever . . . And then . . . I'm so lucky someone's looking after me.

GB: See, I told you.

BG: Yeah, don't be smug, Byrne.

GB: [Laughs.]

BG: This improbable encounter: a woman who doesn't speak English, a boy doesn't speak French. Stunningly beautiful. Ruined man. Ruined, ruined, at that time. And all the spiritual ugliness that comes with that. Why did she like me? Don't know. But, more to the point, you take on four very wounded little girls. You don't have your children yourself, to give them a home. You take care of this loser. That's too much.

GB: Describe that to me: what is that love?

BG: Life without love is absurdity, futility; life without love is meaningless. To live in love is all there is. All I can say is those three inadequate words: I love her. Life is much better with this person. I thought I'd never get this again. And that's the essence of humanity, I think. You just can't be alone. You can't do it alone. I know there's people who find a solidity in solitude and that. I think that's neurotic. I think that these monks and hermits are just objects of neurosis. I mean, to be so hung-up that you can't deal with society, that you have to live in a pair of underpants in a freezing cave to find God. Dude, you've got a problem! Rehab! You know, it's a denial of life. You want to find God? You'll get him, if that's what you believe. He's coming, very soon. He gave you life—get stuck in! Contribute! It's this amazing thing: it's crap, but it's wild. So, what can you do to push the ball along a little? Don't go into a fucking monastery or a convent. Get stuck in.

GB: Suppose the Holy Ghost Fathers were right and you were wrong all your life, and He's up there waiting for you, and you present yourself to Him. What will you say to God, Sir Bob?

BG: "God, you're a surprise!" That's one. And I'd go, "You are so disappointing." I mean, this is all He can do? Spare me . . . !

ANDREA CORR

Corr Values

Andrea Corr doesn't like interviews. For that matter, she doesn't really like fame. So, why on earth would she agree to fly to Dublin, at her own expense, to talk to me about the things that give her life meaning?

Trust is a big thing, and I'm pleased to say that she trusts me. It also helped that she had seen a few previous episodes before our meeting, which had apparently got her thinking, "How would I answer that . . . ?"

When she sat down under the lights—politely declining the assistance of our make-up artist—she looked as beautiful as ever, but far from comfortable. Why was she there? She had recently released a solo album, but understood fully that this was not a promotional interview. In fact, that seemed to be a relief. Self-promotion is obviously painful to her.

All this makes Andrea Corr sound very fragile, almost precious, which she isn't. She is charming, intelligent and funny. But she is also very clear about her reasons for doing what she does. She has talents and, for good, biblical reasons, does not wish to bury them.

The trouble is that music is an industry as well as an art form, and industry requires sales. Since the age of fifteen, when Andrea joined the family firm, she has therefore had to do the marketing as well as the performing. And, boy, did the Corrs prove to be marketable.

Thankfully, those years have given her, I'm sure, a very comfortable cushion on which to sit while she discovers and explores things which matter more to her than record sales. She has married and, since we spoke, has become a mother. Now that's a product she should be proud of.

It is not cool, these days, to express commitment to formal religion, and right now, Catholicism is about as uncool as it gets in Ireland, where the Church leadership sometimes seems to be doing its darnedest to alienate its flock. It is therefore interesting to discover a genuine rock-and-roll star willing to say publicly that she is part of a Church—not an unquestioning or unconditional part, but not cynical either.

After the interview I heard that she had texted to say that this was the first interview she had *ever* enjoyed. If that is true, I am delighted. The audience—our largest to date—certainly seemed to enjoy hearing about Corr values.

GB: The programme is called *The Meaning of Life,* and I had thought to start by asking you what gives your life meaning at the moment.

AC: Well, I suppose what always gave it meaning. I mean, to be honest, I've never been a really ambitious person. I think to live a life and to do something you love, which is music . . . and also I've had a chance to do theatre as well, so I'm doubly blessed. And, you know, my love, my husband, my friends, my family—that's really what it's all about.

GB: Okay. Take me back. Childhood—happy? Earliest memories? Mum and Dad . . . ?

AC: Childhood was very, very happy, thank God. I know I'm very lucky. Our parents were a band, so the house was really immersed in music, and in fact my mother sang for the first time on stage when she was pregnant with me.

GB: Religious?

AC: Yes. Daddy, particularly, was—is! Sharon, at one point [laughs], called him a "religious fanatic", because he gave out to her about not going to Mass. But, yeah, it was religious in that way. I think my mother was a bit nervous.

GB: Nervous?

AC: Yeah, I think the Church made her a bit nervous. I suppose it was different back then. You know, women were told to have baby after baby, and, after being told to have baby after baby, there was churching and that type of thing, which was very, very mixed messages: cleanse the sin of concupiscence, after you've done what you've been told to do, you know. So, yeah, I do feel she was quite nervous about it. But Daddy had enough religion for all of us!

GB: Did the Troubles, by the way, in Dundalk . . . ? Surely, the Troubles *did* have an effect on you somewhere . . . ?

AC: I didn't really feel the effect, other than there were some moments . . . There was one that led to a pivotal moment in my life, I think . . . There was one incident of a caretaker in our school, who we loved, and me and Caroline used to hang around with him in the morning, a lovely man. And then, the next thing, the school was closed because there were arms stored in the roof of the assembly room, and it had been him. And it was an interesting moment, because I still was aware he was a good man, but it's more complicated than that. He had different beliefs. It was quite a growing-up moment.

GB: How old would you have been when that happened?

AC: Very young, actually. Maybe eight.

GB: And you knew that this was a lovely man and you loved him and he was very kind to you . . .

AC: A real kind, family man.

GB: How did that affect you then?

AC: I think it's a turning-point, where you kind of grow up and you see that . . . most of the time, it's not bad people doing bad things. You know . . . And we've all got different beliefs on what's a bad thing. So, I suppose my life got a bit more three-dimensional, and my beliefs and my perspective. At the same time, Dundalk is a lovely place, and I find it very unfortunate that it's tarnished with that reputation . . .

GB: "El Paso" . . .

AC: . . . and is scarred by that past.

GB: What was your immediate reaction, for example, to Gerry Adams being voted in in Co. Louth?

AC: I felt, it's a pity, to be honest . . .

GB: Why?

AC: Because I think that there's a past that is being ignored, and I don't believe that somebody can head something that is willing to hurt and to maybe take lives and everything and then put on a suit and become a figure of respect. I don't think that that's right, really . . . I think authenticity and honesty is very important . . . But, obviously, there's an awful lot of people that don't agree with me, and they've every right to feel like that. That's just my view.

GB: What about school? Nuns?

AC: Yes, it was a convent, yeah.

GB: Were you bright?

AC: Yeah, but not like Einstein. [Laughs.]

GB: Go back now to the music. I get the impression that it was always expected of you that you would be a band.

AC: Yeah, to be honest, it seems like it was an inevitability. And we started the band when I was fifteen. All the time before that, my whole life, I just loved music. I listened all the time; I sang. It's all I cared about.

GB: So when you became a band, who was the boss? There has to be a boss.

AC: Yeah, without a doubt it wasn't the three of us girls. [Laughter.] You know, we were younger. Jim was ten years older than me.

GB: Oh, I see.

AC: But, fortunately, when we became a band we met our manager, John Hughes.

GB: And that worked out?

AC: Incredibly, yeah.

GB: Talking to people about bands, the same thing comes up, that you strive to climb the slippery ladder of fame and fortune, and you're there, and then you start fighting and you split up. You drive each other mad, because you're living so close to each other over an extended period.

AC: Yes, and we worked really, really intensively. I mean, at one point we did four continents in three weeks, about fifty interviews a day and then a show. And we're always stuck on the one couch, so you're touching all the time.

GB: And you're family.

AC: And the thing about family is you pigeon-hole each other. You know, families don't consider that somebody might have developed since they were six. You know what I mean? I might have changed.

GB: [Laughs.]

AC: So, we had to kind of erase the family—and I know that sounds mad. I think other bands *become* a family, and we became a band. We had to, really. "Respect" is the biggest word in it all. It's just absolutely vital. And also space to be your own person. Individuals need to flourish in a family, and I believe we all managed that.

GB: Listening to you and seeing you in various interviews, the weird thought I have is that the older you get, the more nervous you seem to be and more lacking in confidence. Is that so?

AC: Yes, I am nervous ... Basically, the celebrity thing is very uncomfortable with me. As it should be. It's incidental to what I do. You do music and then you see your picture in places. To suddenly see yourself every-where, when you're almost adolescent and your feeling about yourself so self-critical . . . it made me so self-conscious. The only way I could describe it is, like, to walk through a long corridor of mirrors with two mirrored doors at each side. And I think that was probably my youth . . . That only led to making me self-conscious.

GB: Is it shyness . . . ?

AC: No . . . Let me see. Maybe it is shyness, but it's not a lack of con-fidence. I'm brave enough to go for it, regardless of any censoring thoughts that I might have. I think the celebrity thing is quite crazy, and it makes me want to hide in a corner. You know, art is, in a way, pain made beautiful, and what happens these days with the celebrity culture is that we just get the pain. We don't get the art after it. I just feel, the only thing that comes that's good for a person out of fame is being able to give or do something to raise awareness of certain issues. That's pretty much the only good thing that comes from fame.

GB: What comments do you make about Jim's outbursts, from time to time, about these conspiracy theories? How does that affect you? I know you're tied. You don't want to be disloyal to your brother . . .

AC: No, of course. And I don't have disloyal feelings towards him. I don't believe at all in any of the things that he's saying, but all I can say is that he is absolutely genuine, that he believes this stuff. And his motivation for exposing himself in this way is good motivation, as far as I am concerned.

GB: Is this new in his life or was he always like that, when he was in the band?

AC: I think Jim always searched, in a way, but this is over the last few years. I blame the internet, really. You know, things are written on the internet like they're fact, and this, to me, is the casualty of that.

GB: Is it an embarrassment to you?

AC: No, I would never be embarrassed by him.

GB: Are you sad about it?

AC: I'm sad that he has such a bleak view of this world, that it's not the beautiful place it is from my perspective. It's quite a sinister one. I think it just started with 9/11. He didn't get how the towers fell the way they did and—and it snowballed.

GB: Okay. Go back now to the acting. Is it acting or singing from here on for you?

AC: Well, I hope I don't have to choose. I really do love them both. I love singing and making music, but theatre has been amazing, because there's a kind of superficial side of the music world, and it is completely lacking in vanity.

GB: Theatre is?

AC: Yes. And I think it's better for the soul, better for the ego, that if it's a good night you can't replay it. You can't wallow in it. Similarly, if it's a bad night, thank God, you can let that go. Everything is recorded in a band, but in theatre, it's that night—only an audience of four hundred people and you know what happened in there and know what you felt. And I find that it's a really authentic art form.

GB: Did you find it humiliating having to audition?

AC: No, I think auditioning is very important. It's the least I can do. You know, I haven't done my time, as other actors have done.

GB: There would be the feeling that "Here she is, she's a celebrity, and now she's coming in here as a sort of a light-hearted dilettante—'Why don't we try acting for a change?'"

AC: Yeah, and I understand that. But that's what makes me work harder, because that's cringey to me, and that's definitely not where I'm coming from. It's definitely not a spoilt person coming in going, "I want to try this." You know, this is beyond deep-end stuff. This is the ocean that I'm flinging myself into.

GB: Do you *have* to perform? Is there something in your genes that makes Andrea Corr want to get up there and perform, in spite of this— we didn't call it "shyness" . . . ?

AC: I don't really know why I do this, to be honest. I feel very much alive when I'm performing. And I'm trying to give all of myself. I suppose that's it. And I also think people watching feel more alive. It is a celebration of our humanity. I just really love that . . . Maybe it's a chance to admit certain feelings but not call them your own.

GB: Okay. You've been told often enough to have got used to the idea: you're a beautiful young woman. Does that matter to you?

AC: Well, it's obviously complimentary. As I said earlier, I was very self-critical growing up, and seeing yourself everywhere certainly doesn't make you feel beautiful.

GB: It doesn't?

AC: No, I just wanted to hide. It just had the kind of opposite effect on me.

GB: That's odd.

AC: I wonder, is it? I don't think it is odd. I think it would be odd to actually be going, "Wow, amn't I gorgeous?" We never see ourselves as we look.

GB: No.

AC: We don't really know what we look like, and we can't ever separate what we look like from what we feel like. But, at the same time, it's very complimentary for people to say the nice things.

GB: Thank God you are as you are . . . Go back to your mum, who died young and unexpectedly. What effect did that have on you? You were the youngest, the baby.

AC: Yeah. I mean, it had the most profound effect, I think, of anything in my life. The ground beneath your feet moves. It's a totally different world. It just was hard to believe that this was happening. You know, she was diagnosed with the disease in April, and she died in November. And before that, the most vital, healthy woman, with enormous lust for life and appreciation of the moment . . . I suppose you could see how transient it all is, the good and the bad. But, you know, I have faith, and I believe she is with me and she looks after me.

GB: Do you pray to her?

AC: I do, yeah.

GB: About what?

AC: About everything. I believe she knows best, and so sometimes I don't get what I want, but I take comfort in that: she knows best and what's for me won't go by me.

GB: Okay. You are religious, you say . . . ?

AC: Yeah. I believe in God very strongly. I believe in Heaven. I believe my mother is there. The Church is obviously a difficult one. I actually remember one time . . . we got home from touring and I was back in Dundalk, and I went for a walk. And I actually love churches. I find them to be just immensely comforting. You know the idea that all these prayers are in the air and there's not a new sin or there's not a new prayer. I love that in a church. So, anyway, I walked into a church and realised that I was sitting in a queue for Confession. And I hadn't been in, probably, a few years—God forgive me. And so I see this as a sign. I have to go into this Confession. I can't exit stage left now. And so by the time I get into the confessional box, I'm in a state of . . . madly defensive . . . [Laughs.]

GB: Why?

AC: You know! So, I got in and it was an old priest and, God love him, I still remember him. And he starts as they start: "How long has it been since your last Confession?" And then, honestly, he witnessed an absolute tirade from me, because I excused myself for the years I hadn't been there, and I said to him, "Well, to be honest, now, it has been a few years, but, you know, I find it hard to hold my head up high as a woman in this Church." And he was, "Oh . . . oh . . . why would you say that?" And I said, "Well, this really is not a place of respect and love for a woman, this Church."

GB: And he said?

AC: And he was going, "Oh, no, no, no. That's not true. . . ." And I was going, "But it is true." "Oh, no, no, no." And then I realised the effect I was having on him, and I went, "Okay, maybe, maybe not. What have I done wrong? Let me tell you . . ." I felt sorry for him. I probably shouldn't probably have done that!

GB: An experience . . . ! So, you say you believe in God. How do you picture this God?

AC: It is so loving. And wherever love is, I believe God is. And I do believe He is our father and He loves us and wants to look after us. I think it was Karl Marx that said religion was the opium of the masses, and I admit that I would be a junkie if that were the case, because the thought of this life and all we go through, without a divinity and the comfort of that, would be very bleak to me. So, I do believe. You know, you bite into a strawberry and you look at that, or a newborn baby . . . or just the love you feel sometimes in life. There's got to be more . . .

GB: But institutionalised religion, institutionalised Church—not much time for that . . . ?

AC: Well, I suppose it's very poignant at the moment—it's always poignant, but religion and Churches are run by human beings. Human beings are fallible, and if I am to sit and judge I can't blame God for this stuff. I blame our human failings and the corruption of power and greed and all of these things that are our pitfalls as human beings. I suppose the problem with Church, in a way, is that we decided they weren't human, and we decided to give them complete authority and unwavering respect . . . And no voice to say, "Actually, no, I don't think that's right." And that's where it went wrong.

GB: Do you have doubts about God?
AC: No, I don't have doubts about God.

GB: Even when you see bad things happening in the world and bad people doing bad things, or even good people . . .
AC: Good people doing bad things?

GB: . . . doing bad things.
AC: Yeah, there's certain horrors. I believe that this whole life, everything, is borrowed: Heaven and Hell is here sometimes . . . I don't doubt God because of that. In a way, I have to trust that, ultimately, there'll be a reason for it all and that it's going to be so good where we go to—please God—that actually the reason won't even be relevant.

GB: When you say that you have this reservation about the institutional Church—if and when you have children, do you think you'll bring them up as Catholic, or not . . . ?
AC: Yeah, that's the ultimate question, isn't it? I think I would bring them up as Catholic, yes. However—and this might be, to some people, picking and choosing, but I'm the mother, so there you go!—at the same time I will express my opinion on the fallibility of humankind and that some things aren't fair and some decisions made from the wrong motivations.

Fundamentally, if we followed the one rule, "Honour thy neighbour as thyself," or "Do unto others as you'd have done unto you," this would be a utopian world. It all comes down to that. But, you know, I'm happy with what my father gave me, and so I would like to give that too. It's better to stand for something than fall for anything. It's the one religion I do know to a degree, as much as any punter knows. But there are beautiful prayers that help me in my life. You know, all that is begotten and born dies. We need something to help us with that, because that's hard.

GB: And yet was it important to you, when you married your darling Brett, that you did so in a Catholic church?

AC: Yes, it was important to me. Also for Brett. And actually the priest that celebrated our marriage was also the priest that did my mother's funeral . . . I suppose God is watching, wherever you are, but I wanted him to bless it, and I wanted the holiness.

GB: When you met Brett was it instant, *click, bingo,* that's him . . . done and dusted?

AC: No, it wasn't, because I had known Brett for a few years. He was friends with Jim, and so whenever we'd go to London, Jim would hook up with him. So, funnily enough, I said to him, when we got together, "We were in each other's company so often . . . Did you not find me attractive or anything?" And he said, "No, I thought you were beautiful, but I thought you were in the corner, writing poetry about death." [Laughter.] That's what comes from being a bit gothic and—and hiding behind your hair.

GB: There's no answer to that! Now, what and who do you think Jesus was?

AC: Interesting. I do think Jesus was the Son of God. I do think that he was made into a man. But, to be honest, if I found out that was wrong—and God forgive me if I, in any way, seem blasphemous—but if I found that he wasn't the Son of God but he was a very holy person—a prophet—that would be okay too.

GB: But you do think he was divine and he was sent by God?

AC: Yes, I do.

GB: And do you think he rose from the dead?

AC: Yes, I do. I don't know whether it is absolutely how it's written, in that he was physically there again. To me, what the Resurrection meant was an after-life. I don't think it's a physical incarnation.

GB: Okay, if it's all true, what the nuns told you, and you arrive at the pearly gates and you meet God, what will you say to Him or Her?

AC: "Thank you . . . And where's my mammy?" [Laughter.] I think that's it.

GB: That'll do. Thank you.

NIALL QUINN

The Mighty Quinn

It is probably not the easiest time to be setting up a business in Ireland, especially if your name is Quinn. However, as he did so many times in his playing career, Niall Quinn has spotted a gap and gone for it. His company, Qsat, is now selling satellite-based broadband services, aimed in particular at homes in remote parts of the country, where his competitors are unable to lay cables.

Smart move, and not his first.

Who would have suspected that a player who, in previous years, was as famous for his drinking stamina and his "disco pants" as he was for his football skills would reinvent himself as a credible businessman, setting up the Drumaville Consortium to buy Sunderland AFC, and then totally transforming the club?

Who would have guessed that the man Roy Keane dismissed as "Mother Teresa" after their Saipan fall-out should hire none other than Roy Keane to manage the Black Cats of Sunderland—something that proved to be a master-stroke?

Niall Quinn doesn't do the obvious or the expected. He also doesn't appear to "do" grudges.

Let's go back to "Mother Teresa". Only Roy Keane could make that an insult. He chose not to participate in the famous Niall Quinn Sunderland v. Ireland testimonial, where, uniquely, the entire proceeds of more than £1 million were donated to charities, including Crumlin Children's Hospital and Goal. I wanted to know where Niall's motivation for that gesture had come from.

I should have guessed: his mammy. "You'll never outdo the Lord for generosity," she used to say when he was growing up. And it stuck. He even insisted on donating the rather meagre fee for our programme to charity—not something you will find with every businessman running a start-up.

Mind you, the other woman in his life, his wife, Gillian, could pre-sumably veto all these philanthropic gestures. After all, footballers are not noted for their largesse, and most of them seem to regard testimonials as their pension fund. He didn't, and neither did she.

Niall was always a prodigiously talented sportsman. He could easily have been one of the greats in either hurling or Gaelic football, and his GAA veteran dad still regards Niall's three successive long-puck records and his All-Ireland Minor Hurling appearance as his finest sporting achievements. But even he knew that, at Arsenal, Niall stood a chance of making a living out of his talent.

Niall's sporting ability was the making of him, but I suspect Gillian was the saving of him. At a very young age she accepted his invitation to move to England and marry "the mighty Quinn". In the process, she almost certainly averted the downward spiral that awaited his fellow-Arsenal "Tuesday Club" drinking and gambling pals, Tony Adams and Paul Merson.

As I say, Niall has made a few smart moves in his time, but I suspect Gillian is his smartest.

∾

GB: Take me back to when you were smaller, now—the household, Mum and Dad, and family and all of that. Was it a very religious family?
NQ: Yeah, absolutely. My mother was, still is, seven days a week, a Mass-goer. My father, I'd say, has probably never missed Mass in his life on a Sunday. And we were brought into that fold, and, I suppose, until I left for the bright lights of London, I would have been an absolute regular church-goer.

GB: When you were going off to Arsenal—and there you were, sixteen or thereabouts—and your father said to you, "Don't do a Jack Doyle on us ..."
NQ: Yes. [Laughter.]

GB: What did he mean by that?
NQ: Well, when my dad was growing up, there was a famous Irish boxer, actor, tenor, called Jack Doyle, from Cork. He was the first Irish superstar in many respects. He was hanging around with royalty. He was a sportsman. He was set to be the wealthiest Irishman that ever lived. And, of course, sadly for Jack Doyle, he died in a back street in London in the seventies, penniless and destitute, a broken man, a drunken man.

And it was a lovely warning to get. You know, the great song that speaks about Jack Doyle says that he was at the top of the wheel of fortune and got dropped from it from a height. I knew I was going up a little bit of that wheel with where I was going, being lucky enough to play with Arsenal, so it was great advice to get ...

GB: Your father warned you, "Don't do a Jack Doyle." But you did . . . !

NQ: [Laughs.] I did. I had a good look at it. [Laughs.]

GB: Tell me about that period. You really did go mad.

NQ: Well, yeah, I suppose, I had a great couple of years with Arsenal. I was young, single, few quid in my back pocket, got into the Irish team —everything was starting to go right for me. And then it started to go a little bit wrong. Suddenly, there was a manager, George Graham, saying, "No, I've somebody better than you is going to play. But I'm not letting you go anywhere else. I'm going to keep you." Because, in those days, they had the power to do that at football clubs.

And I got frustrated with that, and, of course, when you're not playing a big game at the weekend, instead of going home and going to bed on a Thursday early and a Friday early, I'd go off out with the guys who were coming off the building sites, so I'd have Friday night out, all night. Saturday I'd have another go at it. And then we had a drinking culture within the club, which we used to call the "Tuesday Club". Tony Adams and Paul Merson famously wrote about it.

George Graham used to work us really, really hard on a Tuesday. And the Tuesday Club, after we all did our work and all the running and everything was good, we would all go up to London, and we would have an afternoon on the beer, and it would be last man standing. And the last three were always Tony Adams, Paul Merson and myself. And we could end up anywhere, at any hour of the morning. And, in fact, we often went through till the Wednesday, and I can remember turning up for training one Thursday and we're all in the same clothes we were in on the Tuesday morning.

Now, it consumed Paul and Tony. I was lucky, because I was able to escape out of it with my Irish friends and not be into it seven days a week with the guys . . . It didn't consume me, but I would say it would have gone close . . . I guess I got a lucky break, that Howard Kendall at Manchester City wanted me.

GB: So, going back again to the religious household, your suggestion that when you went to London you lost your faith or you lost your . . . ?

NQ: I didn't lose my faith. I lost the ability to get up out of bed early on a Sunday morning. It was purely just the lifestyle I was leading; and being racked with guilt over it is an understatement. You know, Gillian came over then, and we kind of steadied up a little bit, and then obviously you have children and you look at things a little bit different.

GB: But the drink was bad enough; you got into gambling as well?
NQ: I had a good look at everything, yes.

GB: You said you swam in the river but you never got wet.
NQ: [Laughs.] Near enough. I loved a bet. Some of my most memorable times in London were in bookmakers'.

GB: And it was just horses you bet?
NQ: Yeah. But then, when I went up to Man City, in 1990, and I got my first real, proper wage, I got the Texaco Sports Star of the Year Award for football. And I sat beside Jim Bolger—famous racehorse trainer, one of the greatest I think that's ever lived. And the waiter came round, and I had Guinness, and Jim had water, and the next day I went home with a docket for a horse in my bag. Now, not blaming Jim, because it worked out great: the horse turned out to be the best two-year-old in Ireland that year, and, from earning hundreds of pounds a week, myself and Gillian, who were just about to get married, we had an offer of a quarter of a million old Irish punts for the horse.

So, even though I kind of had three or four years of going to the edge, and at times my mother bailed me out once or twice, suddenly, then, we got this lottery win, if you like, and that's when, funny enough, I started to cop on a bit.

GB: How did Gillian stick it? She went to live in Manchester, and yet you were still on the tear.
NQ: I was, yeah. Looking back, yeah, you'd have to ask her why she ever stayed, because it was difficult. She was very, very young. Gillian was nineteen when she came to live in Manchester.

GB: And you were?
NQ: I was twenty-four. And my mother went around, of course, and had to tell everybody that they were living in digs around the corner from each other. But we actually went under the same roof together. In some ways I was on a roll, and Man City was going great for me. I scored twenty-two goals one year in the top flight, and I was called celebrity around town. We were the kind of people who would get in anywhere.

GB: The dream couple.
NQ: Well, now, Gillian got fed up with that. Gillian said, "This is ridiculous. What are you doing? Cop yourself on." And I was going, "No, we've

got something else to go to." She'd say, "Well, I'm not going," and I'd say, "Okay, I'll be home at eleven." And I'd get home at half four in the morning. I think that's probably where it reached a kind of a point.

And when the opportunity came to go to Sunderland it wasn't so much an opportunity as it was the last-stop saloon, because I'd had injuries, and no other club wanted me. And Sunderland, at the last minute, came in for me, and I took a lot less money to go to Sunderland, but I think it was the best time of our lives together.

GB: Tell me about Norman Whiteside, when he came to visit you in Sunderland.

NQ: Norman, yeah. Norman, of course, was a child prodigy. He was playing at sixteen years of age. He was playing in cup finals. He went to the World Cup with Northern Ireland twice, and he was an incredible guy. And Norman was measuring the feet of all footballers in the country on behalf of some statistics-gathering company, and, look, I don't know what it was for . . . chiropody, of a form.

GB: This was his living?

NQ: Yeah, and Norman stuck his head around the corner and just said, "Did I hear you guys are free for a few hours?" So, we said, "Yeah, it would be great to go with Norman Whiteside for a drink." And we got a young lad, Cliffie Byrne, and a young lad called Kevin Kyle. The five of us went into a little small pub in Durham, and we were having a nice little pint, and Norman started telling some great stories, and Steve Bould and I were in awe of him. And at one stage Kevin Kyle, the young Scottish lad, said, "So, Norman, did you play football yourself?" And it was just an atmosphere where this is the guy who was on his way down, because his career is coming to the end prematurely... For confidence level he probably needed to be in the pub telling everybody how great he was, and then this kid . . .

GB: Innocent . . .

NQ: Innocent, of course. So, Steve Bould was about to sort of give a right hook to this young lad. And that's when Norman came out with the most fantastic line. He said, "No, no, it's okay, son." He said, "I'll answer it like this: Who was the second-youngest player ever to play in the World Cup?" And, of course, Kevin went, "Jeepers! You?" And he went, "No, some fella called Pelé. I was the youngest." [Laughs.] So, straight away, there was respect. But it was also sad, because it was a career coming down, and here was an upstart who didn't know who he was.

GB: And so quick.

NQ: And so quick. I mean, the guy was still in his early thirties.

GB: Tell me about when the tap turns off: your career is over, you're done. Do you think you coped with that well or badly, or in between?

NQ: Very badly, I would suggest. I said, "I'll be fine. Don't worry. I'm grand." And that was fine for three months. And I went off playing at celebrity golf days. I'd be smiley and I'd be happy, and everyone thinks I was a great lad. And then I was getting home . . . And Gillian was going, "What's all this about?" And I got into a dark area there, I suppose . . .

GB: Depression.

NQ: Yeah, yeah, very. You know, people were ringing, and I was getting job offers. I wouldn't even answer the phone to them. The world was crumbling around me, and I was there thinking, Well, you know, I'm not going to do anything about it.

GB: Looking back on it, was this because your entire identity was football and who you were and what you were?

NQ: Perhaps, yeah. Like, any footballer will tell you, you don't prepare properly.

GB: Most people go through the same thing. The only catch is that with sportsmen it happens so much earlier.

NQ: It was ten years ago, and I literally ended overnight—and, thankfully, with Gillian's help, got myself back on track.

GB: You never got so bad as your friend Gary Speed . . . ?

NQ: Gary. Poor Gary . . . Just one of the most beautiful people you will ever meet in your life. And that's why the football world came to a shuddering halt when they heard the news about Gary Speed . . . But football rallied round, and I think we also saw maybe there is a part of football where people do care and where people have got their priorities in order.

GB: The testimonial on your retirement . . . You gave all the proceeds— well over a million—to the Children's Hospital in Crumlin and Goal. What prompted that?

NQ: First of all, I didn't deserve the testimonial. I never counted the money in my pocket—put it that way. And I do believe that if I was to have kept the money I would have got half the crowd, paid forty per cent tax—I'd have got maybe a quarter of the money and a reputation, perhaps, as another player who's creaming it off at the end of his career.

In fairness to Gillian, she's backed me a hundred per cent on everything . . . And, of course, it became big news. So, Tony Blair, in the House of Parliament, thanked me for doing it, because he was my local MP. Bertie Ahern mentioned it here in the Dáil.

But the greatest thing to come out of it . . . I got a letter from a guy in prison who said he was a Sunderland fan. His mother and father are Irish. "Had a bad life, but I want to do something right. I can't attend the game because they won't let me and"—a bit of a ha-ha, but he said, "could you send me a ticket or a programme"—his very words were "a non-attendance ticket" — "and I will send on the money? I work here. I do whatever I do, sew bags, whatever . . ." And we just thought about a non-attendance ticket. And he sparked the idea—a guy in a hell-hole of a situation, somewhere in a prison in the south of England. And we got in excess of thirty thousand people who bought "non-attendance tickets". So we had €300,000 extra.

GB: Tell me about the letter you got from the little girl in India, which you kept pinned up for a long time in your kitchen.

NQ: Yeah. I got one for each player. We were able to give about a hundred thousand to John O'Shea's Goal, who had a street project in Calcutta that needed funding. And, in time for the game, John was able to get a letter from each child in Calcutta to give to the players who were playing for me that night. Now, the normal practice when you have a testimonial is to give the players a nice gift for turning up. So I thought, well, the best thing to keep people in the spirit of this and let anyone who played know what this was all about was an individual letter addressed to each person. So, Robbie Keane, Kevin Kilbane, all the guys in the Irish team would have got a letter—all the guys in the Sunderland team—from young children in Calcutta who, I suppose, the best way to describe is, were heading for a lifetime in perhaps prostitution—all the wrong things that could happen to somebody in those vulnerable situations.

GB: The letter from the girl in India—what did it say?

NQ: It was just "Dear Mr Quinn, I believe you're playing a football match to help me. Thank you very much. I'm now told I'm going to be able to go to school." Thinking about it now, it's close to the bone, you know.

GB: That decision to do that, was that faith-based or just decency . . . or your mother's example . . . or what?

NQ: My mother . . . She has a wonderful saying, and I've kind of lived by it: "You'll never outdo the Lord in generosity." And she's absolutely right. Gillian, of course, was in there as well. She bought into it, and I suppose it was pay-back, too, because we have a lovely life.

GB: Would you describe the household at the moment as a generally religious house?

NQ: Gillian is very spiritual. She would pray a lot. She is a deeper, more spiritual thinker than me. And we're pleased the kids have a relationship with the Lord. And it's their relationship: we don't interfere. We don't push them and make them recite hours and hours of liturgies or anything like that. I'm a proud Catholic. I should be a better Catholic than I am. If somebody turned around and tried to take the Catholic religion out of this household I'd fight very hard to keep it in.

GB: And what's God to you?

NQ: I think He's there. I think He has His eye on me. I do think there'll be a ready-up and He'll balance it up. He'll be like any auditor, sorting my life: anywhere it's gone well, He'll be there to say, "Yeah, I was helping you there."

GB: What do you think Jesus was?

NQ: I think he was a great example and somebody who probably tried to reset the way people's lives were going. He gave the world one more chance, I guess, or gave the world a glimpse of the right path to take.

GB: Do you think Jesus was divine?

NQ: I probably do, yeah. I'd still have that belief that he was the Son of God. I can accept that.

GB: Okay, final question, and it's the stock question we ask everybody: If it's all true, Niall, everything you were taught by the Christian Brothers in Crumlin, and all that your mother believed, and you end up meeting your Maker on the final day, what will you say to Him/Her/It?

NQ: I suppose, it'll have to be some form of thanks in there for everything I've done. I'd be the first to hold my hand up, as there was a lot of things there that weren't right, and hopefully there's not too many more of them to come. I guess, just: "If you're balancing it up, I hope I've done enough on this side to let me in." But it could be a recount. We'll see how it goes. [Laughter.]

SIR RICHARD BRANSON

First Class or Business?

If Sir Richard Branson could work out a way of powering his aircraft using the force of his own personality, not only would he reduce his carbon footprint, but I suspect they would fly higher, further and faster.

Our interview request was almost an afterthought. I was headed to London for the Halloween bank holiday weekend in 2011, to interview Bob Geldof. My thrifty producer decided not only that this would be the time for me to experience Ryanair travel for the first time—with an air coach and a tube at either end—but that we should try to "kill two birds" and record another *Meaning of Life* interview while we were in London.

Not surprisingly, with less than forty-eight hours' notice, the word came back from Virgin HQ that Sir Richard was not available. He was in Brazil. But then, within an hour, we got another call—this time from his Belfast-born PR, Jackie McQuillan: "If Richard were available for no more than thirty minutes on Friday evening, would that be enough for you?" He was flying from Brazil to India and could make a brief stop in London.

Oh, what it is to own your own airline! I wondered whether to tell him that we were flying Ryanair to meet him.

True to his word, Richard arrived at his West London office on time, looking radiantly healthy and without a trace of jet-lag. The magazine *Hello!* that week was full of pictures of his Necker Island hideaway, which had been burnt to the ground in a conflagration that could very well have claimed the life of Richard's mother, but for the heroics of Kate Winslet. Even that trauma hadn't wiped the smile off his face.

His wife and daughter had taken "powerbike limousines" from their Oxfordshire home to come and clink a glass of bubbly with him before he jetted off again. He was wearing a white cotton shirt and jeans and had no baggage, so he had to borrow my producer's jacket to avoid shivering during the interview in temperatures that were markedly lower than in Brazil.

We had met before, on *The Late Late Show*, when, I remember, he quickly found his way to the audience's heart by giving free transatlantic flights, impromptu, to the family of a previous guest who was in need of medical treatment in America. You could simply call that good PR, but Richard has a talent for making his PR seem uncynical.

He is not a formally religious man. His PA was clearly astounded that he had agreed to give us an interview about his faith and morality, since she was not entirely convinced that either figured high on his list of priorities. In fact, Richard had agreed to the interview primarily because he wanted to talk about the Elders, an initiative he dreamed up with Peter Gabriel (of course!), to which he managed to recruit an A Team of elder statesmen and women, including Nelson Mandela, Archbishop Desmond Tutu, Jimmy Carter, Kofi Annan and our very own Mary Robinson.

That's what gives his life meaning. He now wants to use his considerable wealth and energy to make the world a better place, and he was only too happy to accept our invitation to explain how.

❧

GB: I know that you have come hot-foot from Brazil, where you were attending a meeting of what the *New York Times* called "a diplomatic league of superheroes", the Elders. Could you start by giving us a quick run-down of what and who are the Elders?

RB: Well, the Elders was set up by Nelson Mandela and Graça Machel, his wife, and he basically chose the twelve men and women that he felt had moral authority, who were maybe in the last—I'm not sure Mary would like me to say this—the last ten, fifteen years of their lives, so they put ego behind them—people that the world could look up to, who could talk out about issues like global warming, poverty and the other major issues in the world. So, the reason I was there was that myself and Peter Gabriel came up with the idea originally.

GB: They don't have power within themselves, but presumably the people who do have the power listen?

RB: Yes, they have no legal power, but if you are a young leader some-where in the world and Kofi Annan rings you, and then Nelson Mandela also is on the line, and Archbishop Tutu is on the line, and Mary Robinson is on the line, and President Carter from America, he's on the line as well—it's going to be difficult for you to refuse to take the call.

GB: And by small, incremental steps they can have an influence and get things done…?

RB: Yes, I think sometimes by small steps and sometimes by large steps. I mean, they've taken on the rather unfashionable subject of childhood marriage. Something like ten million children get married every year around the world, and they've taken that up as a cause. But, at the same time, President Carter has said to the Church, "Look, if you're going to set an example, you should be allowing women to serve in your Church, and you shouldn't be getting out there and talking about women's rights, but at the same time not allowing women to serve as pastors." I happen to believe he is right on that subject.

GB: It would be a major breakthrough indeed if the Vatican and the Pope listened to him.

RB: Yes, it would be a major breakthrough, but it's not going to stop him, in his lifetime, trying. And I think it would be good for the Catholic Church. I mean, some of the problems that have taken place within the Catholic Church would not have taken place if there had been women serving in the Catholic Church. And so I think if the Catholic Church is going to have a long-term future and serve its people, I think it ought to open its door to women.

GB: Amen. What has been the effect on you personally of rubbing shoulders with these fine people, do you think?

RB: Well, I hope I am the better person for rubbing shoulders with these people. I mean, it's a tremendous privilege to be sitting at their feet . . . I write every word down, as I don't want to miss a word. And Archbishop Tutu, who chairs the meetings, has got the greatest sense of humour of almost anyone I know alive today—the greatest stamina. I mean, you know, eighty years old, he flies to Rio; he flew back to South Africa the same day that I flew here. In five days' time, he's flying back to Rio again.

President Carter, eighty-seven years old, he'll be going to Sudan soon; from there to Korea. Just unbelievable, their stamina and their commitment and the difference they want to make . . . I was brought up in an agnostic family, but if anyone was going to convert me, the Archbishop would, and it's just a real pleasure to be in his presence.

GB: Now, the question is, why did you, Richard Branson, become involved in it? Was it a question of conscience or morality or ethics or what?

RB: I think, quite strongly, that if you find yourself in a position to make a difference in life, you've got to do your best to not waste that. I think that, as an entrepreneur, you can see problems in the world perhaps in a different way than social workers can see them or politicians can see them.

GB: Why?

RB: Because of your experience of trying to tackle big issues. I mean, I've looked at global warming and thought, "Why is nobody out there tackling global warming?" and so felt, "Well, then, what would Churchill do about this? And if it really is as big a threat as World War I and World War II put together, how would he address it?" And so, I thought, "Well, the first thing he'd do is set up a war room, where you could concentrate the firepower against the enemy, which is carbon." And so that's exactly what we did. We've set up a war room with the idea of working with the twenty-five major industries to get a giga-ton of carbon out of each of those industries and to come up with imaginative ways of getting that carbon out of those industries that benefit the industries and don't damage the industries.

GB: Just about the global warming, the quick, smart-alecky reply to you is that if you stopped flying your planes around the world, that would make a major contribution to lessening the thing. And your answer to that is . . . well-practised and well-rehearsed by now—yes?

RB: [Laughs.] Well, it's a fair comment. Of course, if we did stop flying planes, British Airways would rub their hands and replace our planes tomorrow . . .

GB: [Laughs.] Why didn't I think of that . . . ?

RB: . . . But what we have done is pledge to put a hundred per cent of all the money that we take out of our airlines and try to develop clean fuels, and, between the carbon war room and Virgin Atlantic, we have come up with quite an exciting aviation fuel. I was actually standing four days ago in New Zealand, in a steelworks, where we have our first test plant. Basically, all the rubbish that goes up the chimneys of steelworks and aluminium plants and coal-fired power stations, we're now syphoning that off and turning it into aviation fuel. This genius engineer has managed to work a way of turning it into aviation fuel. And so in a couple of years' time, you know, we will be flying planes on fuel that is sixty per cent less carbon than our current . . .

GB: Go back to that point about where you see the need, you want to become involved. Is that from a religious point of view or a moral point of view, or just a social point of view?

RB: I think it's a moral point of view. I was brought up to care about other people. If I ever said something bad about somebody, my mother would make me go and stand and look in the mirror and say this reflected badly on myself. So, I think, throughout my life, I've looked for the best in people. Most of my life is now spent on setting up not-for-profit organisations and trying to address some of the bigger issues of the world. And I get tremendous satisfaction from doing that, and I think it's the right thing to do.

GB: Okay. Go back to your mum and dad. Your mum, happily still alive, and in no small part thanks to Kate Winslet. And Dad died in March—Edward—Lord rest him. How much religious foundation did you get as a child?

RB: We didn't get a lot of religious education, as such. We got an enormous amount of love and the teachings of religion: love, purity, unselfishness, honesty—you know? We certainly knew what was right, and we knew what was wrong. But conventional church-going was not something that happened in our family.

GB: School?

RB: I stayed in school until I was fifteen, when the headmaster told me to either stop running my magazine or leave school and run a magazine, and I chose to leave school and run a magazine.

GB: Do you think your dyslexia forced you on to be a success?

RB: If I hadn't been dyslexic I would have stayed at school and gone through a conventional education . . . And being dyslexic made me realise that I was hopeless at school, but I knew what I wanted to do. And that was very good for me.

GB: Church of England school, was it . . . ?

RB: It was a Church of England school. And, you know, I read the New Testament. Being a bit of an analytical person, I would compare, you know, Paul with Mark with Matthew with Luke and try to analyse different paragraphs and to see . . .

GB: Even then?

RB: Yeah. I wanted to believe. My parents didn't believe, but I was certainly questioning and trying to work out whether the Bible had been written by one person, whether it was real, whether it was not real. But what I started to really believe in was just the magnificence of the world we live in, the magnificence of evolution, and, as I got older, I was worried a bit about these different religions. Just the fact that one's born in Ireland, you know, why should the Catholic Church be correct? Or the fact that you're born in England, why should the Protestant Church be correct? The fact that you're born in the Middle East, why should the Muslim faith be correct?

I mean, I think there may be a God up there. Gandhi said, "If there is a God, he didn't have a religion." And I think that we have one people in this world, and those people need to be treasured and reared and protected . . . I can't see why one religion should be superior to another religion.

GB: Dad died in March. Do you think you'll ever see him again?

RB: My father was ninety-three when he died. He has lived on, I think, through his children and his grandchildren. And we were an incredibly close family, and tons of love in the family. And he's with us every day. He certainly didn't expect to see us again—it would be a wonderful bonus if he's mistaken.

GB: But you don't think...?

RB: I don't know. I don't think any of us really know. The important thing is to live life today as if there isn't a future, and give life a hundred per cent. And that's what I plan to do, and that's what he did. . . . When we, finally, on our deathbed, feel that we gave life its best shot, if there is a superior force out there that is going to take us into their bosom, you know, let's make sure that we can go to that force with a smile on our face.

GB: And does Archbishop Tutu ever try to influence you, or Jimmy Carter, towards their religious beliefs?

RB: They are Christians through and through, and everything that is the best about Christianity beams through them.

GB: And you admire that?

RB: I admire it enormously and wish I could have that faith, because it's nice.

GB: Do you? Do you wish that you could have that faith?

RB: Good question. Yes, I think it would be wonderful to feel that, one day, I could say hello to my father again . . . Personally, intellectually, I think it's less likely than likely . . . I pick up the phone to talk to him occasionally, but then, sadly, put it down again . . . But, anyway, he's a hundred per cent in my heart, and I'm in his heart.

GB: One last question. Just suppose that what they taught you in school, the fine Church of England theology, was all true and you come to meet God. What will you say to him?

RB: Christ!

GB: That's a good opener. And then?

RB: Oh, dear—I'm sorry . . . No, I would say, "I got it wrong . . . ! I would like the opportunity to go back to earth and let people know that I was mistaken . . . Anyway, thanks for a great life, basically."

MARY McALEESE

When in Rome . . .

"I hope yous have brought a big box of tapes." With his softly spoken, dry Belfast wit, Mary McAleese's husband, Martin, warned us, on arrival at the former President's private home in Roscommon, that this, her first interview since leaving the highest office in the land, was unlikely to be a short one.

For fourteen years, Mary McAleese, one of the most opinionated people in public life, was effectually gagged—a situation that, in fairness, she accepted with good grace. It is the job of the First Citizen to speak the people's mind, not her own, and so all her private opinions—on religion, law, politics, morality and any number of other subjects—were carefully placed in storage until the day she left office.

Now, however, there is no reason why she cannot say exactly what she thinks. And she thinks, and says, a lot.

Mary McAleese was never one for standing on ceremony and, characteristically, she insisted on all the crew sitting down to coffee and home-made scones on arrival, and then to lunch before we left, all the while buzzing around the table to wait on us.

She and I have a connection. My daughter Crona was, for a while, nanny to her children and got along famously with them. Even so, I was surprised and deeply touched on the day I announced that I would not be standing for the presidency, in 2011, to receive a very supportive call from Mary, from Rome, where she was studying.

When we met for this interview, in the summer of 2012, she was back from Italy for a few days in the house for which, she admits, she and Martin paid "acres of cash" at the height of the boom. They were always uneasy about the greedy excesses of the Celtic Tiger era, but neither of them anticipated the crash, and so they too are now caught in the negative-equity trap. For a former President's home, the house is surprisingly lacking in presidential clutter, because Mary McAleese made a point of giving to the nation every single gift she received during her years in office. It was a historic presidency, full of rub-your-eyes moments, book-ended by the Good Friday Agreement and the Queen's visit. But the day she left the Park, Mary McAleese moved on.

Having embarked, while still in office, on a part-time postgraduate course in canon law at the Milltown Institute in Dublin, she headed to Rome, in 2012, to complete her doctorate. Our interview was prompted by the publication, by Columba Press, of her first thesis, under the title *Quo Vadis?*.

For the sake of anyone seeking a riveting page-turner for the beach, I should probably say that this isn't it. *Quo Vadis?* is a forensic analysis of the laws, codes and traditions that determine the structure and governance of the Roman Catholic Church. And if that précis leaves you none the wiser, don't assume that reading the book will have any different effect. I know. I did. The nub, if you are looking for a short-cut, is contained in the foreword and the last half dozen pages, in which Mary McAleese first of all explains that it is not only her right, but also her canonical duty, to offer respectful criticism of faults in the Church if, with an informed conscience, she perceives any. And then, in a rather unexpected gloves-off finale, she nails her ninety-five articles to the doors of St Peter's, spelling out the dysfunction and inconsistency that, she believes, prevent the institutional Church in Rome from living up to the vision of its founder. Now, that *is* worth reading.

You don't mess with Mary McAleese. And she is not messing with the Vatican. However, she knows that there are figures in the Curia who will dismiss her with a wave of the hand, unless she takes them on on their own terms. Hence, adding to her already considerable civil legal expertise and credentials with a canonical qualification from the Catholic Church's own Gregorian University.

Why is she doing it? Because her Catholic faith is at the core of who she is. It is not only what gives her life meaning, but what nourishes and sustains it. The daily disparity she perceives between Christianity and mere *Churchianity* is therefore, to her, an obscenity, a blasphemy even, that she is willing to dedicate all her energy and talent to redressing.

Will it work? Will our former President succeed in persuading a Church that prides itself on "thinking in centuries" to hurry up and change? Personally, I doubt that she will live to see the ordination of women, which she so craves, even though she would undoubtedly make a magnificent cardinal herself. Perhaps even a pope. As for a Vatican rethink on homosexuality, which she sees as a simple matter of justice, well, that really would take a miracle. However, as Mary sees it, working and praying for miracles is part and parcel of being a Catholic, so don't expect her to give up soon.

❧

GB: *Quo vadis?* The quotation comes from the Acts of St Peter ... Peter, confronted by the crucified Christ, on the way out of Rome, escaping Nero etc., is asked to go back and face his destiny ... So, tell me about the book.

MMA: The book is a study of collegiality. And collegiality was one of the two really big buzz-words that came out of Vatican II. Collegiality was about the governance of the Church, and Vatican II said emphatically that the bishops, what we call the College of Bishops, was to co-govern the Church with the Pope. The idea was that, in involving the bishops more in actual governance of the Church, they, in turn, right the way down the line in their dioceses and in parishes, would encourage greater collaboration with the rest of the Christian faithful, with the laity.

And, effectively, what happened at the end of Vatican II was that they, yes, embraced the notion of the College of Bishops co-governing with the Pope, but in fifty years they've never met. The Pope continued to govern in a solely, exclusively primatial way. And I think some people definitely planned for a reversal of Vatican II.

GB: In order to keep power up there?

MMA: Yeah, I think some people made a very clear decision that they in no way wanted the Pope to co-govern with anybody else. And we've had major problems that are very evident in the Church, particularly in Ireland, in recent times. A lot of those problems have come through silence, through not encouraging the kind of debate or the kind of openness that might have helped us to deal with some of the problems at an earlier stage, before they became embedded in dysfunction.

So, the lawyer in me always wants to really examine that carefully, to see is there something we could do by way of making that structure work in the way that it was supposed to, to give a better end result.

GB: So, the question for you, Mary McAleese, is, *Quo vadis you?* Where are you going with this book, and what do you hope to achieve?

MMA: Well, I'm studying canon law and thankfully, now, I'm a qualified canon lawyer. So, *Quo Vadis?* actually asks the question directly of the Pope, in a way, because he's the only person who can kick the log-jam, the only person who can change the rules. I'm not talking about democratic structures within the Church, because the Church always balks at the idea of being regarded as a democracy, but rather structures that allow for legitimate debate.

We've arrived at a time where nobody is really terribly clear any more where are the boundaries for discussion. At what point do you become regarded as a heretic? At what point do you become a so-called dissenter? What are we allowed to talk about? What do we have to accept by way of handed-down views, particularly at a time when those who are handing down views to us lack a certain credibility, in the light of their own embedded practice?

We know, for example, how embedded bad practice was in relation to the reporting of child sex abuse or clerical child abuse. And that has given many of us pause for thought about—well, if they could be so dreadfully wrong, and take so long about accepting how wrong they were, what else could they be wrong about?

I've never in the past had any difficulty stating my opinions on some things that I know the Church leadership has different opinions on: clerical celibacy, gay rights, women in the Church, particularly women's ordination . . . And we seem to have arrived at a time when actually those views, which in no way touch on what you might call the core deposit of faith, have almost been sucked into an area of creeping infallibility . . .

GB: About everything.

MMA: About everything.

GB: When you were involved in *The Tablet*—your beautiful piece in *The Tablet*, in '93, '94—did you not have correspondence with JPII?

MMA: I did. I wrote to Pope John Paul at the time, saying that I was a cradle Catholic. I loved the Church. I had watched, in my native Belfast, as people died, literally, for their faith, and where religion was such a mess. Christians were killing one another, and every day, I had to ask myself, "Is it worth this? Is membership of my faith worth this?" And I had come to the conclusion that, yes, it was worth it.

But now, here in my own Church, I felt a stranger, and I felt that, possibly, I was no longer in communion with the Church, because that's what *it* seemed to be saying: that if you couldn't accept its teaching, then you were out of communion. So, I wrote and I just asked the question, "Am I a member of this Church? Am I in communion with this Church?"

GB: And he said . . . ?

MMA: And I have to say I got a lovely letter back, written on his behalf. It said, "The Holy Father instructs me to say to you, 'Yes, you are a full

member of this Church. Yes, you are in full communion. Try to understand: this is the teaching of the Church. You don't have to believe it,
but you do have to accept that this is the teaching.'"

So, I persuaded myself then, yes, that I could stay within this Church.
And, to be honest, if I'd had to walk away from that I think my life would
have been really diminished. And then I wrote to the Archbishop of
Dublin, who was Cardinal Connell at the time, and I said to him, "Look,
could you give me a reading list?—the theology that excludes women
from priesthood." And he did. And I read everything on it. And I found
nothing in it that impressed me, and a lot of stuff thoroughly *depressed*
me, because the scholarship was so wickedly poor. So, that's where I left
it. And I would say to my children, "I don't think we are expected to
accept things that we have, in all faith and conscience, tried our very
best to understand—tried our very best to believe—but cannot."

GB: It strikes me that during your time in the Áras you must have been
driven demented, not being able to participate in these controversial
and contentious issues?

MMA: No, funny enough not.

GB: No?

MMA: I had no business in the role of President, using it to express my
own private views. So, that never bothered me. In fact, the only time it
really, really bothered me was when I had a most dreadful encounter
with Cardinal Law of Boston, when he told me that he thought I was a
very poor Catholic President and I was very distressed.

GB: He said that?

MMA: He did, indeed, yes. And in front of an audience too. And I took
him on. I said to him, "Excuse me. I'm not a Catholic President. I'm a
President of Ireland. I'm a President of people who are Protestant,
Catholic, Jewish, Agnostic, Muslim, Orthodox; all sorts of people. And it
happens that I am a Catholic and I've tried my best to be a good
Catholic." And I said, "I really don't think it's any of your business to tell
me whether I am or whether I'm not either a good Catholic or a good
President. I don't think that's your business." And we had a really
appalling discussion, to put it frankly.

GB: What an inappropriate thing for him to do?

MMA: You asked a question earlier about are these people stupid . . .

GB: Yep.

MMA: ... and the answer I would give you is no, but they have an arrogance at times and a self-righteousness, some of them, that is inculcated, that is so embedded that they don't see things through the same prism that you and I would see them. What I would regard as inappropriate, they think is appropriate. What I regard as appropriate, they see as inappropriate.

GB: Apart from being extremely upsetting, who do you think won that encounter?

MMA: Oh, well I won it, hands down.

GB: Did you? [Laughs.]

MMA: Absolutely hands down, as those who are witnesses to it will tell you.

GB: Was there a sequel to Cardinal Law?

MMA: There was. Because Cardinal Law had been invited to Ireland by the hierarchy or, I think, I'm not sure, by Cardinal Daly. He was promptly uninvited.

GB: Well done. Take me back now to the Leneghan family. The eldest of nine. Mother from Maghera, father from Co. Roscommon. Sure, ye were all cross-border initiatives from the very beginning.

MMA: [Laughs.] My mother and her siblings between them have sixty children. I used to say my family thought they had to increase, multiply and fill the earth entirely by themselves ... and they came very close.

GB: I presume it was a very Catholic home ...

MMA: It was, of course. There was daily Mass, because we lived beside the church, Saturday Confession—went to Sunday school. We were in the Legion of Mary, the St Vincent de Paul—you name it.

GB: So, a happy childhood ... ?

MMA: Yeah, really very happy ... Ardoyne is nowadays regarded as a kind of Catholic ghetto. I grew up in the Protestant side of Ardoyne. We were the only Catholics. My best friend in those days was a girl called Florence Maxwell. She married a British soldier. My sister, Nora, was their bridesmaid. We went to that wedding at a time when Catholics going to the weddings of soldiers was an open invitation to be tarred and feathered, but nothing happened to us, thankfully.

GB: Then everything went wrong, and the place was burnt down, and your brother, profoundly deaf, was beaten to within an inch of his life by people, and no-one has ever been charged with that . . . ?
MMA: No.

GB: When that horror struck you, were you at any stage tempted to join in, retaliate, revenge, have a go?
MMA: Many's a time.

GB: You were?
MMA: I was. I was young and very headstrong.

GB: You were eighteen-ish when the thing started. Did you actually ever throw a stone or throw a petrol bomb?
MMA: Thanks be to God, no, I never did.

GB: Were you tempted to?
MMA: God, I was tempted to many's a time. But I didn't, thank goodness. And I remember at one time, when there was a bunch of lads who were throwing stones, a big confrontation going on right across the Crumlin Road, where we were living, between Catholics and Protestants. This was just shortly before the army moved in. And I came racing up to our house to get the milk bottles, to bring them down, either to throw them or to give them to the guys . . .

GB: To make petrol bombs.
MMA: Yeah. I wouldn't have been making them, but some of the guys would have made them. And, oh, my father . . . ! There was no way. When he saw what I was doing, there was war. And I'll never forget what he said to me: "I did not rear a rabble. A rabble." He said, "You will stay in the house." And my mother was saying, "You'll stay in the house and you'll say your prayers." So, that's what we did.

GB: Was that a pivotal point . . . ?
MMA: That's when you get good guidance and you're helped and guided to make good choices. Friends around me didn't. And I'm talking about friends on both Catholic and Protestant sides, regrettably. And they made, I think, dreadful choices that were to limit their lives and change their lives, and certainly limit the lives of others.

I mean, my next-door neighbour joined the UVF. He subsequently killed—murdered—five people. He intended them all to be Catholics, but, as it happened, the one who was walking down past the chapel that he killed turned out to be a Protestant . . . Now, he got angry. That young man got angry, because so many of his friends were being killed by members of the Provisional IRA. And because of his politics. He, in his indignation and anger, joined the UVF.

But my parents—I never, ever heard a sectarian word uttered. Never. The values of the family, the Christian values, stayed the same. You did not kill. You did not get involved in paramilitarism. If you had a problem, you discussed it. You prayed about it. If the politics were so glued that you had no faith in them, you prayed about them. I mean, we prayed for Paisley. And I remember when, first year I was President, and I went on retreat to the Poor Clares in Ennis—I told Ian Paisley subsequently that I had the holy nuns in Ennis praying for him. And he was delighted.

GB: Now, I'm not going to—well, I *am* going to gloss over your legal career. Suffice to say you did pretty well, didn't you? I mean, called to the Northern Bar at twenty-two. Then you headed south, where you inherited Mary Robinson's Reid Professorship at Trinity College, at the age of—what, twenty-four?

At twenty-eight you even wavered slightly and you joined RTÉ. What strikes me is that people in that line of profession—law, academia and so on—they generally keep their religious beliefs and their prejudices and their biases pretty close to their chest, whereas you were very publicly Catholic and nationalist and Fianna Fáil and dedicated to a whole rack of causes. Was that by accident or by design?

MMA: [Laughs.] I don't know how to answer that. It was just the person I was. One of the causes that I got involved in very early on, in 1975 I think, was when, along with David Norris, I was a co-founder of the campaign for gay rights. And you know that *wouldn't* have been seen as a very Catholic thing to be doing at that time . . .

GB: Not very Catholic!

MMA: . . . or even today, for that matter. I just didn't like . . . I've never, ever been comfortable around injustice and, in particular, comfortable around silence around injustice.

GB: Just going back to your espousal of gay rights . . . Now that it seems the entire world is calling for gay marriage, how do you feel about that, Mary? What would you be anti, for, whatever?

MMA: Wouldn't have a problem with it at all . . . I mean, some people talk about it as if, the day there's gay marriage, it's now going to be compulsory, and we'll never, ever again have heterosexual marriage. [Laughs.] I mean, don't get me wrong: I'm a big supporter of marriage. I'm a big supporter of family. But I have a very strong view that, for centuries now, gay people have lived in a really bleak, dark, secretive world that has regarded gay people, to use the expression that some-times is used in the Catholic Church, as "intrinsically disordered."

GB: Evil.

MMA: Their *activity* is evil . . . What is it like to live your life always in fear? To never have the opportunity to live with a partner who loves you and will love you from now until the day you die; and when you're dribbling, as an old person, will wipe the dribble away, as my mother does for my father now? Not to have that opportunity in your life— that is what life has been like for gay people for ever.

I just think that people have this obsession, somehow, around homo-sexuality, with the idea of sex, forgetting what it is . . . that family and partnership is about love. And it's about being there for another human being, building them up humanly and living out that great Gospel commandment.

So, that's where I'm at with this debate. I'm just thrilled that anybody would want to get married now. I do think that marriage—the bond of marriage, the lifelong commitment, through thick and thin—it's a great grace.

GB: Speaking of marriage, taking you back to 1976, let us fasten on Martin McAleese, a young dentist, whom you married. Do you think, Mary, that there is one person for us all in the world and that faith and/ or prayer or hope will bring us together?

MMA: No, I don't. I mean, he wasn't the only person I ever fell in love with, but he was the only person I ever fell in love with, I think, that I could have made a lifetime's commitment to, and stayed with that commitment for life, too. Martin's personality really suited mine. His characteristics suited mine.

GB: What are those characteristics that he has?

MMA: Infinite patience and forgiveness, I think. I'm the world's champion huffer. I like to have a really good huff the odd time . . . And it drives him nuts. But, over the years, the huffing period has got shorter and shorter, because I know I'm going to be with him to the day I die anyway, so what is the point in huffing any more?

GB: Okay, so now we have a young, loving mother with a loving spouse, and you have a good career. What on earth made you want to be President?

MMA: It was a window that opened up at the time that . . . I had no notion of being President . . . Bear in mind it was 1997, before the Good Friday Agreement, and I had been involved before that in talks between John Hume and Gerry Adams in a pastoral ministry that was run by the Redemptorists, by Father Alec Reid.

So, in 1997, when Mary Robinson decided that she was not going for a second term, a friend of mine came to me and said, "I think that you should think about this, because you know the South very well: you've lived there. You know the North very well: you were born and raised there. We're at a time now when there is a huge amount of work to be done on the bridge-building front, and people are beginning to be open to that, and the presidency would be a perfect vehicle for that bridge-building work." And he persuaded me that I had the kind of insight and vision and the commitment to be able to do something useful in that space.

GB: That's what made you run. Would you give me a pithy comment, having been through what you went through, and having worked—and Martin having worked—on that whole, amazing thing . . . ?

MMA: Well, on the day we went into Áras an Uachtaráin, in 1997, I said to Martin as we walked through the door, "We're going to know, some time, whether the great Commandment, to love one another, really works, because that's what we are going to try and do here." And I have to say that, leaving Áras an Uachtaráin last year, I said to Martin, going through the door, "I think that we may have been able to show that the great Commandment to love one another *does* work."

GB: Okay. Look back a brief moment, then, to the moment when you received Communion in Christ Church Cathedral, and your Archbishop described this as "a sham" and all of that. What are you feelings about that now? Just regret?

MMA: Dreadful regret at *his* remarks. And I think that Archbishop Connell regrets them too, you know? I stayed very friendly with him. And no priest, no bishop in Ireland ever castigated me for it in private. But I think it showed us the fault lines that existed—all the elephants that were in the room that we still had to deal with, in terms of ecumenical endeavour.

GB: And was it not your aim, in doing that, to point up the inclusiveness rather than the exclusion?

MMA: Correct. I was the President of all the people. I had been invited to a Eucharistic celebration and I could not walk away from that Eucharistic table. I couldn't, when I had been invited to their table to share *their* food.

But, actually, part of my problem, even with my own Church, is the fact that so many people *are* excluded from that Eucharistic table. Because I regard it as the Father's and Mother's table. It's our family table. And even though my own parents, you know, they've nine kids, and we fall in and we fall out, but around that table, everybody is welcome. You never arrive at the house and are told, "Well, you go and sit over there, now, because the rest of us are going to have this big meal, because you got divorced or because you're in a gay relationship, you can't have this food."

GB: But in your mind—is it the same meal, in your mind?

MMA: I didn't ask those questions, and they're questions for theologians to argue the toss over. One of the ways, for me, of trying to understand the many, many different faces and interpretations of God is that I'm the oldest of nine children. If you were to ask any of my brothers and sisters to describe our parents and their relationship with our parents— and these are the *same* parents—you would not think we came from the same house. Because I inherited my parents when my mother was twenty. She was thirty-eight and banjaxed when she had my youngest brother, Clement. And I kind of think that that's the way we are with this God-Parent person.

For me, we're baptised. We share the Baptism. And indeed, in the Catholic Church today, thankfully, we have moved quite considerably towards inter-communion with other Christian denominations—regrettably not the Anglican tradition. I think it's one of the biggest regrets for me, and one of the biggest hopes, that we will move on that axis.

GB: Okay. About your beliefs: in your book you describe yourself as "one of Christ's faithful." Now, does that mean that you adhere to all the Catechism and theology of the Catholic Church, or does it mean something else?

MMA: I believe in a God and I particularly love the story of Christ: the intervention two thousand years ago of someone who allowed us to understand the healing power of love . . . And I don't understand how we would ever have got that narrative in without the intervention of Christ. For me, that's really what it's about. It's Christ's words and his great Commandment; the Beatitudes, the beauty of that; his sacrifice; the replicating of that sacrifice through the Eucharist, so that it's ever present to us, ever available to us as a resource to help change minds and hearts and soften stones. When I say I'm a member of the *Christifideles,* that's what I mean.

I'm also a member of the Catholic Church. That's a different phenomenon. I didn't voluntarily join the Catholic Church; I voluntarily stay in it. I was baptised into it by my parents, but I have stayed with that denomination from adulthood, through choice.

I think it has done wonderful work in the world. I *don't* think that its story has been an unbridled narrative of good. The work in education—I wouldn't have got an education without the Church—the work on health care, the work on charity, the moral stance, Catholic social teaching. There is still a world of work to be done in the Church and through the Church, and I think it's still a very powerful vehicle for change in the world. It's also a dreadful frustration at times. But I've learned to live with that and to be patient . . .

GB: Okay, you've spoken about regular Mass and the Eucharist and your meditation. Do you meditate every day?
MMA: Every day. It could be five minutes and it could be twenty-five minutes. It depends on the time I have.

GB: Who are you talking to, Mary, when you pray on these occasions?
MMA: Well, prayer is just turning to God. It's a conversation with God. I might have an image of Christ that would come to me from all the pictures that we've seen over the years, but actually that's not what would come to me in prayer.

GB: And so Christ is an ongoing presence?
MMA: Utterly, absolutely. And that's why the Eucharist is so important to me, because the Eucharist is Christ present. It actually just gives me the most wonderful rush of joy. I'm never happier in my life—literally, never happier—than when the Offertory starts at Mass. I feel peace, and I know that, by the end of it, whatever I'm facing through my day or my week or my year, I'm going out a little bit stronger.

GB: But do you believe the consecration brings about the Real Presence, body and blood?

MMA: Oh, absolutely. I believe that what happens in that moment in the Communion draws us into the sacrifice that was made two thousand years ago and, in some way, allows that sacrifice to be ongoing. I just see it as the space in which we come to realise that love is by far the most important, influential and wonderful gift that we have as human beings. It is transformative. All the misery that we have in the world that is man-made, we can actually redress and stop and prevent or heal, by and through the use of love.

And I'm fascinated by other religions and other perspectives on God, including agnosticism, including atheism, because every one of them offers to me some other way of looking at this unknowable, unfathomable mystery that I subscribe to. And I don't have any great desire to stand up and say, you know, that I'm a Catholic because my religion is best. I'd die sooner than do that . . .

I don't know what lies beyond death, incidentally. I have no idea. But I do believe there is something beyond it. That makes a bit of sense to me. In fact the whole Christian narrative, the narrative of Christ himself, makes sense to me. Which is why I still hang on to it . . .

NOEL GALLAGHER

Sorted

In 1995 the self-proclaimed "biggest band in the world" played an enormous gig at Slane Castle. I was one of the few people in Ireland who were *not* there to discover whether Oasis were—as their songwriter and lead guitarist, Noel Gallagher, had been telling anyone who would listen—better than the Beatles.

I did, however, get to meet him, on *The Late Late Show,* thanks, I'm told, to his Mayo-born mammy, Peggy, who told him, "If you do one interview in Ireland, go on *The Late Late Show* with Gay Byrne."

And, like so many working-class Manchester boys, Noel does what his mother tells him.

I knew all about his Irish connections, but I don't think he knew anything about my Manchester ones. In 1962, I presented a show there for Granada Television called *People and Places*, and my duties included introducing the first TV performance by a new four-piece band from Liverpool who would go on to become—well, nearly as big as Oasis, if Noel is to be believed.

Fast forward to the summer of 2012 and a rather humbler Noel Gallagher is in Dublin and has agreed to meet up again. In 2009, after yet another bust-up, he and his brother Liam finally realised it was impossible for them to stay in a band together. The trouble is, as every good geographer knows, once you leave Oasis you're in the desert, and they have both been there ever since. So, with the Eucharistic Congress packed up and de-rigged from Croke Park, and the Red Hot Chili Peppers moving in for their one night at the GAA mother-ship, Noel Gallagher's new band, High Flying Birds, had been booked to support. A stadium gig, yes, but surely a come-down from the days when the even higher-flying Oasis could have sold out practically any stadium in the world.

If Noel feels any regret about this turn of events, however, it doesn't show. Bang on time, he turned up for our interview and said a well-mannered "Hello" to everyone in the room. The famous excesses of drugs and alcohol are now a thing of the past. He's a happily married father and, as they say in Manchester, "sorted".

He is never short of opinions, but is not famous for having much to say on the subject of religion. I therefore decided to break the ice with a rather tangential subject, which I knew would bring a smile to his face.

GB: I'm going to start with a small miracle which happened in May, when Manchester City, in injury time, slapped one in and gained the premiership over a crowd called Manchester United for the first time in forty-four years.

NG: That's right.

GB: And I want you to tell me, what did that mean to a young fella from Burnage?

NG: Everything! Supporting that team since I was five or six, for forty years, I haven't seen them do anything, really. It meant the world.

GB: And on a scale to do with marriage and sex and having a child and a Number 1 in the charts and everything else, how does it compare? Up there with that?

NG: Absolutely, yeah. And my wife understands that. It's like your family is one thing . . . I wouldn't give up my kids and my family for City winning the league, but I'd give up a few Number 1s, for sure . . . Well, I've had nine. I'd give up four of those. Four of them weren't the best.

GB: Okay, take me back to Burnage and the household you lived in. Peggy and Thomas. Was it a very Irishy Irishy house?

NG: Yes. Little wind-up cottages that played *Danny Boy* and stuff like that, you know? And we always spent our summer holidays in Co. Mayo.

GB: And Irish nights in St Kent's, Chorlton Irish Club—that kind of thing?

NG: Oh, yeah! Oh, yeah, St Kent's. I used to play for their football team . . . How do you know about that?

GB: I did my stint in Manchester as well, you know . . . Your father: much has been written about his alcoholism and his violence and . . . mother doing a skip in the end and all of that. You seem to play that down as if it was sort of average for the area and the times.

NG: Well, I don't think he was an alcoholic: I just think he was a bit of a rubbish husband. But, I've got to say, all my friends who were my age, *all* their families were split up. So, it was kind of par for the course. The seventies was a tough time in Manchester, not only for working-class people but for Irish people, with the Troubles . . . But I don't look back on any of that time with any regret or sadness. It kind of makes you what you are.

GB: It didn't mean that you were an unhappy child?

NG: Well, I discovered music. There was a guitar in our house, for some reason. Once I picked that up, that was my escape from everything, no matter what was going on at home . . . And I still, to this day, can sit and pick up a guitar and I can be gone for hours.

GB: You don't see your father.

NG: No.

GB: It must have been bad then that you have no contact with him . . . ?

NG: Well, no. See, after my mam and dad split up, we still seen him—only lived about two hundred yards up the road. So, my mam never said anything like "You can't see him." And we still did a bit of work with him. But then, very soon after that, we kind of became men, and then that was the end of that . . . It's not shocking for families to became estranged, particularly a family of boys.

GB: Did you and Paul have a stammer?

NG: I did. I think Paul did. We used to go to speech therapy. Fabulous.

GB: And you got over the stammer?

NG: Eventually.

GB: Eventually. Okay, tell me about religion in your house. Your mother and father must have been traditional Irish Catholics.

NG: Yeah. My mam would take us to church every Sunday until, I'd say, we were teenagers, and then we just stopped going. Religion plays a massive part in an Irish upbringing. Then there's a point, for me, where it was just like "I don't really buy into this" . . . My mam goes again now.

GB: She's praying for you and for the rest of the family and everybody else?

NG: [Laughs.] Well, one would hope, yeah.

GB: So, you stopped going . . . and that was a relief—Thank God that's over?

NG: Well, not really. I haven't got anything against . . . It doesn't work for me. My wife and her mother and father, they go to church and sing the hymns with great enthusiasm. I kind of envy people that have that with religion, that they can insert it into their lives and it guides them through whatever path. I genuinely wish I had something like that. I don't believe that, but I don't scoff at people who believe that at all. I kind of envy them. My path is different. And my wife will undoubtedly bring the boys up in a certain way, and I guess I wouldn't be against that.

GB: Okay, now, when you arrived on the scene with a big bang and Oasis, you were 27-ish, which is kind of advanced for a budding rock and roll star.
NG: That's when everyone starts dying, in the musical annals, is at twenty seven . . .

GB: You weren't behind the door telling people how good you were and how great you were going to be, and you were fairly cocky about the whole thing, were you not?
NG: Well, it wasn't the time for wallflowers. You know? We were out to inspire a generation.

GB: What is it, do you think, that appeals to so many people in what you do? Thinking of football crowds singing tender love songs like *Wonderwall* and . . .
NG: Yeah, I truly don't know, and I genuinely have no interest in finding out, because I think if I did, I'd know what it was. And if I knew what it was, I'd just do it all the time. And I'd be very cynical about it . . . I just put it down to magic . . . But when I'm coming off stage, every night, I'm always mystified by it.

GB: Drugs . . . Is it absolutely essential that rock and rollers need drugs? Does it absolutely have to happen?
NG: [Laughs.] Well, er . . . yes! Ha.

GB: Okay.
NG: Not really. No, evidently, you don't need them. I was doing all that stuff before I was even in a band . . . So, when you become a rock star and you have money and a big house, you tend to stay in, and you get bored. And you surround yourself with like-minded people. But there came a point for me, in 1998 . . . I went to bed one night thinking, "This is the greatest thing ever. I am living the dream. I'm like the new Keith Richards." And I woke up the next morning and I thought, "This is boring. I hate all these people. I'm not doing it any more." And I've never done it since.

GB: And when you were on all that stuff, did it improve your creativity or you musicianship?

NG: Not in the slightest . . . I've got to say, we were doing the wrong drugs. We were doing the one that's historically known to destroy any creativity. There are psychedelic drugs that evidently help. You know, *Sergeant Pepper's* wasn't made on drinking tea, was it? . . . But everything that we ever did when we were in the studio, out of it, late at night, thinking, "This is better than the Beatles! Wow! Wait till you hear this." You get up the next day and listen to it when you were straight, and you go, like, "That's diabolical!" And you'd have to quickly wipe the tapes and pretend it never happened. We had a lot of those scenarios.

GB: Was it easy to stop?

NG: No, because trying to kick illegal drugs leads you to prescription drugs. And they're worse, because you can get those and you're not breaking the law. And doctors, they're quite willing: they'll sell you anything, if you've got the money . . . I remember, I went out one night and I thought, "I'm giving up drinking and everything." And I just looked around the people I was with, and I thought, "I don't like you. I don't like you. I don't like your missus. I've *never* liked you. I don't even know what I'm doing with all these people."

Well, that's just me. That's the way I am. It's all or nothing. Luckily for me, quite soon after that, I met Sarah.

GB: Fantastic . . . The high that you get from whatever it is you're on, does is it equal the high you get from going on stage in Slane or Maine Road or Croke Park . . . ?

NG: No, there's nothing—and I've done it all, and you've got to trust me on this—there's nothing in the world that, when you walk out on a stage, before you've even played a note, you've only got to put your arms out like that, and that's it, game over. Can't beat that. That's why we still do it. That's why Paul McCartney still does it, and the Rolling Stones. Lord knows, they don't need the money. They're not doing it for credibility . . . They're doing it because it is the ultimate high . . . It can never be replicated, and it's something you want to keep and keep and keep.

GB: Are we talking to you at a good time in your life? You have Sarah, and you have Sonny and Donovan, and it looks like you have marital harmony . . .

NG: You mustn't forget the girl, Anais, she'd kill me.

GB: Yeah, Anais.

NG: But, yeah, you've talked to me at the best time . . . Because it was my first wedding anniversary about a week ago, although we've been together for, like, twelve years, and my wife is still my best friend in the world . . .

GB: By the way, going back to all the trauma between you and Liam— and it went on and on—did Peggy get involved?

NG: Oh, yeah, of course . . . Well, this Christmas just gone, she said, "Call. I've told him to call you, and I'm telling you to call him. So it's about time you spoke . . ." And we exchanged texts on Christmas Day and stuff like that . . . See, Liam doesn't have a phone, 'cause he's always losing them, so you've got to text his missus's phone.

GB: Yes.

NG: My mam doesn't take sides, but she's quite calm about it now. She's like, "It'll be all right." And it will be all right . . . And we were never a Christmas Day kind of family anyway. So to start forcing that now would be just weird.

GB: But there's no question of you all getting together as a band?

NG: Oh, no . . . Publicly, there's things been said. Privately, I can assure you, nobody wants it.

GB: As we speak, you're going on Croke Park tonight. You spoke about the high of going on to face that crowd. Is there any semblance whatsoever of "Here we go again, get it over with . . ."? Do you feel nervous about tonight?

NG: I've never felt nervous. When I go on at festivals or at my shows, the people are there to see me. And there's only one person in that crowd—only one person here today—who's the expert at being me, and that's me. So, I can't fail. I can sing, I can play, my band are great, I write songs that they all love. That's it. If I can't enjoy that, I retire . . . I never, never think, "This is just another gig." You know, people have paid money to see it. It'd better be good.

GB: You're never afraid of making a mistake playing, or forgetting the words . . . ?

NG: Oh, no, I do forget the words sometimes. But a quick "La-di-da" will get you through that. Luckily for me, I write songs that people like to sing . . . But now, with the advent of YouTube and all that, you can get found out. People will say, "Ever seen that thing on YouTube of you forgetting the words to *Don't Look Back in Anger*?" And I'll be like, "Oh, shit, I thought I got away with that."

About two months ago I was away for a couple of months, and we'd had a new kitchen put in in our house. And I was just playing a song one night I'd played a million times before, and I just found myself just drifting off. And I was thinking, "I wonder what it looks like," 'cause I hadn't seen it, 'cause my missus had sorted all that out. And as I was kind of thinking, "I hope they've not put the dishwasher in a stupid place . . . I hope they've moved the sink from under the window," and the rest of my band were falling around laughing. I'd completely forgotten where I was.

GB: Come back now . . . We covered church. What about God? Would you describe yourself as believing in God or not?

NG: Again, it's a complicated thing, because I believe in the power of love and humanity and real things. If you're asking me, do I see the hand of God at work in the world, I'd have to say "No," for the simple reason that, if God as a real thing exists, with all the things over the last decade that have been—terrorism and wars are fought in His name, or in Its name; all the innocent people that have died in the name of God—wouldn't you think now would be the right time for some kind of global sign? And, of course, that opens the argument of faith, and then repeat that argument to fade out to grey, and it goes on for ever, doesn't it? To believe in God is for faith . . . I live in the here and now, and I go back to what I said at the beginning: I wish that I believed in that. People that believe in it strongly, I envy them, in a way. I *don't*. I believe the end is the end, you know?

There's a line in one of the songs off my latest record, and it's a song I wrote about my wife, and it says, "You're the only god I'll ever need." If I do believe in God, I believe it's here somewhere, in everybody . . . My wife is an angel to me, and a real one, because she appeared out of the smoke in a nightclub when I was at my lowest, and I've never looked back since then . . . But she's not a heavenly body: she's real. I can touch her. And I do, regularly, and it's great . . . For me . . . not for her. [Laughs.] And God is in *me*, I think, and God is in her, and God certainly is in my children. So, that's what I believe in.

GB: Last question. Suppose everything they taught you in St Bernard's, way back when, is all true. When you get there to the pearly gates and He/She is standing in front of you, what will you say?

NG: I'd say, "You've heard *Don't Look Back in Anger,* right?" And He'd say, "Of course." And I'd say, "Well, look, it's me. Let us in. I can play you a tune. I robbed some stuff, I took a lot of drugs, but I'm all right. I can write a song. Let us in . . . I can't play the harp, though!"

GB: Thank you.
NG: Thank you very much . . . Nice one.

SINÉAD O'CONNOR

Mother Knows Best

There are those who dismiss Sinéad O'Connor, out of hand, as a fruitcake. I am not one of them, although I do acknowledge that, from time to time, she supplies this particular constituency of ditch-hurlers and mud-slingers with all the ammunition they need.

I am more inclined to look at the family tree. Sinéad and her brother, Joseph, and sister, Eimear, seem to me an exceptionally gifted and creative trio. Over the years, I have got to know them all fairly well and found it an immensely rewarding experience.

Sinéad gets the headlines. She's good at that, and pop stars need headlines to remain pop stars. Occasionally, I will read something that makes me worried for her well-being, but then I meet her and realise she is fine. Occasionally troubled, occasionally furious, but generally fine.

She was certainly fine on the morning when we recorded our interview, in 2009, in her seaside home in Co. Wicklow. A carved Renaissance statue of the Madonna stood vigil like a chaperone over the interview in Sinéad's front room, her presence part devotion and part irony, I suspect. Sinéad has a very dry and knowing wit.

During the interview I found myself—as, no doubt, a few viewers did too—trying to read what was written on her hand, in case it was significant. It said, "*Piano lessons.*" As soon as we were gone, she needed to find a piano teacher for one of her children. Nothing significant, but still important.

Some journalists wonder how Sinéad O'Connor's musical career has lasted as long as it has. The answer is that it *is* a musical career, not, as some might think, merely a celebrity one. Sinéad silences her critics whenever she opens her mouth to sing. She is, quite simply, a magnificent singer.

Why? Because she means it. Every word and note is felt and *meant*.

That is why, however much they might be inclined, or even entitled, to dismiss her grenade-throwing rhetoric, the Catholic Church leadership should pay attention to what she says about the real root of the clerical abuse problem: those responsible, and those who covered up what they did, just didn't believe that God was watching.

It's a simple thought, but it stops you in your tracks. She's good at that, Sinéad. Do stop in your tracks, once in a while. And listen.

～

GB: Now, in your new album, *Theology,* you start with a rather surprising admission. You admit to stealing a Bible. What's the story there?

SOC: Well, how can I put it? I stole a Bible, basically . . . I was going through a rough time in life, and I wanted a small Bible that I could keep in my pocket, for "clinging to" purposes. I was very heavily pregnant and it was Christmas Eve, and I had a big bag on each side of me, weighed down, and I was about to give birth. And then, when I looked along the bookshop, there was this long queue, and I said, "Okay . . ." Had a chat with God about it, and we figured it should be free anyway. So, I said, "Okay . . ." but I'd make up for it by doing something good with it.

GB: Excuses, excuses! Okay, did you make use of it, then?

SOC: I did make use of it, very much so. I ended up giving that Bible to a guy I know who had done some pretty terrible things in his life. I reckoned he needed it more than I did.

GB: And do you think it did him any good?

SOC: I do, in terms of a comfort.

GB: What do you find attractive about the Old Testament?

SOC: I think that maybe the Old Testament appeals to someone who is of a kind of artistic or emotional kind of nature. It's very emotional, it's very dramatic, it's very poetic. And I like the books of the prophets, especially. I was just always very moved by them . . . They are people who lived thousands and thousands of years ago; the stuff that they were saying is just as relevant nowadays as it was in those days . . .

GB: Tell me about your early upbringing and religious teaching. Was it conventional?

SOC: Pretty conventional. I was born in Ireland, which was a Catholic theocracy . . . which had good points and bad points. My father used to take us to Mass every Sunday. I would think I'm one of the lucky people, insofar as I didn't soak up any of the negative aspects of Catholicism. I fell in love with it. You know, I was very happy with it, although I noticed that the priests seemed very unhappy. They didn't come across to me as if they were taking any joy out of what they believed, either out of Catholicism or out of God. It was all about suppressing your emotions and suppressing your thoughts and trying to control what you thought.

And, to some extent, to be a good Catholic you had to have low self-esteem. You had to think of yourself as being a bad person. It was a sin to think you were a good person. Therefore, you were only going to be *unhappy*, because you told yourself what a complete waste of space you were, all the time.

When I was growing up I seemed to already have a sense that God and religion were two separate things, and it was quite important to understand that.

GB: Do you think, looking back on it now, that you were particularly holy?

SOC: I don't know that I was "particularly holy", 'cause I was a little devil, obviously. But, yeah, I was religious. I was in love with the whole idea of *me* from the second I was born. And I prayed all the time, and, yeah, I guess, I wouldn't say that I was "holy", but I was religious.

GB: Go back now to the difference between God and religion.

SOC: Well, before there was religion there was God. You know, if religion wasn't there, there would still be a God. And I think, sometimes, it thinks it is God. So, often, I think perhaps its problem is, it doesn't believe in God. There is a crisis of faith. And I do believe that when it came to the Catholic Church, during the years of the sexual abuse and the subsequent years of trying to unravel that, they had a crisis of faith: they didn't believe in a God that was watching.

GB: In one of your hymns on *Theology* . . . this is you talking to God:
> And I've heard religion say you are to be feared,
> But I don't buy into everything I hear,
> And it seems to me you're hostage to those rules
> That were made by religion and not by you.
> And I'm wondering, will you ever get yourself free?
> Is it bad to think you might like help from me?
> Is there anything my little heart can do
> To help religion share us with you?

Kind of unusual vision of God, that this omnipotent, omniscient being is, in fact, a prisoner of religion . . .

SOC: Yeah, well, when I was a kid, the way I used to see it was, they told me that the Holy Spirit is like a bird, but yet they thought that the Eucharist was also God and Jesus. But they would have it in this cupboard, in the tabernacle—a cupboard that they would lock and unlock; and *they* would say when we could have . . . be with it. And I used to feel I couldn't breathe properly with the idea of this bird, or this thing, being locked up in a cupboard.

There is an awful lot of dictating by religion as to who God can love and who God can't love. For example, there is an attitude in the Catholic Church towards gay people: that they're not allowed to receive Communion, that priests will shake hands with them but won't give them Communion. But my attitude is, well, God made gay people, and who has the right to say who God can love?

God is the most libelled character in history. If God were actually here, He or She or It would be suing a whole lot of people for libel.

Religion teaches a version of God as being this aggressive kind of punishing, judging, negative character, and I never believed that, and I felt really strongly—on God's behalf, actually—that people need to stand up for God against that rubbish.

GB: Well, what is your image of God? When you're making that prayer, that hymn, that song to God, what's in your head?

SOC: It's complicated, isn't it? 'Cause the way we're brought up, we're brought up to believe that there's the Trinity—God the Father, God the Son and God the Holy Spirit. And, to me, I have relationships with God, I have relationships with Jesus, but my main relationship would be with what I would call the Holy Spirit. To me, it's a spirit. I can never understand it, because I'm a human being, and human beings are limited. So, none of us knows and no-one, except Jesus, has ever come back to tell us what it's like.

GB: All right. Jesus asked his Disciples, "Who do you say I am?" What is your answer to that?

SOC: Well, to me, when it comes to Jesus, I don't know whether that man ever existed or not. I don't know if the story is true. And, to me, it doesn't matter whether that's true or not, because I've always believed in Jesus the spirit or the energy.

GB: Why would you doubt that such a man existed? Because it's fairly reasonably well established that, whatever kind of person he was, the four Gospels give a reasonable account of the places he lived in and the philosophy he taught.

SOC: Yeah, well, I suppose it's not that I'm disputing that. All I'm saying is that, from the time I was a kid, that never mattered to me, whether he was real or not. He does exist as a spirit that you can communicate with and have a relationship with . . . and I did have a very deep relationship with, and still do.

You know, it's widely known that I had a very difficult upbringing . . .

GB: Yes.

soc: . . . and there were times in my life where I really did have to depend on Jesus; and the thought of Jesus and the image of Jesus, the actual image of the Crucifixion, got me through a lot of things when I was a kid. I would close my eyes and focus on the image of the Crucifixion. There would be Jesus and there would be the Crucifixion, and there would be blood coming from Jesus' heart down, down to the ground and into me. And somehow that gave me strength.

GB: What I'm getting is that you don't believe in a personal God?

soc: What is a personal God, before I say whether I don't believe it?

GB: The man with the white beard who answers your prayers and is listening to you and keeping an eye on you.

soc: No, but I do believe there *is* a God. I don't know what It is or what It looks like. The best I can guess is that It's an energy, a life force, which exists beyond, and also within, us.

GB: More than most people I've ever come across, especially in show business, you have been searching all your life . . . You've delved into Hinduism and you've delved into the Jewish faith . . . And I'm wondering, what do any of those beliefs offer you that the Catholic Church that you were born into does not?

soc: Well, they offer me the same things. It's all the same God to me. It's just different cultures express it differently.

GB: But no-one has the real secret? No-one has the truth?

soc: No, nobody. Because we are limited as beings. We're trapped in a human body. I think when you die you probably find out what's the truth.

GB: The Blessed Virgin . . . One cannot escape the beautiful statue behind you which you brought especially from France . . .

soc: Yes.

GB: You didn't nick that as well, did you? I hope not . . .

soc: I couldn't put it in my pocket. [Laughs.] It's *very* heavy. Well, again, because of the Ireland I grew up in, the Virgin Mary was everywhere. But I was born on the 8th of December, which is the Feast of the Immaculate Conception. And, in those times, if you were born on that day and you were a girl, every time it was your birthday someone would give you something that had the Virgin Mary on it. So, since I was young, I collected Virgin Mary things. I've got zillions of them.

GB: And what is your belief about her? How do you see her?

SOC: Well, I suppose I'm kind of a hodge-podge, and I've created my own little theology. And I see her, Jesus, God, the Holy Spirit, as all the same thing. Again, I don't know whether there was this woman and there was this virgin birth—I'm not saying there wasn't; I'm not saying there was—but it doesn't matter to me. She is someone I would pray to and think about, and I find myself, all the time, saying, "Holy Mother" this or "Holy Mother" that. And that's one of the things I liked from studying different theologies: the idea that God is a mother as well as a father.

GB: You don't see her as an intermediary between you and God in any way, no?

SOC: I do sometimes. But other times I just take the direct line . . .

GB: Okay. Do you believe you have a guardian angel?

SOC: I believe that we have spirit guides who hang around us and influence us. I wouldn't call it a guardian angel.

My granny, my mother's mother, was my godmother also . . . and I used to say to her, "Well, how are you going to look after me, if you're dead before my parents?" And she said, "Well, I'll be up whispering in God's ear and telling him to make sure you're all right and look after you."

GB: And has she?

SOC: Ah, well, I don't know. I won't know till I get there. But I like to think that she has. But I do think there are spirit guides around, definitely, who guide you in the right way, if you're actually paying attention . . . Because, of course, God made a big, big mistake, which was free will. Right?

GB: Why do you think free will was a mistake?

SOC: Look at the state of the world! Look at how we treat each other, how we deal with each other, how we look after our environment . . .

GB: You haven't, clearly, formally, left the Catholic Church ... ?

SOC: No, I consider myself to be a Catholic person, by culture and by choice ...

GB: And your children are being baptised ... ?

SOC: That's because they can't make their Holy Communion *unless* they get baptised. That's the only reason I'm getting them baptised. I don't see why there is a need to feel that, without the Church, the child doesn't belong to God. The child already *is* God, as far as I'm concerned—came from God and knows more about God than the lot of us put together. Do you know what I mean?

So, the only reason I would baptise the boys now is because they all have to get baptised to make their Holy Communion. They want to make their Holy Communion, because they don't want to be different to other kids.

I am a mass of contradictions, but I consider myself proudly Catholic—by birth and by culture and by nationality. It isn't necessarily that I *chose* to be Catholic or that I believe in all the rules and regulations, or that I go to Mass or la, la, la, la. But in my DNA, I'm a Catholic person.

GB: If there was one thing that you would try to change in the Catholic Church, what would it be?

SOC: It would be that, instead of using the image of the Crucifixion, I would use the image of the Resurrection. It's so much more joyful and hopeful. And, it seems to me, if the man did exist and he went through all of that trouble ... then to raise himself from the grave, to show us that there is no need to be afraid of death—which is what I think Jesus was all about—there is no need to fear death.

GB: When you look back now—and I remember the day very well when you were ordained: this was a schismatic Church—basically, looking back on that now, do you regret that ... ? Or what is your attitude?

SOC: No, I'm really proud of it. I don't like to talk about it. In a way, I regret *ever* talking about it. I should have kept it private, but it's something that's very precious. To me, it was a calling. I always, from the time I was a kid, I knew I had a vocation. I used to pray to God to make me not want to be a nun ... I was that worried about it ...

GB: Why?

SOC: Well, why do you think? [Laughs.] The obvious reason, do you know what I mean?

GB: Yeah.

SOC: But I knew there was something there. And I felt very strongly about it. And had it been legal for there to be women priests, I would have been the first one at the door, before being a singer or before being anything else.

So, then, obviously, when I heard that there were a couple of bishops who were willing to ordain women, I was going to be first at the door.

What I'm attracted to in the Rasta movement is that they use music as a priesthood. And since I obviously am not allowed to be, officially, a proper priest, doing the work that a proper priest would do, I'm interested in using music as a priesthood. So, that's a vocation, definitely, the same as a priesthood is.

GB: Let me go to your talent . . . Do you believe that you were given this talent to make music and that it is a sacred duty to use it as such?

SOC: From the time that I knew I had music inside me, which is probably when I was about four or so, I associated it with God. That music was something that God gave me, which would get me out of the particular situation that I wanted to get out of. And I made a deal with God, at a very young age, that I would, in gratitude for that, use my voice and use my music to do whatever I could to represent that Spirit.

GB: And can you remember clearly making that promise?

SOC: Yeah. Absolutely, yeah. I made this promise to God one night in bed. And I remember it distinctly, 'cause I used to pray in bed, and I always said that "Glory be . . ." prayer. And I said, "Yeah, when I'm bigger I'm going to use my voice and my singing in my music to do whatever I can to pay you back . . . you know, for being there for me."

GB: What about evil?

SOC: What about it?

GB: Do you think there are evil people in the world or do you think there is a concept of the Devil rambling around, seeing who he can destroy? What do you think about that? You've encountered evil and badness in the world, of course you have . . . ?

SOC: Yeah, and luckily I also *haven't,* thank God, encountered evil. To me, evil is child-killing—people who steal people's children and use them sexually and kill them. You know, that kind of thing to me is evil. I don't know if there is a Devil as such. I don't really believe there is. But I do believe that the word "evil" is the word "live" backwards. You know: life gone the wrong way around can be an evil thing.

And I think there are certain people who *are* that way. They absolutely have to be taken off the street. Child thieves, for example. But I don't know if they come from the Devil or what makes them like that.

You could argue that the Devil has been through the Catholic Church, given what's happened with the sexual abuse thing. My mother used to always say, "The Devil dresses as a priest." So, I think, to some extent, there was some type of evil spirit that went through Catholicism in the years where that was happening to children.

GB: What do you think happens to the Hitlers and the Stalins of the world—all those atrociously, appallingly bad people? Do they somewhere get a come-uppance?

SOC: From what I have studied, between the College of Psychic Studies and looking at Scriptures, I don't believe in Hell. I believe everybody goes to God . . . But what I do believe is that, if you have someone like Hitler or someone like any of us, if we die and we have caused hurt to anybody, I do believe that our spirit has to hang around and do its best to try to make up for that damage.

GB: It kind of falls into line with the idea of Purgatory, doesn't it?

SOC: I wouldn't even put it like that, because I don't believe there is anything negative about it. It's not punishing. I believe, and it says in Scriptures, all people go to God, and God loves everyone, and that the person that God goes looking for is the lost person—the sheep or the prodigal son or whatever.

I believe, when you die, you become pure compassion. Therefore, you think, "Oh, my God, look at this terrible stuff I did. I have to do what I can to fix it." It may take some time for someone like Hitler. You know, it's hard to know how someone like that would ever actually make up for what they've done.

GB: Do you think Granny and your mother and other loved ones will be waiting for you on the other side when you die?

SOC: I do, yeah.

GB: Do you think about death?

SOC: Oh, all the time, yeah. Every day.

GB: Why?

SOC: I think most people think about death every day, but just we don't say it. It's the great pink elephant in the room, isn't it? No-one really discusses it. We're all afraid of it. We've been conditioned to be frightened of it and think of it as a terrible thing.

GB: And are you?

SOC: I'm half and half. Half of me is terrified of it, and the other half is completely calm and confident. I'm hoping that the way I go is that I get some illness or something, so that I know I'm on the way and that I'd somehow be able to enjoy the journey.

I would like to have enough trust and faith that I wouldn't let my fear overtake me, because fear is human. And some part of me has been with God since before we were born, and some part of all of us knows that that's where we are going back.

COLIN FARRELL

Just a Man

"I thought I'd missed you, man."

Colin Farrell and his lovely sister Claudine had just flown in especially from LA, at their own expense, to record a deeply probing interview for a new and untried RTÉ series that had a budget of zilch to pay its contributors. And yet he greeted me with a huge hug. He was clearly up for it.

Because the period of Colin's biggest career success came after my period at the helm of *The Late Late Show*, he was missing the "Interviewed by Gay Byrne" medal and certificate from his collection of accolades and was apparently delighted to tick the box. Only marginally more significantly, he had also just added a Golden Globe to the mantelpiece, for his performance in Martin McDonagh's deliciously black comedy thriller *In Bruges*. He was a megastar again, after a few years in which his many demons had nearly succeeded in dragging him to oblivion.

Colin Farrell is gorgeous. There's no other way of putting it. He's a beautiful human specimen. I happen to know that his ex-footballer father is another head-turner, but one who contents himself with health-food retail rather than Hollywood. And Claudine provides yet more evidence that beauty genes are unfairly distributed. Some families simply get more than their fair share. But Colin adds something else to his looks: vulnerability. He came into the Four Seasons, Ballsbridge, on a cold winter's day with unlaced Dr Martens and an unbuttoned shirt and instantly had half the staff reaching for sewing kits. People will do that for Colin: they'll fall in love with him and come to his rescue.

Which is just as well, because he's needed quite a bit of rescuing in his time. But only because, for a long time, he hadn't fully worked out how to save himself.

As we talked, for well over an hour, I discovered an extraordinarily bright, lucid and thoughtful man, totally honest about his behaviour, his flaws, his passions and his values. In the end, we ran our intended half-hour programme at twice the length. To hear Colin speaking so candidly about the self-destructive lows of his addictions—to drink, sex and drugs—and the highs of recovery and fatherhood was simply compelling.

Two years later, at Christmas, I bumped into him again, in the same hotel, and it was like meeting an old friend. That's the privilege of the job I do: if you create a safe space and opportunity for people to share their deepest thoughts and experiences—and don't abuse that trust—they will become your friends. Forget fame. It is always trust and truth that matters.

∽

GB: At time of going to press, congratulations on the award for *In Bruges*. Throughout all the awards ceremonies, you kept your family very much to the forefront and gave them all a mention . . . Tell me about how important they are to you.

CF: Very important . . . and always have been a great support system. You know, families, what is it? It's the first society that you're aware of. You have your first experience of status, your first experience of envy, your first experience, certainly, of love . . . And it does shape you.

GB: Tell me about the childhood and your *rearing* . . .

CF: My rearing? My rare oul' times? As you know, grew up in Castleknock, which is probably one of the more affluent areas of North Dublin, and I seem to remember having a real easy childhood. A lot of football—*lot* of football! School, I went to St Brigid's.

GB: Was it a Catholic upbringing . . . ? You weren't an altar boy, no?

CF: I did two Masses!

GB: [Laughs.] And . . .?

CF: And I was so *fucking* bored! The only reason I did the two Masses was to get off class, and then I chose class ahead of it, because it was so dull.

GB: But apart from that, you were brought up a Catholic?

CF: Once a week, Saturday evening Mass in Castleknock. We'd go to see the girls . . . But it wasn't a particularly Catholic upbringing, no, not that I remember.

GB: So, what about the moral guidance that you were given at that age?

CF: Moral values. You know, at certain times in my life, certain behaviours of mine would lead people to believe that there was absolutely nothing, no moral or no value. No positive virtue.

GB: You were a bold boy . . .

CF: You know, I was the youngest of four—very diplomatic way of saying yes . . . !

GB: Castleknock you didn't like very much . . . ?

CF: I didn't like Castleknock College.

GB: Gormanston—you didn't like . . . ?

CF: I *didn't* like Gormanston. [Laughs.] Seeing a pattern here . . . ? I just got ill at ease with it . . . A system, by its very nature, was something that was to be pushed against . . . I mean, I had terrible results in school after fourteen. Never did my homework. Never studied. I couldn't. It was the practical thing of not being able to figure out how to study . . . I didn't know what the itch was, but I started to scratch it in kind of acting out and being a bit mischievous and bunking off, and started smoking and simple stuff . . .

GB: And were you expelled from Gormanston?

CF: From Gormanston? No . . .

GB: I think you hit a teacher. You put him up against a wall . . . ?

CF: No, that was Bruce College.

GB: Oh, that was Bruce College, was it?

CF: Yes. I didn't hit him. I didn't follow through. 'Cause he put his hands on me. And it wasn't the first time a teacher had put his hands on me. It was the first time a teacher put his hands on me and I was bigger than him [Laughs] . . . So . . . I threw him against the wall and said, "You little fucker." You know, I was thrilled the day that I was asked to leave.

GB: Okay, well, come forward now . . . You found acting . . . ?

CF: Yeah.

GB: Was it fame you were after or was it the *act* of acting . . . ?

CF: Fame . . .

GB: You wanted fame?

CF: In the beginning, sure . . .

GB: You auditioned for Boyzone?

CF: Yeah, yeah . . . I went along and I sang. He says I got in. Louis [Walsh] *still* says. I didn't. I remember the phone call I got from Castleknock saying, "You're actually a *really* bad singer, and it's not going to work out."

And the acting thing . . . I think the idea of fame brought me to acting, but fairly much that was substituted by a curiosity, which was ignited in the first acting class I ever did . . . And I couldn't understand it—still defies my attempts at explaining what it is. But it was what I wanted to do.

GB: But once you were in, then, you went from zero to sixty in four point two seconds: from a bit part in *Ballykissangel*, you were mixing with the Hollywood stars . . . Why do you think that was? Was that luck or work or talent?

CF: Erm, all of the above, and I don't know what percentage of what. Again it defies too much thought. There's no answer why this should happen to me. There's better-looking fellas than me out there. There's better actors than me out there. There's fellas that would probably have more luck if they sat at a table in Vegas. There's fellas that work harder than me out there. I've no idea why. I just know that it happened to me. And I carried that . . . It lent itself to feelings of lack of worth, or "I don't deserve it." And then I made a decision: you know, I'm *not* going to change . . . I'm going to stay the same to prove that maybe I'm not any different. You know, I kind of orchestrated my own arrested development, in a way . . . It's not natural at twenty-two . . . So you press pause on any potential for growth as a human being that you may have. It's—it's bizarre.

GB: Okay. You were never exactly a good boy, but when this fame and fortune happened to you, it was like being given the keys to the sweetshop. And I'm talking about booze, sex, drugs, all of that . . .
CF: You got it in the wrong order, you got it in the wrong order . . .

GB: [Laughs.]
CF: Two to number 1 . . .

GB: I haven't much experience in this field—you'll have to forgive me. But, anyway, you grabbed at them, and I want to know why . . .
CF: At the end of the day, it was a young fella having a good time . . . I've always had a propensity towards addiction.

GB: Oh.
CF: Always. And I got into what I would call, personally, "trouble" with booze and drugs, the first time when I was nineteen . . . Before I ever

left Ireland for those shores, I was in trouble, and I was already seeking help for the amount of stuff that I was doing and, and somehow not being able to stop doing it, even as it was making—kind of cementing—this sadness that I was feeling.

I had a blast of a time. I went over to Los Angeles and it was handed to me on a plate . . . And I was very much of the mind: make hay while the sun shines. And I remember saying, you know, "If I'm not going to take advantage of this experience, they should give it to somebody else." . . . And the negative aspect was loneliness—never figured it in. Missing my family and all my friends. Never figured it in, this very clear and very pronounced severance from that life. And so, I simultaneously had an amazing time and incredible adventure and, bit by bit, started to be chipped away at. And I didn't even know it.

GB: We're so used to hearing about people who take drugs, that they're more creative . . .

CF: Horseshit, for me. I mean, I fully subscribed myself to the belief that that was true—that only out of a certain amount of pain and darkness and reaching those dark recesses of the soul could creativity be born or could anything worth creation be—be given breath . . . And I found that to not be the case . . . I was filling myself with a clatter of stuff, you know, I was putting into my body . . . and I couldn't stop, and I just knew I was really sick.

GB: Were you becoming unemployable?

CF: Yeah . . . And I had people that were in my life . . . who were very concerned—not for whether I was employable or not—for whether I was going to be alive. And they got involved. And family had to get involved . . .

GB: This was a closing in?

CF: Yeah, it was a long time coming. I remember my sister saying to me, or maybe my brother, suggesting that they were going to sign me in; and being so self-centred and so dogmatic in the pursuit of what I wanted to pursue, which was oblivion, that I remember saying to him, "Try it! Get the people with the white coats and see if I don't fucking stab them all! Do it! See what happens . . ." And so, by the end, as I had to do, I—I relinquished, you know. I gave up. I just realised—I found myself in that very humble position where all was nearly lost, and I had no idea who I was or what I had become.

GB: You described it as a "spiritual malady".

CF: Yeah, it was . . . I was fucked, man . . . I was heartbroken . . . I just had a broken heart . . . Nobody would know but those that were very close to me. On the film set I was most the fun. I was gregarious. I'd make the crew laugh, and nobody would have any idea. But I was heartbroken. And yet I was aware that I had all these beautiful things in my life, and I had this beautiful son that was three years of age, and I had friends that were incredibly dear to me and a family that cared about me, that I cared about inordinately, and this career, this—more important than a career—this job, this vocation, this whatever it is.

GB: So, there came a moment, then, when you said to your brother or your sister, or your mum and dad or whoever it was—you said, "Yeah, I give in . . ."?

CF: I said, "I'll go in, yeah." A man flew down to Uruguay, where we were shooting *Miami Vice* . . . We got to the end of *Miami Vice*, and they said, "That's a wrap," and I went straight from the set to a plane, and I woke up two days later in a fucking rehab place going, "Oh, no, I've just come full circle in the world of clichés: I have the sex tape and now I have the rehab."

GB: [Laughs.] The twelve steps of AA and rehab are rooted in spirituality . . . How does it work?

CF: I don't know the twelve steps, 'cause I don't do it any more, and I only got to step 4 in rehab . . . But step 1 is realising that you're power-less. And I was. But, by Jesus, you remember rehab: the first two weeks I was kicking and screaming, saying to all the counsellors, "No, look . . . My passport has a harp on it. I'm Irish. I'm not giving up drink." I said, "I just want to get off the other stuff." And they were like, "All right, fine." And then two weeks into rehab I was like, "Why the fuck am I fighting so hard to keep this thing in my life, this little bit of liquid, you know, that's never taken me anywhere good? Yeah, it has given me some great nights—as I said, howling at the moon—and great memories of the lads, but it has really caused me, personally, just a lot of torment. Why am I fighting to keep that in my life?" Now, that was about two weeks into rehab, and then, the next day, I was like, "My name is Colin, and I'm an alcoholic!"

This is part of the process, to look really, really into yourself and find out about who you are, what you are . . . You know, it was kind of like,

"All right, I have an identity. I'm a bad boy . . . and I fuck as many girls as I can, and I drink as much as I can, and I'm the last person standing," which I was, most of the time. And then that's all, all gone. Silence. Who the fuck am I? Literally. Wow. Who am I?

GB: So, who were you?

CF: I was, I was . . . I had such a liberating moment when I realised how many fears I had . . .

GB: Fear of what?

CF: Fear of judgement. Fear of failure, you know? Fear of inadequacy. Fear of being a bad father, bad friend. Fear of being bad in the sack. Fear of being a bad actor. Fear of not being the last man standing in the bar. You fucking name it. And for years I had said, "The only fears in my life are spiders and flying." Horseshit that was again. You know, so, who am I? I don't know. Just a man. Just a man. No more, no less than that. No weaker, no stronger.

GB: The twelve steps ask you to make a decision to turn your will and your life over to the care of God, as you understand Him.

CF: Uh-huh. I don't know if I *do* understand Him . . . Do you know what? I copped out . . . and made my son, like, my God. I made *him* the absolute force of benevolence and goodness and something that I aspired to.

GB: And is that because you couldn't identify God?

CF: It's because I was already making a big leap by being in there, and I wasn't ready to . . . just go, "Okay, I'm in this situation. Now, I'm going to adopt all of your ideas about everything."

GB: No. Did you go so far as to say He's not there at all?

CF: No, I didn't. I did when I came out. I tried to be an atheist. I tried hard. I didn't have the faith.

GB: [Laughs.] Figure that one out. That's either very deep or very mad . . . You didn't have the faith to be an atheist. Good one.

CF: I just didn't . . . !

GB: So, if you didn't find God on the twelve steps, then what's your state of spirituality today . . . ?

CF: I believe in a connectivity. I believe in elements of the spirit transcending the physical form. I really do. I believe in energy, both positive and negative. I believe it's contagious. I believe it travels great distances, you know? I believe in thought. Thought is incredible, both in its destructive and constructive aspects. Do I think there's one Creator? Don't know. Language, as beautiful as language is, it's too limited. Everything is transient, and life is transient, and I believe there is a possibility that the spirit goes on, when the physical form, you know, relinquishes and dies.

GB: The twelve steps also recommend that you pray and meditate. Presumably you don't pray?
CF: I don't pray . . . No.

GB: Do you meditate?
CF: Still. Yeah, absolutely.

GB: And then, in 2003, little James came along. Now, was that a seismic change for you?
CF: Should have been. Again, resisted it. Resisted it, you know? Wasn't going to change me, man. I was going to be the "Friend-Daddy"—was going to be his pal and . . . and I was still going to have my life the way I wanted it . . . But it did change things, yeah. And it probably . . . I mean, he . . . I don't know if I'd be here talking to you, if I haven't had him. I mean, he was a huge, a huge part of me going in and making certain changes in my life, you know?

GB: 'Cause if you hadn't made that change you would be dead by now?
CF: Yeah.

GB: Tell me what he means to you.
CF: . . . He's just a really, he's a really, really, cool human being. He is nothing but light, and there's no darkness at all there, which is not to say there is no pain. He cries. He has what's termed an affliction, and yet I see it somehow as a gift.

GB: And he draws love and . . .
CF: God! And gives it . . . He is just light.

GB: Is he like you?
CF: Physically, I say no, but, but he certainly is the best of me, and then not the rest, you know? He's like the upgrade, and then some! But I don't even feel, at times, like he's from me. I know he's from me physically. I was in the room when he was conceived. I get it. But at times he

doesn't feel like he's from me. He just feels very much like his own little creation.

GB: Do you play with him?

CF: Yeah, loads! Deadly fun. We wrestle a lot and, and just . . . yeah . . . A lot of touch, a lot of sensory stuff. He has no language.

GB: Does he make sounds?

CF: He makes *loads* of sounds. Oh, my God, like birdsong, yeah, like, you know . . . the botanical garden . . . He's a cheeky little fucker as well. You know, you can see sometimes a little look in his eye if he's trying to get away with something . . .

GB: And do you resent the fact that he wasn't born normal?

CF: No. Not at all . . . The more and more I live, and the more I experience people and life, the less understanding I have of what the perceived "normal" is. I really don't. He is completely normal, as far as I'm concerned, *for him* . . . I only know him one way. He only knows himself one way.

But, you know, I've seen it too much for me to think that my fella's journey is not anything but a gift.

GB: When you talk about James as a gift, are you implying that people like him have some special spiritual value or influence?

CF: Yes. Both. The influence is certainly one of the values. Specifically to James, because of his, erm, we would call an intellectual disability: his levels of cognitive working are different from most of us. He seems to be devoid of an ego. I don't think he misses me—which is brilliant. He lives incredibly in the present . . . And it's not that I wish he missed me. It's great, because it just means that the only one that misses, maybe, is me.

GB: Since you don't believe in God, then, you're not railing against God for letting this thing happen to James?

CF: No, and you know . . . of course when one questions the presence or the potential presence of a Divine Creator . . . makes me sick, and, fuck, man, like there is so much hideous stuff that seems to happen as a result of, of nature. How can that be if this God is benevolent? How can it be? . . . Where is the compassion? Where is the understanding? Where is the humanity? If man is made in your form, is he made in your form physically or is he made in your form spiritually? And if that's the case, and you ask decency of your flock, where is your decency?

So, those things, in moments like that, come up. But I may think something different tomorrow. If I do, I'll text you ...

GB: [Laughs.]
CF: But I don't need to believe in a God as offered to me by anyone. And I certainly don't need to disbelieve it because it's offered by anyone. But I will really believe in goodness ... the power of goodness. I believe in the power of decency.

GB: Is it something akin to the old theology of grace?
CF: Erm, yeah, yeah, yeah, yeah. Absolutely, absolutely, you know? Absolutely.

GB: Do you believe in Heaven and Hell?
CF: Nooooo.

GB: Do you believe Heaven and Hell are within yourself?
CF: Absolutely, yeah.

GB: And do you believe you've been in Hell in yourself?
CF: My own private Idaho. I mean, my own little private Hell I created for myself, yeah.

GB: And compared with that, is this Heaven, where you are now?
CF: I'm so grateful to be here and chatting with you, man, and, yeah, loving my work like I never did.

GB: And have you lost this loneliness that you spoke about?
CF: No, not fully, but I'm okay with loneliness now. That's the difference.

SIR TERRY WOGAN

I Believe in One . . . Blank

I knew there would be letters. There always are. "You must not call Terry Wogan 'Sir Terry,' as he is an Irishman, and his knighthood is honorary." Twenty-six minutes of verbal cut-and-thrust, and all they could think of was what I had called him at the start.

Besides, they were wrong. The knight himself told me that, because he was born before the Proclamation of the Irish Republic, in 1948, he had been assured by some thrice-gartered Sergeant in the College of Arms that he is perfectly entitled to use his title at will—even to joust on Mitcham Common, if he so chooses. So far, he has not exercised that privilege.

By way of symmetry, he is also a Freeman of the City of Limerick, although, as far as I know, he has also yet to exercise his right to drive sheep over Sarsfield Bridge. Terry Wogan wears his titles lightly, as every true gentleman should. *Noblesse oblige.*

For many a year, Sir Terry—as I shall continue to call him—has, to all intents and purposes, been a loyal, tax-paying subject of Her Majesty the Queen of England. In 2006, however, he was surprised to discover that this was something of a reciprocal arrangement. "I'm a TOG," she declared on meeting him in the foyer of Broadcasting House, on the eightieth anniversary of the BBC. TOGs—as only his listeners would know—are Terry's Old Geezers (and Gals). At least, that is his polite euphemism for a senilescent club of more than seven million ne'er-do-wells, who for decades accepted his invitation to "Wake Up to Wogan" on BBC Radio 2. He wore *them* lightly, too, which is why they adored him and why they still miss him.

Let's face it: Sir Terry wears everything lightly, including his Jesuit learning. Father Brian D'Arcy once told me that Terry was as likely to converse with him in Latin or Irish as in English before Brian's "Pause for Thought" items on the Radio 2 breakfast show—something that left his English producers scratching their heads and sniffing for conspiracies. You see, for all his avuncularity and jocularity, Crescent College in Limerick and Belvedere College in Dublin clearly instilled much into Britain's favourite Irishman.

Ah, but had they succeeded in their true mission: giving him a faith for life? In a friendship that had spanned more than fifty years, beginning when he mitched off his banking job to audition as a Radio Éireann continuity announcer, I couldn't remember ever discussing matters of religion with him. Which is why, when he contacted me to say he would like to interview me for his BBC television series *Terry Wogan's Ireland*—now there's a presumptuous title!—I agreed, but only on condition that he *also* record an interview for RTÉ about the things—human or divine—that have given his life meaning.

Touché.

~

GB: Let me take you back to Limerick and your mum and dad and that household. What were they like, and how religious a household was it?

TW: It was 18 Elm Park, Ennis Road, Limerick. It was just me and my brother, Brian. I was an only child for the best part of seven years, which is what marks you, makes you what you are. I quite like my own company best.

I was educated by the Jesuits, in Crescent. I became a Pioneer, as you had to . . . and I gave that up as soon as I could, of course. But in Limerick, my mother and father, they followed the normal thing, which you *had* to. It was a rule: *everybody* went to Mass. But they weren't religious in the same way that my friends' families were religious. My father had a somewhat, well, cynical attitude to religion—the priest-hood in general, not necessarily to God. They were believers—my mother was as well—but they didn't have that kind of deep religiosity that you could find among Irish families—my wife's family, for instance. When I came to Dublin and I met my wife and I went to her house one evening, I found myself on my knees, saying the Rosary.

GB: Are your memories as vivid as mine of the repressive nature of the Catholic upbringing we got and the punishment and the guilt and the darkness about the whole thing?

TW: I was conscious, in Limerick particularly, of being very religious: the Redemptorists would come to town, and there'd be what was called a mission. Now, the mission—the job of the missioner—was to frighten everybody to death. Everybody was going to Hell. There was this incredible idea that everything you did was a sin.

But when you look back you think, "Did this in any way stunt your growth? Did it make you more self-conscious? Did it make you repressed sexually?" I don't think so. [Laughs.] I think we Irish boys and girls, we grew up *despite* the kind of severe Catholic education that we had to endure, because human nature keeps bursting through. And I think the Catholic Church ought to remember that and be a bit more sympathetic about it.

I always feel, you know, the worst sin, of course, was sex. Second sin, vanity. And I always wondered how any of us managed to get out of there with any kind of self-regard at all.

GB: [Laughter.] It comes back to guilt . . . It stopped you going too far, though, didn't it? Ah-ha!
TW: Well, now, to be quite frank, when it came to sex, neither I nor any of my friends got anywhere near it.

GB: Not at any stage?
TW: No.

GB: Because of the guilt and because of the instruction and because of the fear of damnation that hung over your head . . . ?
TW: And yet romance . . .

GB: Blossomed . . .
TW: Romance is better than sex anyway.

GB: I think we'll cut out that statement and pin it up on a board somewhere, probably over Limerick.
TW: No, honestly. The unfulfilled sexual urge is much more satisfactory than the actual act.

GB: I see.
TW: It's less of a disappointment for an awful lot of people.

GB: Did the Js teach you about the birds and the bees . . . ?
TW: No.

GB: Never a mention?
TW: Not a word.

GB: Even in Belvedere?
TW: I suppose, when we moved to Dublin it was tougher for me, because I was fifteen, and, you know, sinfulness, of course, dominated our lives. Sin was everything, wasn't it?

GB: Guilt!

TW: Always! You were *always* committing sin. You know, pick your nose, you're committing a sin. And you remember, when you were a little chap, going in to Confession: you used to make up sins so that you weren't wasting the priest's time. Ridiculous!

And the shades fell from my life years later, when I finished in Belvedere and we went to a Jesuit retreat. And the priest who was lecturing, he said, "Now, listen." He said, "Remember, young men, as you go out, it's almost impossible to commit a mortal sin."

GB: "Be ye holy . . ."

TW: The whole world changed for me. I'd been committing mortal sins for years. [Laughs.] And I was condemned to Hell for ever. And it was a big change for me. I thought, "So, what was it all about, then, all this supposed sin?"

GB: One man making one statement to you . . .

TW: Yes. The watershed. And I thought about that: Original Sin. What sort of an idea is that, that when we're born, we're born with a sin. Where does that come from? I don't remember Jesus saying that. So, these are the kind of little things that undermine your faith. If you think, "Wait a minute now: all this stuff I've been taught, how much validity has that?" So, that's why you question.

GB: And apart from that one priest saying it's almost impossible to commit a mortal sin, was there any other stage that you remember being a watershed in your belief?

TW: I don't think I can remember a specific day. I don't think I ever had what we call "the gift of faith". I always think that I questioned, perhaps too much. And if you have faith, then there's a point where you stop questioning, because you put logic aside and you believe. I didn't have that gift. And my mother always said it was the Jesuits that put me off believing. [Laughs.] That's not true.

GB: Can you ever shake that off, do you think, that brainwashing, if you want to look at it that way, or that early inculcation . . . ?

TW: No, you can't shake it off.

GB: It's in there?

TW: I know so many friends who, for instance, would never go to Communion if they hadn't been to Confession. And I remember going to Communion, because a great friend of mine had died. We had a memorial Mass and I thought, I'm going to make a tribute to him, obviously. He was totally scandalised, my friend. I hadn't been to Confession, and yet I was receiving Communion.

GB: Since you've mentioned the subject, what do you think the Host is?
TW: I was *taught* to believe that transubstantiation meant that's the body and blood of Christ. I personally don't believe that, but who am I to turn up my nose and say to people, "Oh, you shouldn't believe that"? Religions all throughout the world believe all sorts of strange things. If people wish to believe it, if it gives them strength, then it will help.

GB: Who do you think Jesus was, or what?
TW: I think he was an extraordinary man, who *thought* that he was the Son of God, who was an extraordinary preacher, who said the most remarkable things that hadn't been said before, along the lines of "Turn the other cheek" and "Love your neighbour" and all those things that nobody had ever said before. Extraordinary. But he said them to the Jews, and it was St Paul who took the idea a lot further. It was St Paul who spread it to the Gentiles. It's debatable whether Jesus meant this message for anybody other than the Jews. But if he was God, obviously he did.

The thing that worries me *always* about Christianity, and most religions, with the exception perhaps of Buddhism, is this thing of "Go out and convert." That has created so much suffering.

GB: Whether they want to be converted or not.
TW: Yes. If Jesus had just not said that, it might have been a bit better.

GB: Go back now to Crescent and, particularly, Belvedere. Were you not introduced, in Belvedere, into your show-business thing, insofar as you took to the stage and operettas and Gilbert and Sullivan and that class of thing?
TW: It was very strange, yes. They kind of held an audition in my first year in Belvedere, and it turned out I could sing. People will argue with that now, but it turned out *they* thought I could sing.

GB: Did you not realise you could sing before then?
TW: I used to sing a little bit. My father used to sing very loudly in the bathroom every evening as he shaved, waking the neighbours in Limerick. And singing such crowd-pleasers as *Dead for Bread* and

Valentine's Goodbye from *Faust,* and indeed *The Floral Dance,* which is where I learned *The Floral Dance* and then was able to sing it on the radio, to the offence of so many people in Cornwall.

GB: Quite! . . . Okay, now come back to *you.* Suddenly, Belvedere decided this fella can sing . . .
TW: Yes.

GB: Did you enjoy the applause? Did you enjoy the experience?
TW: Yeah, I'm not big on applause. It's nice to have people applauding you, but it didn't become a thing where I said, "Now, this is my life. I must have applause wherever I go." No. What I do is I talk to a microphone or I talk to a camera. So, when I'm required, as indeed *you* would be, to speak for a corporate thing or speak to a number of people, that's the most difficult thing I can do. It's not something that comes naturally to me. I'd never be a stand-up comedian, because I don't *desperately* want people to love me. I'm not craving their applause. That's why I like talking to myself on the radio or the television, because I'm always assuming that people out there are smiling.

GB: So, take me back, then: you got the great big job in the bank. Was that an ad? Did you answer an ad for that?
TW: No, I didn't, no. The Royal Bank of Ireland—which is a small, mainly Protestant bank—had a quota of Catholics that it would allow in from the better schools. My father would have liked me to be a doctor. I couldn't see that I could spend seven years studying—couldn't see that at all. Didn't particularly think I should get a BA, and I thought, anyway, they'd spent enough money on me, on education. So, up came the opportunity to get a job in a bank. I did the exam, and I achieved a position of clerkship in the Royal Bank of Ireland.

GB: And did you like that job?
TW: I loved it. We were all young men there, and, you know, we had an enormous amount of fun, tremendous fun there. You know, you'd be taking in a lodgement from a particularly pretty girl, and the next thing a wet sponge would come flying across the bank and hit you straight in the eye. All that kind of stuff. That went on all the time. It was "Christmas Day at the Workhouse" there, really, most of the time. So, I had a really happy time.

GB: Yes.

TW: So, I don't know why . . . Saw an ad, I think it was in the *Irish Independent* . . .

GB: Radio Éireann . . .

TW: As Gaeilge and Béarla. Radio Éireann requires announcers, newsreader-announcers . . . So, there must have been ten thousand people applying for this. For some extraordinary reason, which I can never fathom, I get called to do an audition. I did the audition, and, blow me down, about a couple of months later, I was called for an announcers' training course. So, I would work in the bank all day, off to Radio Éireann in Henry Street. After a month or two of that, they offered me a position. They offered me a job.

GB: And did you realise that broadcasting is what you wanted to do?

TW: Oh, yes, almost from the beginning. "This is it, lads. I can do this!" This is where I wanted to be.

GB: And at what stage did you decide you wanted to go to the BBC— you wanted to leap across the water?

TW: I don't know. I'd always been listening to the BBC. It's the same old thing: you want to see whether you can do it elsewhere. You want to see whether you can do it for a bigger audience. It was kind of, I don't know, "I'll give it a go. I'll see." I made a tape, sent it to the BBC. They liked it, and it started from there.

GB: Did you find it difficult as an Irishman to settle down in the UK or the BBC . . . ?

TW: No, not at all. I took to the BBC like a duck to water. I was lucky. The public took to me. So, that was fine. It was easy. I left in 1969. Now, as you know, the Troubles, the euphemistic Troubles, started in '68 and, of course, the terrible Birmingham bomb came, where innocent British people were killed in a pub. Now, I came up the morning after that happened with a cheerful Irish voice . . . But that's what I was *supposed* to do. I never found it necessary to, in any way, hide the fact that I'm Irish—proud to be Irish. All this is not being done in my name or in the name of any decent Irish people that I know. And I hope I helped the Irish people in Britain by this attitude, because some of them, subsequently, over the years, have come to me to say that I did. And that's perhaps the greatest compliment I've ever had.

GB: You never got any nasty post or any nasty phone calls, or any Provo nastiness or anything like that? You were not subjected to any of that kind of thing?

TW: No, I wasn't. And it wasn't vetted, so I would get it. I never got anything from the British public. I did have a bomb sent to me . . .

GB: Sure we all had that.

TW: . . . in Broadcasting House. And all the traffic was blocked in Oxford Street, Regent Street, Oxford Circus. A bomb . . . ! He couldn't have been a great listener, because I was on holiday at the time.

GB: [Laughs.]

TW: [Laughs.] Unbelievable! Not much of a fan, then.

GB: Nobody ever said they were the brightest people.

TW: No, exactly.

GB: Now, we've skipped away a lot, because I want to hear about *la belle Hélène*. I want to know where you met her, how you first laid eyes on each other, and was it love at first sight?

TW: Erm . . . yes.

GB: Saw each other first where, when?

TW: Some enchanted evening, there across the room was this plain-looking girl, and I thought, "I'll talk to her. She's probably lonely."

GB: This plain-looking girl . . .

TW: [Laughs.] Yes. So . . . No, what happened was, there she was, standing there, statuesque, incredibly beautiful . . . Now, if I had been Michael Terence Wogan, the simple old bank clerk, I'd never have approached her in a million years.

GB: You would have been bashful and shy ?

TW: Well, no, I would have felt inadequate. I'm not going to talk to this goddess. But I was Michael Terence Wogan who was on the radio and the television.

GB: Let her scoff at that . . . !

TW: So, I crossed the room.

GB: And that was it.

TW: Yes. Forty-five years later . . .

GB: There you both are.

TW: ... still together.

GB: So, you and Helen got married, and you went to live in England. Now, I know this is sad, but your little girl, Vanessa, when she died, did any of the remnants of the religion that you had been taught, in Crescent and in Belvedere—did any of that constitute any kind of consolation to you ...?

TW: No. Our first child died when we were still living in Ireland, a year after we were married, about '66. And Helen gave birth after a very, very difficult labour, and our daughter had a fault in her heart, and she died after about three weeks ... No, I didn't flee to God. I was extremely resentful.

GB: Resentful ...?

TW: Absolutely!

GB: Of God ...?

TW: Of fate, of life, of the unfairness of it.

GB: Did you rail against it?

TW: To myself, yeah.

GB: Not to anyone else?

TW: No. Certainly not to Helen. Helen had to get over far more than I had to get over. So, you know, I kept it to myself.

GB: And do you think Helen had recourse to consolation in religion?

TW: Yes, she did, because she has what we called earlier on "the gift of faith". She believes. She goes to Mass and she is a Catholic.

GB: That resentment about Vanessa, is that still with you?

TW: No. No, I've got over that a long time ago. But you remember a little bit of the pain, because that never goes.

GB: And you think of her?

TW: Yes, absolutely—never forget that. You ask why it should happen to you, of course.

GB: And then the answer comes: why not you?

TW: Exactly. As you go through life you realise that it's a lottery anyway and that I've been luckier than most in my life. I'm not going to knock it. Lots of people have had to go through a great deal worse than me. So, you learn proportion, and you also learn that life is not fair, and you have to take the rough with the smooth. It's a very important lesson that everybody has to learn.

GB: Now, I know you've had this conversation with Father Brian D'Arcy on many occasions. In the end, did you decide that you do *not* believe in God, or otherwise?

TW: Yes. I don't believe in God. I know it's arrogant. Better men than me have believed in God, far more intelligent people than me. But at this stage of my life, let me put it this way: that I don't—I can't—accept the logic that there is an all-seeing God. There is too much evidence, in my book, to the contrary.

GB: Okay, so, this programme is actually airing in Positive Ageing Week, which RTÉ, in their wisdom, have designated "Coming of Age Week". Do you, Sir Terence, believe that you're ageing positively or just positively ageing? Which would you go for? [Laughs.]

TW: [Laughs.] I think a shrewd combination of the two. I think more likely positively ageing.

GB: Positively ageing, yes.

TW: Particularly when you find yourself half way up the stairs and you don't know why you're doing it, or why you've opened the fridge door with a hammer in your hand. [Laughs.]

GB: [Laughs.] It comes to us all . . . ! We get around to asking, to what do you ascribe the success of your life in broadcasting? Let me preface that by saying that I've always believed that you had one wonderful gift over the rest of us—*one of the* wonderful gifts over the rest of us—and that is that you were born, it seems to me, with a naturally sunny disposition.

TW: I've said before that, if you really want to succeed in this country, learn how to listen. A good listener is worth millions in this country, because everybody else is talking at once.

For me, the greatest attribute and the most important thing you can bring to a marriage, the most important thing you can bring to a family, the most important thing you can bring to anybody, is kindness. Kindness is the most important thing. In the old Church word, "charity". So, it's a combination of love and charity. Kindness: that's the word.

GB: This programme is called *The Meaning of Life* . . .

TW: A fairly portentous title!

GB: Indeed, it is. Perhaps a little over-reaching in its ambition. Nonetheless, what do *you* think the meaning of life is?

TW: Gosh, what a question! It's an existence. I was born. I'm living. I will die. My life, if you ask me about *my* life and the meaning of *my* life, it's been absolutely wonderful. I've had the most wonderful time. I've had a lovely family, I've had a loving wife, I've had success in the material world, I've done something I wanted to do. I've had an ideal life. So, I can only tell you what it means to me, which is happiness.

GB: So, let's round up. Do you think about death?

TW: Yeah, yeah. I'm old now, you know. But then there's a lovely song by Gretchen Peters—there's a wonderful line in it that says, "When you are old, death no longer makes you weep." You don't worry about death as much as you get older as you did when you were young, because you were always worried about your mother and father dying. Do you remember that?

GB: Uh-huh.

TW: But now, no. It's a kind of acceptance. Hopefully, I'll cling to the wreckage as long as I can.

GB: Indeed. And when you die? [Clicks fingers.] Gone?

TW: Yeah.

GB: Okay. Come-uppance?

TW: I don't believe in Heaven, and I don't believe in Hell. I don't believe we're going anywhere. I think this is it. And one of the reasons I would think this is it is because my life has been so, if you like, heavenly. I've had an absolutely wonderful time. I can understand why people whose lives are dreadful, whose lives are poverty-stricken or painful, why they would feel and hope that there was some eternal reward that they could go to, where their spiritual life would be a great deal better. But, certainly at this stage of my life, I don't need that. This is it.

GB: Last question. Suppose it's all true, what the Js told you in Crescent and in Belvedere: when you meet that great Director-General in the sky, what will you say to Him?

TW: I'll look around a bit, and I think I'll say, "Where am I?" And then, "You're having me on. I don't believe this." [Laughs.] And I'll take it, if it's there! [Laughs.]

GB: [Laughs.] Won't we all, dear, won't we all!

BONO

One Man In The Name Of Love

I t was a polite, but very definite, "No", and for the best of reasons. Bono had seen and liked some episodes of *The Meaning of Life*, but word came back that his wife, Ali Hewson, felt that so much of their life together is already lived in the public glare that some private areas have to be guarded.

You can't argue with that and I wasn't inclined to try.

So, what had changed his mind? Here he was, sitting down in a room at his local, the Fitzpatrick Castle Hotel, Killiney, with no pre-conditions, knowing full well, given the nature of the programme, that I would want to ask him about deeply personal subjects: faith, family, music, morality, love, death and taxes.

Yes, taxes. Fiscal matters aren't usually a subject for my *Meaning of Life* questions, but U2's tax affairs have become such a preoccupation for anyone from tabloid hacks to government ministers that it was obviously something I would have to raise. In some ways, I actually got the impression that Bono was grateful for the opportunity to discuss his taxes, himself, rather than have them talked about by others, in order to set the record straight and, hopefully, close the matter.

He knew as well as I did that that was about all that Irish journalists would write about, but we both have enough faith in the discernment of Irish audiences to know that, in an hour-long interview, they would absorb some of the other stuff, too.

I would not say that Bono and I are close exactly, but having known each other for over thirty years, I like and respect him. Hopefully, that feeling is mutual. Just as importantly, in this context, I believe he trusts me: not to soft-soap or to schmooze him, but not to stitch him up either. Bono has long been aware that, whatever he says, there will always be some who will scoff and sneer at him. They call it Tall Poppy Syndrome. Thankfully, he has enough "sticks-and-stones" toughness and tenacity to say his piece anyway about the things that matter most to him.

Bono and I first met in the early 1980s, when he and Ali came on *The Late Late Show*. U2 were on a mission to conquer the world, but even then, there was a sense that this would be more than egotistical, unit-shifting empire-building: they wanted to conquer the world in order to change it, which was either a very noble and lofty ambition or a mad one. Or both.

Ali was not part of the band, but she was clearly a vital ingredient in U2's chemistry: part muse, part wife, part surrogate mother to one of the most visionary and talented young stars in the business. She was, undoubtedly, the person who protected Bono from his own worst excesses, but without ever treading more than softly on his dreams. Forget U2 for a moment, I don't think he would have lasted this long without her.

One of the reasons why he seldom agrees to the sort of interview we were about to record is that, however nuanced your answers in one context, they can quickly be reduced to absurdity in another. U2 have never hidden the fact, for instance, that they are a Christian rock band. What they have resisted, however, is the naff, unhelpful stereotyping that goes with that happy-clappy tag.

Christian beliefs and ethics, Bono once claimed, are like "a fish drawn in the sand" in U2's lyrics. To those who look for the camouflaged turbot, it is there, but you can just as easily focus on the waves and the sand in their songs.

So, again, I couldn't help wondering why he was choosing, now, to let the turbot break cover. My challenge, though, was to reel it in.

∾

GB: It just occurs to me that I am greeting the product of what used to be known in Ireland as "a mixed marriage": Iris Rankin, your mother, Protestant, married to Bob Hewson, Catholic, your father, and I often wondered, at what stage do you become aware that your family, in that context, is unusual?

BONO: It's hard to imagine it being unusual now isn't it?

GB: Incredible.

BONO: Yes, there are a lot more interesting marriages going on now than Catholic and Protestant, but I guess in the '60s and '70s, in Ireland, that was pretty extraordinary. And if I'm honest, we did feel it was a bit different to have my father drop us off, my brother and I, with my mother, at a little Church of Ireland church, St Canice's, in Finglas, and not come in with us; and then be waiting there for us when we came out.

GB: So, your father, do you have a sense that at some stage he regretted not seeing to it that you were brought up Catholic . . . ?

BONO: No, I don't think so. He was one of the first people to wake up to this rather ridiculous family argument in the Christian family. And of course, these things were made more vivid by the troubles in the North and sectarianism. But I think everyone was waking up to the fact that religion was probably the enemy of God and that God was a bigger subject than religion.

GB: I want to come back to that later. Meanwhile, around about fourteen, your grandfather died, and then almost immediately, your mother died suddenly.

BONO: Interesting, yeah. My mother died at her own father's funeral, right at the side of the grave, which I guess is an unusual way to die. She had a stroke, so it was a few days later and eventually we gathered around the bed in the Mater Hospital and said goodbye to her.

GB: So now, you're fourteen and your Dad is left with you and your big brother, Norman. How did you all cope with that, can you remember . . . ?

BONO: Irish males are a piece of work, are they not? And I'm sure it was very difficult for my father. I think he really did his very best to be the sergeant-major and get myself and my brother into shape. But I was "Enter Chaos." You have your big tantrum, don't you, with God and the universe, because you're fourteen, just come into puberty and you don't know why you feel the way you feel. You have some rage, let's put it like that, and they had to live with that.

GB: The parallels with Bob Geldof are amazing. He was left alone with his father, who was away most of the week, unlike your father . . .

BONO: I'd *wish* my Dad would be away all week . . . [Laughter.]

GB: So, you're at loggerheads with Dad?

BONO: Yeah, but it's my fault. And I realised that later in life. I had quite an epiphany and I realised that he was really doing his best.

GB: So, then, Mount Temple, co-ed, non-denominational. You liked it, yeah?

BONO: Yeah, this extraordinary oasis in education in Ireland. You know, it's co-educational—we have boys and girls—great! There's no religion in the formal sense, great. And later, when we joined the band, they kind of moved things around for us then. Couldn't have been better.

GB: Okay. Now, let me move on to Ali Stewart. At what stage did she come on the scene?

BONO: Well, I dated Ali the week I joined U2. That was a very good week for me. And she had a very special way about her. She was completely un-self-conscious, I thought. The most beautiful girl I'd ever seen. She wore wellington boots, a tartan skirt and a jumper her mother made for her. She just looked elegant in anything she wore, but she didn't think about what she wore. And she was very bright—she was in the same year as Edge—the two of them were the smartest people, the top of their class and I was a year ahead of them. And I remember, I was going on the back of somebody's motorbike, leaving Mount Temple, and I saw her crossing the schoolyard. And something just snapped inside of me and I just saw her as this very special presence that I just needed to hold on to and never let go. So, that's what happened.

GB: Was she resistant?
BONO: Yes. She still is!

GB: How long did it take?
BONO: It took . . . minutes! [Laughter.] I mean, I was at her for years really. I had tried to sort of get close to her maybe a year earlier and she did brush me off quite seriously, and it was a friend of hers who said to me, "I think you should try again." And I said, "Well, what's the point?" And he said, "I think you should try again. I think there's something there . . ."

GB: Now, I don't want to go through the early days of U2 all over again, but it seems to me you were setting up a Christian rock and roll band. Now, if ever there was a kiss of death on any enterprise, that had to be it?
BONO: No, it wasn't really like that, though. Remember, punk rock was breaking out... and we connected with those kind of art rock groups. We did not start the band to go save the world. We started the band to go save our own asses and try and impress people like Ali Stewart.

GB: [Laughs.] Quite. Yes. But then Dave Fanning paints a picture of you reading the Bible on the bus, and the Shalom Fellowship.
BONO: Yes.

GB: What was that?
BONO: Well, there are revivals. You read about them. It's a kind of wind blowing through and people are moved. And at that time, '76, '77, a lot of things were happening. You had Bob Dylan's conversion to Christianity. And it was happening in Mount Temple a little bit. And there was a fella called Chris Rowe, who ran a Christian meeting called Shalom. And this fella really understood the Scriptures and he could really unlock them.

And I had always been fascinated by the Scriptures. I mean, you can't be a fan of blues or Bob Dylan or folk music and not really understand the Scriptures. So, we became very interested in this and they, at first, appeared to appreciate that we were different and didn't want us to change the way we looked. But then it started to dawn on us that, in the end, they thought that rock and roll was a kind of distraction from what was really going on in a broken world. And it sort of crescendoed with Edge leaving the band. It was Edge and me, but he said to me, "It's right, you know. The world is a broken place and there's a lot of broken lives and this is really not the way to go about anything useful with our life."

So, we both left the band. And we go and see Paul McGuinness, the Winston Churchill of Rock, and he's sitting there and ready to meet them on the beaches. And we say, "Paul, we're done and actually want to do something useful with our lives and maybe rock and roll isn't it." And he goes, "So, God told you to do this?" And we said, "No, not exactly, but we're deeply conflicted here." And he said, "Well, would you mind speaking to God about the commitments I've made on your behalf to another tour? Because I presume that breaking your contract wouldn't be…"

GB: . . . In accordance with God!

BONO: And we kinda go, "Oh, yeah . . . Right. Okay, just one more tour." And so, we do that tour for that album. And Edge actually just starts writing this song, *Sunday Bloody Sunday*. And somehow, we started to realise that our music was the way that we spoke to the world. These were prayers of a kind. And what are we doing, hanging out with these people who didn't understand this? They'd somehow turned God into a very retail relationship: everything had to have a "Christian" sticker on it. I don't understand that. Does a tree have a sign up saying "Made by God"? No. It's there. It declares itself. The creation does. So music does, poetry does. And more importantly, the problem with gospel music is, a lot of the time, it's in denial of where we're really at. It's trying to brush things under the carpet… The blues, Robert Johnson, *Hellhound On My Trail*, starts to speak the truth. Now, if you know anything about Scriptures, you know it's the truth that sets you free. So, we started to see the lies in all this happy-clappy stuff. And of course, rock and roll is the combination of blues and gospel: the highness, the headiness, of gospel and the mud of the Mississippi Delta, or indeed the Liffey or the Mersey. And that is where our music really comes from.

GB: Okay. Moving on to 1984 and Bob Geldof comes along and says Band Aid, Live Aid . . . And it would have been in accordance with the track you're already on.

BONO: Right. That's true. And it's funny, because the Boomtown Rats couldn't be on a more different tack. You know, *Looking After Number One* and all of that. So, I thought it was rather odd to get a call from Bob Geldof saying, "We have to do something about this famine in Ethiopia and we've got to look to music, because people aren't responding fast enough." And I was like, "Well, yeah, I think you're right." And I do think God has a great sense of humour, to have Bob in charge of this.

GB: [Laughs.]

BONO: First, because he doesn't believe in God . . .

GB: In anything . . . !

BONO: . . . But surely, I can tell you God believes in him. And also, Bob is not famous for throwing it around. You know, as the band will tell you, he's frugal. And so, the idea that this instrument of peace would be Bob Geldof is just one of the most beautiful ironies. This is the divine comedy. And here is a man who profoundly changed things . . .

GB: Profoundly.

BONO: . . . in Ethiopia and in the activism that grew in the UK, in particular, and indeed me, because afterwards, myself and Ali went to Ethiopia for a month and a bit, just under the wire, no cameras, and that changes our lives. So, I owe Bob big time for turning my life upside down . . . or right side up, depending on the way you see it.

GB: That took you into the whole area that you've been working on for so long now and I can understand the need of Bill Clinton and Tony Blair and various presidents to be seen photographed with you, but did you ever think, mixing with any of these people, that you were supping with the devil?

BONO: No. I feel when I go to meet, particularly, a head of state, and people ask me if I'm nervous, I always say, "No, I'm not. They should be." Because they will be held to account for their decisions they made in office. And I've met so many heads of state now, who, when they leave office, say to me, "I wish you'd harangued me even more." Bill Clinton, who is my hero, led on debt cancellation and he is right out in front in the fight against AIDS since he left office. But it's a real deep regret of his that he didn't do more on the AIDS pandemic while he was in office.

GB: So, the strategy is: don't antagonise them and don't harangue them . . . ?

BONO: Oh, *do* antagonise them.

GB: Well, don't fling mud at them from the rooftops.

BONO: Don't take the obvious route; and understand, when you go to a meeting, that the meeting will be longer if you can solve their problems for them. So, when George Bush's heart wanted to respond to the AIDS emergency, there wasn't much support on the right, particularly religious support, strangely. You would think that AIDS would remind people of the leprosy they read about in the Scriptures, but it didn't. And Evangelical Christians at that time, they weren't responding. Getting support for President Bush on his right was part of our strategy, making it possible for President Bush to do what he did. And you have to say this: he led the largest ever massing of resources against a single disease in the history of the planet. And we were part of that and part of getting him there. There's eight million people now on antiretroviral drugs, largely paid for by the United States of America. God Bless America.

GB: God Bless America.

BONO: You know, I just had one idea, really, when it came to activism: don't let it be a creation of the left. Don't leave the right out, in terms of the political spectrum. Try to find a radical centre, because why divide the audience in half? So, when I go and see an economist, when we were doing Drop the Debt, for example, I'd ask to see a conservative economist as well as a liberal one. I was very happy to spend time with George Bush, as I am with, say, President Hollande of France or whomever it takes to move it along.

GB: So a quick recap, then: well nigh on thirty years after Live Aid and Bob Geldof and this turning point in your life, a quick précis of how has the world improved?

BONO: Oh, it's remarkable. And the great indicator is infant mortality, under 5's: in twenty years, there are 7,000—let me get this right—7,256 less kids under 5 dying, every day.

GB: Every day?!

BONO: Yeah. And these are figures released by the World Bank and the

World Health Organisation. And you can plot it going forward. So, if we keep doing what we know how to do: vaccinating young kids against Pneumococcal, Rotavirus, names you can't even pronounce, but they're killers. I mean, we have the science and we really know what to do now. Biggest problem, biggest killer of all, it's not a disease, it's not HIV/AIDS, it's not malaria, it is corruption. But we have a vaccine for that too. It's called daylight, transparency. What we are working on now with the ONE Campaign is pushing transparency legislation in, for example, extractive industries, so that people have to declare what they've paid for those mining rights. Because normally big mining companies, oil companies and gas companies, they don't have to do that. And by not declaring it, it allows somebody in those countries to take a payment and declare a different one and then that's where corruption starts.

So, I would say I'm very optimistic indeed. By 2030, it is possible, if people hold tight to their aid commitments—and Ireland is doing that, what a heroic thing. Broadly eighty per cent of Irish people are behind the Irish aid commitment. If we all keep concentrating, the sort of obscenity of those pictures that inspired Bob Geldof to put on Live Aid, you won't have to see them again and that gives me incredible faith in people and incredible gratitude to God.

GB: To God?

BONO: Yeah.

GB: If I don't ask you this, I will be criticised and if I do ask you this, I will be criticised, but since you've touched on the subject now, the subject of U2's taxation arrangements, whereby people are expressing their wonder at what they call your "hypocrisy"—not my word but their word—"hypocrisy" of haranguing us all and asking us to pay more for international aid, at the same time as you shift your company overseas in order to save taxation?

BONO: Yeah, but it's very hard for Irish people to be critical about this, because the shock-horror moment here is U2 behaving like a business. We live on a small rock in the North Atlantic and we would be underwater, were it not for very clever people working in government and in the Revenue, who made tax competitiveness a central part of Irish economic life. That's the reason why we have companies like Google or Facebook, and indeed, I helped bring in those companies, because of this tax competitiveness. So, it's more than churlish for Irish people to say, "Well, we don't want an Irish company involved in that stuff, but we do want everyone else." It's not being very fair to your own. I mean, we do pay a lot—I want to say *a lot*—of tax, but we are tax sensible . . .

GB: As every business must be by law.

BONO: And why is it, because I'm involved in these, what some people think of as idealistic things, why can't U2 be tough in business? I mean, Bill Gates, one of the reasons I admire him so, it's not just he's giving all his money away to fight against extreme poverty, it's that he's put his tough-mindedness to work on the subject. George Soros is another hero of mine, he has done the same. This thing of the "warm fuzzy feeling", I'd like people to get over that, because that's not who I am. I may sing from a very private and intimate place and I make art, but I'm tough-minded and I'm intellectually rigorous, I hope. And I think U2's tax business is our own business and I think it's not just to the letter of the law, it's to the spirit of the law in Ireland.

GB: In that context, do you feel that you are removed from the ordinary, everyday lives of people, in Ireland, especially today?

BONO: That must be true. I mean, all of us who live in the northern hemisphere live incredible lives, as far as the world's poor are concerned, but I have to accept that mine is different. And in Ireland, especially at this moment, when, really, people are hurting so badly and are being deeply affected by problems they had no part in creating. And I'm amazed at the intelligence of the Irish people in realising that you have to attract jobs: we have to get through this. And I think it's heroic . . .

My kids go to a regular, non fee-paying school. I don't think of myself as removed. But, to answer your question, I probably must be.

GB: Could we get back now to religion and faith? You are obviously a believer, but not in the Church. What is your complaint about the Church?

BONO: Oh no, I *am* a believer in the Church. I just don't think there's loads of different Churches. There's *one* Church. It's just smashed into loads of different pieces. And I think that the Holy Spirit is much more anarchic than we think. You don't know where it comes from, you don't know where it goes, Scriptures say. Religion is a slightly different thing and I think people have got to be very careful of thinking they have a monopoly on the truth.

There's a thing that everyone reads out at their wedding, that beautiful scripture in Corinthians: "Love is patient, love is kind, love bears all things, love believes all things." Then it says, "Faith, hope and love and the greatest of these things is love." Well, why is that? Why is love more important than faith? And the answer is found just a few verses later, in that beautiful passage—especially beautiful in King James—where it goes, "For we see through the glass darkly, but then we shall see face-to-face. We know in part, but then I shall know even as I know myself, even as I shall be known . . ." The reason love is more important than faith is we don't have a monopoly on truth. We see through the glass, darkly. And whenever you see religious people, where their faith is more important than love, they've got it the wrong way round, in my view. I mean, the Scriptures are very eloquent about love and I can't really figure it out how people have so maligned Christ. We don't even know that Christ ever intended to set up a religion.

GB: Okay, you said somewhere that rock and roll is your religion . . .
BONO: No.

GB: You didn't say that?
BONO: I don't believe that. I think rock and roll is an art form and that is, for me, how I choose, and band members in U2, to figure it all out. As it happens, I do believe there is a force of love and logic behind the universe and I do think it's extraordinary that it might have chosen a single point in time, in a small impoverished community, to express itself. I love the idea of this baby born in shit and straw. How do we understand God? How do we understand this force? It must be unfathomable, if you believe it's behind the universe. And then you see it describe itself as a child in that vulnerability and that fragility. There is such genius to that for me. I just go "Wow!" And that child would teach us how to love, by laying down your life for your brother.

GB: Well, you did say, "Most rock bands start by singing about girls and end up singing about God. We just did it the other way round." [Laughs.]
BONO: [Laughs.] Yeah, I might have said that.

GB: Have you tended to ease down on the religious lyrics, of late, or are you still proceeding with that?
BONO: When I write about romantic love in lyrics, I constantly get it mixed up with eternal love. We continually get girls mixed up with God. And we have only one word for what the Greeks have three. They have Éros, Philia, Agápe. We just call it "love." It's really handy for a songwriter.

GB: Okay. So, tell me about your configuration of God?

BONO: Christ is my way to understand God.

GB: Do you pray?

BONO: Yes.

GB: And what do you pray for?

BONO: Pray to get to know the will of God, because then the prayers have more chance of coming true. [Laughs.] I mean, we don't do it in a very lofty way in our family. It's just a bunch of us on the bed usually. We have a very big bed . . . !

GB: Yeah.

BONO: We just read the Scriptures. We pray. It's not even regular. Sometimes, if we go to church on a Sunday, we go when the church is ended and we'll just go in on our own as a family, for peace and quiet . . . And we'll pray, usually, about people that we know who are struggling with something...

GB: So, what, or who, was Jesus, as far as you're concerned?

BONO: I think, it's a defining question for a Christian: who was Christ? And I don't think you're let off easily by saying "a great thinker" or "a great philosopher", because actually, he went around saying he was the Messiah. That's why he was crucified: because he said he was the Son of God. So, either, in my view, he *was* the Son of God or he was nuts. And I find it hard to accept that all the millions and millions of lives—half the earth for two thousand years—have felt their lives touched and inspired by some nutter. I just don't believe it.

GB: So, therefore, it follows that you believe he was divine?

BONO: Yes.

GB: And therefore it follows that you believe that he rose physically from the dead?

BONO: Yes, I've no problems with miracles. [Laughs.] I'm living around them. I am one . . . The miracle of just being in U2 is mad. I mean, we were the crappest band, we were useless, but we had the spirit between us. We found the best in each other. Love, if you really push it, what is it about? It's about realising your own potential and realising somebody else's potential. That's the job of love; that's what God wants from us: to realise your potential, to be what you can possibly be. And the greatest sadness to me on this earth is the waste of human potential. That's why I do the ONE Campaign, Drop the Debt and Make Poverty History.

GB: I have long thought that you are realising *your* potential more than most people that I know?

BONO: Well, I came into the world with some average talents.

GB: You've leveraged to that, as the Americans would say.

BONO: With poor materials [laughs], I've been very blessed.

GB: Your own not very good relationship with your father... to what extent does the *Our Father* . . . ?

BONO: Aaaaah! You have an unusual mind for, clearly, the most probing question: how do people who have a difficult relationship with their father deal with the concept of a male, father-like figure? It's an interesting question. My father was great and the bit about him that wasn't great was the bit I didn't like about myself. Classic enough. And I told you, sometimes, as a family, we just go when the church service is ended, because we don't want to hear anything. And I went in a little church in the South of France. We were just sitting there one Easter. And I had been quite angry after my father's passing. The rage, which is in me anyway, was just back. And I just got on my knees and I asked for forgiveness from my father, because I realised what an ass I'd been. And it was a fantastic thing to let go of that. I'm not sure if he was listening, but I knew God was listening. And it was important. I had gotten the relationship the wrong way round. And with that, I think, came one of the steps towards some kind of spiritual maturity, which I haven't got to yet, but that was definitely a step for it. And an amazing thing happened. My voice changed and I've been singing like a bird ever since, in his tenor voice.

GB: He was a useful singer?

BONO: He was a *really* good singer. And now I've got his tenor voice. Now, that could be, you know, when we let go of things, when we surrender, we are released to be ourselves more. Most people, even people who don't believe in God, would say that. A therapist will tell you that: you let go.

GB: Do you go to Confession?

BONO: I write songs.

GB: No. Do you go to Confession?

BONO: You think I'm joking! They *are* Confession to me . . . And believe me, I have a lot to confess.

GB: Am I right in saying that the overall message that your father, Lord rest him, used to give you was one of pessimism: that to dream is to be disappointed.

BONO: That's exactly right.

GB: And how did you overcome that?

BONO: My revenge on that idea, God help us, was to have the most impossible dreams. And that was a way of getting back at him, because he could have done anything: he was a beautiful painter; really fine singer; he could write perfectly; extremely bright. And it's just fear, perhaps, because, coming out of poverty and Dublin in the '50s, he got a job in the Post Office . . .

GB: For permanence and security . . .

BONO: Probably. Fear was a part of that and, of course, faith is the enemy of fear, isn't it? And I had a lot of that. And I believed in my friends and I believed in the band and I believed, if you're around really smart people—number one, your partner, your wife, then your colleagues, your partners, your friends—they make you smarter, they make you better. And I think that's how these sort of impossible ideas and bigger ambitions got dreamed. Had I been left on my own, I would have been just like all the people I don't like: people in the corner of a bar with big ideas that never came to anything. And I'd probably be looking at somebody like me now, having my wine turn to vinegar.

GB: Now, you did write two beautiful songs about your father: *Kite* and *Sometimes, You Can't Make It On Your Own*. You knew he was dying, very seriously ill in hospital, there's no way out and you came back regularly to spend the night with him . . .

BONO: Well, my brother was a much better caretaker of my father's illness, because he was home. We were on the Elevation Tour, but I would fly home, whenever I could, and take over from my brother and I would sleep beside my dad in the hospital. And I just drew my father, which was a beautiful way to spend time just looking at his face. I wrote to him, I read to him . . .

GB: What did you read?

BONO: I'd read the Psalms to my dad and my dad would be looking at me with the hairy eyeball. You know, like "Take it elsewhere, son . . ."

GB: Completely compos mentis, of course . . .

BONO: Yeah, but attitude to the end. And I don't know if I should say this, but the night before he died, he woke up. And he had Parkinson's at this point, as well as everything else, so he was whispering. And I couldn't really hear him, just sort of sibilance, and so I called the nurse. And I'm going, "What's up, Dad?" She's got her ear down and I've got my ear down and I'm just here [mimes putting his face down listening] And . . . "Fuck Off!"

GB: [Laughs.]

BONO: And he goes, "I just want out of here. I just want to go home." And that was his last words. What a great exit! And I'm sure he is at home and I'm sure it will be a lot more of a home than 10, Cedarwood Road was, without my mother.

GB: Dear, oh dear . . . ! Do you think you will see your mother and father again?

BONO: Yes.

GB: You believe in the Communion of Saints?

BONO: Yes, I do.

GB: You believe that there is somebody there keeping an eye on you, do you?

BONO: Yes. I believe God is interested in us, in the detail of our lives, and I think that's remarkable. But I accept, it also sounds preposterous to a lot of folks.

GB: Final question. If it's all true, when the time comes and you pop your clogs and you present yourself at the gate and meet Him, what will you say to Him?

BONO: Well, first of all I won't be wearing clogs.

GB: [Laughs.]

BONO: I'll be wearing some Cuban heels probably. And you know, it might be the first time in my life I don't say anything. I think I might just shut up. And wouldn't that be a great thing?

GB: That's a profoundly disappointing answer.

BONO: [Laughs.] I'm so sorry.

GB: [Laughs.] Thank you. God bless you.

BONO: Thank you, Gay.

BRENDAN O'CARROLL

Knees Up, Mother Brown

"**G**ay Byrne? I'd paint the Liberty Tower yellow for Gay Byrne. 'Course I'll do it."

Brendan O'Carroll's reported response to our invitation to take part in the series is a clear sign that he and I have formed a Mutual Appreciation Society. Beware.

Mind you, that was before his IFTAs and BAFTAs. Perhaps he wouldn't give me the time of day now, as he rides to his Florida mansion retreat on a litter carried by fawning BBC and RTÉ producers.

I knew Brendan in the forty years *before* he became an overnight success. Like we do for a lot of comedians, we gave him a break or two on *The Late Late Show*. But that's all you can ever give a comic. They will only succeed if the people in the seats out front laugh.

Brendan spent all those years in theatres, clubs and studios working out *exactly* what makes those people laugh. And it's not always what, or who, you'd expect. The success of *Mrs Brown's Boys* is attributable, not to the Boys, but to the Mrs Browns of this world. Women of a certain age, in whose mouths butter generally wouldn't melt, will howl at the potty-mouthed guilty pleasure that is an episode of *Mrs Brown's Boys*. And, as any family household at Christmastime will show you, if Grandma is happy to laugh at smut, it's okay for the rest of the family to do so, too. No-one wants to be the dirty-minded loner, laughing at saucy jokes, if the rest of the family is sitting in stony silence. Brendan's genius is to get people laughing together.

That laughter is what gives him the self-confidence to challenge accepted thinking in television circles. "A live show, in front of an audience, with hammy asides and mistakes left in on purpose?" The Sebastians of BBC Television Centre must have had a fit . . . until they saw the viewing figures, at which point, they got their dinner suits cleaned in readiness for the BAFTAs, IFTAs etc.

But Mrs Brown didn't spring from nowhere: she is steeped in the culture and values of working-class Dubliners, who, as Brendan has discovered, are pretty similar to the working-class people of Birmingham, Liverpool, Glasgow and, for that matter, Mumbai.

So, what are those values? What makes the man who makes Mrs Brown tick tick?

～

GB: Can we start with your childhood? Where? When? How many of you? All of that . . .

BOC: Eleven of us. But it never seemed like eleven, because by the time I was born I was the baby, so I had sisters who were twenty-one, twenty-two years of age.

GB: You were doted on, were you?

BOC: Yeah. My dad died. My mam retired from politics. Most of them had emigrated, so it was just me and her, and I got the undivided attention of this genius, who told me every day, "You can be anything you want." I can sit down with members of my family, and they talk about a woman that I don't know when they talk about my mother. And I talk about a woman that they don't know when I talk about my mother. And it's because they would remember a woman that they'd hear on the radio decrying the fact there was so many children coming out of school illiterate, but yet wouldn't be there to help them with their homework.

GB: Is it true that she had been a nun?

BOC: Yes, she was, in Galway. I'm not even sure of the order. Gortnor Abbey she went to, and she went to Galway University . . . She took her final vows and then had to fight the Vatican to get out of the convent.

GB: And did she leave because she fell in love with your dad ?

BOC: Well, no, she was sensible enough to have doubted her vocation anyway. And I think, once she graduated, she found out very quickly, actually, "I wouldn't mind a bit of a man." And so she did the right thing, but it was difficult for her.

GB: So, she became a TD. She was the mother of eleven. She was the Chief Whip. And she was more than partly responsible for women being accepted into the Garda Síochána . . . ?

BOC: Yes.

GB: She must have been quite an outstanding woman.

BOC: Yes, she was so far ahead of her time.

GB: Now, is Mrs Brown based in any way on your mother?

BOC: I used to say, "Absolutely not," because Mrs Brown, I believe, is a collage of all those women I knew in Moore Street. They have a great optimism, and that's what I tried to put into Mrs Brown. But the more I've done book readings around the world, and the more I've spoken about Mrs Brown, the more I'm starting to see that, you know, I think Mrs Brown is my mam . . . without the education, but she is my mam. Or there's a possibility that Mrs Brown was the mother that I wanted to have.

GB: Do you remember it being a religious household?
BOC: To a point. We said the Rosary . . . up until my dad died.

GB: Every night?
BOC: I think it was every night. And my mother used to do this thing about "The family that prays together stays together." It was just complete ****. I mean, as soon as they had a chance, they were gone. But when I stopped going to Mass, there was no objections, and I was about thirteen.

And my mam said, "You haven't been to Mass the last couple of weeks."

I said, "No, Mam, I haven't."

She said, "Why not?"

I said, "Well, the purpose, for me, of going to Mass was to get Communion." I started masturbating at that stage, and I wasn't going into a box to tell anybody that I was masturbating. So, because I couldn't get a good Confession, I couldn't be in a state of grace, and I couldn't get Communion. So, the whole thing seemed pointless.

So, she didn't say to me, "Well, stop or you'll go blind." She just went, "Ah, well, if that's what you feel, that's what you feel."

She did once—and this came out of the left field—just before I got married, she asked me to get Confession. And I did . . .

GB: You did go to Confession?
BOC: Well, I did and I didn't. I went down to a well-known church in town that was supposed to have quite open-minded priests, and I went into the confessional and I said, "Bless me, Father, for I have sinned. It's been nine years since my last Confession."

And he said, "Right, let's get started. I suppose you've been drunk."

I said, "I don't drink, Father."

"Don't lie to me!"

I said, "What?"

"Don't tell me lies."

I said, "I'll tell you what: stick it." And I left.

GB: End of Confessions . . . Did that turn you off your faith and religion for ever more?

BOC: I never identified with Catholicism, really. I don't know why. In my teens, I started to read the Bible, would you believe, and I found it very interesting. One of the passages I always remember was a thing that Jesus said: that the closer you are to religion, the further you are from God. And I thought about that. And I'm not talking about Catholicism. I'm talking about organised religion in general. I started to look at what I believe were money-making machines. How come, in Finglas, we are poor, but we have one of the biggest churches in the country? And we all paid for that, door to door.

I thought the Pope being infallible was something that was given to St Peter by Jesus. And then you realise it wasn't. It was a Pope that woke up one day and decided he was infallible. So, I started to question organised religion, but I never lost my faith in God.

GB: How did you end up in Daingean?

BOC: [Laughs.] I was caught stealing. I was the worst thief in the world. It was a roll of Sellotape, a bicycle lock and two Oxo cubes and a biro . . . And I had the stuff, and I looked and I thought, "There's the door . . . There's me . . . Door . . . Me." And I nearly made it.

GB: And?

BOC: It was very peculiar. I didn't think I would get punished for it. My mother didn't think I would get punished for it. But I'm not sure that the judge and herself had, in the past, politically, seen eye to eye . . .

GB: Ah!

BOC: And they thought a period of minding might do me the world of good. I think it was my tenth birthday.

GB: What sentence did you get?

BOC: Three months, I think it was.

GB: Three months in Daingean! For that!

BOC: Yeah.

GB: Was it bad?

BOC: No, it was actually very lucky . . . When I was being checked in, the brother that was checking me in asked me when was the last time I got Mass.

I said, "Yesterday morning."

He said, "Yesterday morning? And what about before that?"

I said, "The morning before that." And I could serve the Mass in Latin . . . Well, I became a star! I served Mass every day, and I was minded.

GB: And do you think you were treated softly because of that?

BOC: Without a doubt. Some of the guys there . . . terrible times.

GB: Did you learn your lesson out of Daingean?

BOC: Yes, I swore I'd never get caught again.

GB: Now, what age were you when you left school?

BOC: Either eleven or twelve. You see, I'm dyslexic, and when you're dyslexic you feel like you're stupid, but I was also living with a genius who didn't think I was stupid, who had this theory: never confuse education with intelligence. And she said, "You obviously can't learn the way the others are learning, so we're going to have to find a different way for you to learn."

GB: Is it not extraordinary that your mother, having been educated and having been a nun, and being the woman she was, that she didn't encourage you to stay on in school?

BOC: There you go! None of us went past primary. She thought education didn't teach you, it didn't prepare you for life.

GB: Is there spirituality in your life, Brendan?

BOC: Yeah, I give it off to everybody I speak to.

GB: Explain that to me.

BOC: Brendan Comiskey—that Bishop Brendan Comiskey—I knew him. He actually christened my daughter, Fiona—I know he had his woes—and one of the greatest compliments he ever gave me, he said, "Brendan, you're one of God's people. You don't just talk the message of God: you live the message of God." And that's what I hope . . . My home is the place of God, my heart is the place of God, my car is the place of God. I do more talking to God in my car than I've ever done in a church, ever.

GB: At times of turmoil, do you pray?

BOC: All times: turmoil, celebration. Every time I've asked for help, or peace . . . After my son died I got very, very down, very disillusioned with life, because I was very young, and I had everything prepared in my mind: white picket fence, swing in the garden, you know, take him to the zoo, take him to all the football matches. I had everything planned and then this happened, and the plans all went out the window. And I just couldn't find peace in myself. I just couldn't be peaceful. And I asked for peace, and it came. But with people, with friends.

GB: Now, tell me about Brendan. The child died at what age?
BOC: He was only a couple of days old . . . It nearly killed me. It tore my heart out. And it still does.

GB: How old would he have been now?
BOC: Thirty-five.

GB: And did you rail against God at that stage?
BOC: No, not at that stage. I didn't blame him; I didn't think it was his fault. I did later on, at different, other things. "God, what did I do? Was I so bad that I deserved this?" Brendan was spina bifida. His head was enlarged so much that in order for him to be born they had to operate on him while he was still in the womb. So they had to remove some fluid from the brain, and every time they removed fluid from the brain it would damage him. So when he was born he was blind. Then, next, he was paralysed. Then it was a gradual disintegration. And I remember kneeling and begging God to take him, for selfish reasons, because I didn't think I could cope . . . And then, of course, when God did take him it was my fault. "What did I do that for?"

The doctors were amazing, because, first of all, I didn't want to see him, because he had no longer become the baby I had pictured in my head. He now was a monster. And they got me round. And when I did see him, he was beautiful. Ah, God, he was just beautiful . . . And I held his little hands. And then, of course, bravado kicked in, and I said, "So, when can I have him home?" and the doctor said, "Mr O'Carroll, you'll never have him home." He said, "Brendan could live for three days, three weeks, three months. And, for your sake, I hope it's three days." So, he lived a little bit more than that.

GB: You once said that the greatest gift your mother made you was that she died.
BOC: Yeah.

GB: What was that all about?
BOC: She used to say, as a kid, "You're special, you're special." So, you keep telling yourself, "I'm special" . . . But *this* doesn't feel special. So I

kept trying different things, and she would say to me, "Brendan, this is not going to end well. End it quickly." And I would, and she was right. And because of that, I never failed. I never truly failed. Things . . . I wound them up, and I went on to the next thing.

After my mother died, God, everything I touched just turned to muck . . . And that's what I needed more than anything else in my life: I needed to fail, because there is no lesson in *not* failing. There's only lessons in failure. And I learned so much about myself, about my own character, about my ability . . . to be an honourable person. I learned all of that through failure and had she still been alive, she would have been showing me how to avoid the failures. I'm very lucky that I have a success now that I am very, very pleased with. But, by God, I feel I've earned it.

GB: What failures are you talking about?
BOC: Oh, God—well, my marriage.

GB: That was a bad split-up. . .
BOC: Well, it's not so much as it was a bad split-up. We were very young: we were thirteen when we met. So, you're getting married and you're wondering, are you marrying because you're friends or are you getting married because you're in love? And I reconciled it with myself at the time: "Well, it doesn't matter why you're getting married. If you stand up there on the altar and make your promise, you keep your promise. That's what I do." Until you get a bit older and you say, "No, I expect to be happy." We were great friends, but there was just something that wasn't there.

GB: And when you broke up, did you feel guilty about it?
BOC: Oh, God, yeah. First of all, the manner in which we broke up . . . But it's very difficult. I was also very arrogant. I thought, "Well, I can't leave, because if I do, she'll fall apart." Which is terribly selfish and arrogant of me. She far from fell apart: she's extremely happy and living with a lovely guy. I could have done it earlier, so I'm sorry I delayed that. I'm sorry I held her life up. And, as well as that, I just wish it hadn't happened for the kids.

Jenny was in my life at that stage, and certainly there was a perception that I was leaving Doreen for Jenny, which couldn't have been more wrong. The fact that I did fall in love with Jenny was amazing, but I didn't expect it. And here we are now—what, fifteen years later—

And now I'm remarried and absolutely head over heels.

GB: You do feel that way now?

BOC: Oh, God, yeah. I tell you something: God sent her to me, whoever or whatever He is. Somebody looked down on me and said, "That little ****** needs a minder," and He sent her to me. I'm blessed.

GB: You mentioned karma earlier on. Do you believe in that?

BOC: Oh, big time! It comes in many guises and forms, but, beyond any shadow of a doubt, it's there, because I know, I know: I've seen people who I've thought, "My God, that person has tried so hard, so hard, so hard, and they're so good, and they're not going to get a break." And then they do. The problem is hanging in there.

And, more than ever in our history, the people of Ireland need to just hang in there. Don't quit. Most people quit a yard from the finish line. They don't realise that they are close to the finish line. Don't quit! Tomorrow is another day. Every twenty-four hours the world turns. Remember that when you are in the bottom of the world it turns every twenty-four hours. It's important to remember when you are on the top as well!

GB: Do you think that you're going to go to Heaven?

BOC: Of course! Are you kidding me? First of all, they need a few laughs, and, second of all, anyone who reads the Book of Revelations will know that the God of Revelations is an all-forgiving God. You couldn't offend Him, Gay Byrne. I couldn't offend Him. No matter what your misdeeds are, and no matter who you are, He will find a way to forgive you. That's what an all-loving God does.

GB: Do you believe in Hell?

BOC: No! . . . I think come-uppance happens usually right here on earth.

GB: In what way?

BOC: Listen, I was having a dinner in a restaurant in LA with a very well-known producer, and just as we paid the bill everybody in the restaurant got up, and they all left together. And it was because O. J. Simpson was coming in for a meal with somebody else. The entire restaurant got up and left. And the producer turned round and said to me, "That's his Hell. That's his prison." You know, I really don't think that there is even a remote possibility that there is a Hell.

GB: Getting back to Mrs Brown, what is astonishing to me is that, in the Olympia for your show, seventy-five per cent of the audience, it seems to me, are lovely, respectable, blue-rinsed, middle-aged women, enjoying every single moment of it. What is that about?

BOC: That's not just in the Olympia. That's the same in Glasgow, Liverpool, Manchester, Sunderland, Newcastle, Birmingham. You know, what Mrs Brown says is funny. "F" doesn't make it funny, and taking out the "F" won't make it less funny. It's funny. The woman that I have in Mrs Brown is an authentic woman. She's not something I made up. And, for me, taking the "F" word out would be like taking every second word out of a Wordsworth poem and thinking it would still have the same rhythm. It doesn't. And if you notice, in the TV series, nobody else says it: not one other actor on that stage or in that TV series says the "F" word. Only Mrs Brown. Do you know why? Because she wouldn't have bad language in her house.

GB: [Laughs.]

NORAH CASEY

The Magic Dragon

There is a deeply unfair question I sometimes ask people in this series: "Do you think of your partner as *the* love of your life or *a* love of your life?" Who could ever admit the latter? But there is a serious point to the question. So much romance depends on the idea that there is some *one* out there, somewhere, for everyone, if only we have the good fortune and good sense to find them.

What total guff!

And then you meet Norah Casey and wonder if all that "guff" might just be true. Because she did find her *one*—the yin to her yang, the person who completed her life: Richard Hannaford.

And then she lost him. Or, rather, he was brutally taken away. In a matter of weeks, cancer silently breached his defences and overwhelmed his body like a marauding horde. He died at the age of just forty-nine—no age to die, and no age to be a widow. No wonder, as Norah told me, that their then twelve-year-old only son, Dara, has flirted with atheism since. At the very least, you would want to shake your fist at the Big Guy Upstairs. Perhaps disbelieving in Him is an even better way of getting your own back.

God was only just beginning to figure in Norah's life again when we spoke. She, too, had shaken her fist at Him, but then she found herself being unexpectedly comforted by the calm cadence of ritual and Rosary, which her native Catholicism had at the ready during the worst of her grief. Was this faith? She wasn't sure. But when she needed something, Catholicism was there like an enfolding blanket, softening the biting cold of grief.

I interviewed Norah in the week of the first anniversary of Richard's death. I am still not totally sure why she agreed to do the interview, especially at that time, although she told me afterwards that she has got huge support from the way people respond to her talking publicly about Richard's death. She has discovered, through the written embrace of hundreds of strangers, that she really *isn't* alone.

That said, when I asked her if she felt Richard as a presence or an absence, she was very clear that, right then, he was an absence: there was a Richard-shaped hole in her life, which she was busily trying to fill with too much work. And Dara.

Dara will be Norah's strength and her salvation, as the psalmist puts it. I know that without even meeting him, just from the way she spoke about him. The love of her life is still there, every day, in the life their love created, and she knows to be grateful for small miracles. She also has the good sense to mother Dara, but not to smother him.

Of course, given the timing, our conversation was partly about death. But perhaps, more than most, and for that very reason, it was also about life: truly, the *meaning* of life. Every human story, as Philip Larkin once observed, has a beginning, a muddle and an end. Without the end, it would just be a muddle. In his life and his death, Richard Hannaford taught Norah something terribly important about the meaning of life. It is a lesson, I am sure, she still wishes she had done without, but I am grateful to her for having the generosity to share it.

GB: You met Richard. He was working for the BBC . . . Was that an immediate attraction . . . ?

NC: Yeah, it was . . . I met Richard at a media dinner, and, yes, I will be honest, I told a number of good friends afterwards that, if I ever married, it was going to be to Richard Hannaford. And he was such a charming, nice, intelligent person . . . There was a big connection between the two of us. I'll also say to you that we had a year of very old-fashioned courtship. We got to know each other in a way that didn't involve holding hands or kissing. And I knew everything there was to know about Richard at the end of that first year, and he knew everything that there was to know about me, so that when we did finally kiss it was quite magical.

GB: It took you a year to kiss?

NC: Yes. [Laughs.]

GB: [Laughs.] Well, I've heard of nerves in my time, but a year to kiss?

NC: Well, looking back, I can only say that it was the perfect foundation, because within a month or two of us kissing, we wanted to get married. There was no doubt in either of our minds.

GB: Wonderful, romantic story.

NC: Yes.

GB: Now he became a Catholic.

NC: Uh-huh.

GB: Was that a cursory thing, in order to marry his darling Norah, or was that a conviction thing, do you think?

NC: I'll tell you the honest truth. He grew up in a household that was Church of England, so didn't really have anything like the kind of up-bringing that I had. He would come to Ireland with me regularly and just absolutely loved the community spirit of the Church. He loved the fact that we'd spend so much time in church. He loved the fact that when people were sick or ill, that we said the Rosary—that we bonded together. And it was really *that* he wanted to buy into. He just felt that if he was going to marry me, and truly that we were going to connect and get married in a Catholic church, that he had to absolutely believe in it.

GB: Did he ever come back to you and say, "What about this? Do you really believe this?"

NC: All the time he challenged me. I mean, I grew up with Hell and damnation and lots of rules, and he was being taught a totally different view of God, like a really benevolent God. So, he was challenging my thinking, definitely.

GB: And then you were married, and I know you were disappointed about having a baby for a long time, and then—dah-dah!—along comes Dara.

NC: Yes, and like when you find, you know, Richard was the absolute love of my life, and the only thing we wanted was a child. And it didn't happen that way.

The irony for me was I *did* get pregnant, but couldn't retain the pregnancy, and in fact my mother and father had come over when they heard that I was going through this terrible miscarriage. And I left St Thomas's Hospital, bought a bottle of brandy and two hundred cigarettes. Went home with my mother, and I said, "That's it. I'm going to enjoy my life."

And then, over the course of the next five or six weeks, the professor in Tommy's, he did a scan and he said, "You won't believe it. You are pregnant. Totally naturally, one hundred per cent pregnant, and here it is." And I went straight from a miscarriage to a normal, healthy preg-nancy, which was miraculous, and delivered my big, bouncing ten-pound baby nine months later. I still, to this day, don't know how that happened, because there were physical reasons as to why Richard and I couldn't get pregnant.

GB: Wonderful. Wonderful story. Brandy and two hundred fags.

NC: Stop!

GB: So, why the move back to Dublin?

NC: I was running a company in London, and my boss in Paris flew in and said, "Would you run the Dublin company?" I had been in London for eighteen years. It was always my ambition that I would return home. And this was almost the perfect solution, because he didn't want me to live in Dublin: he wanted me to commute. And I thought it would be real easy to do . . . But it was dreadful.

GB: A recipe for disaster . . .

NC: Yeah. It was the most difficult decision we ever had to make, because one of us had to give up the job. At the time I was earning much more than Richard was, and he took the big decision then to leave the BBC and to come and live in Ireland with myself and Dara. And I'll tell you, from Day One, he loved Dublin. And it was magical, because all of a sudden, after eighteen months of us going through this very difficult time, we were suddenly all together again.

GB: Well, it sounds a wonderful life . . . And then disaster.

NC: Yeah, it's like somebody just side-swipes your life. I'll be honest with you: we were out partying the night before he got sick. He was really fit and healthy. The next day he was cooking lunch for my mum, and he said he had a terrible pain in his back, and I was joking with him that perhaps he'd had a little bit too much to drink the night before. And then within a couple of hours he was lying down, saying, "No, I really have a *very* bad pain in my back." And subsequently, over the course of a week, they diagnosed him with a kidney tumour . . . Unfortunately for us, the story didn't end there: about two weeks later they did a scan and discovered he had three cancerous tumours in his liver, and it was then a rollercoaster of bad news for us. We never had a break, not once.

As well as the liver cancer, they discovered that he had some on his spine. So, fairly quickly, they decided to do radiotherapy in St Luke's, and it actually fractured his spinal column . . . So, my vibrant, lovely young husband who was joking and partying with me, about four weeks later, was in a wheelchair. When they went to check about whether they could do spinal surgery on him, they discovered even more cancer.

GB: Did he fight it, Norah?

NC: Yeah. "Fight" is an odd word, because in fact you're completely powerless. We were very much in other people's hands . . . We managed to get to August, and we went in one day. Richard had a terrible pain in his side. We were about to have chemo, and the doctor said, "Let's just get you checked out. You might have a little bubble in your lung." And he went down to x-ray. Hours later, we found ourselves sitting in front of that doctor, and he said, "I'm sorry. You have cancer in your lungs now, and that's the end of the treatment." English wasn't his first language, so it took a little while for me understand that what he was saying was actually "That's the end of the road."

GB: Jeepers!

NC: So, when we left there, I actually couldn't even drive. And I went to see my mum. You know, my mother's such an amazing woman. She just . . . I don't know . . . She put us together, I think . . .

GB: Was there prayer involved here at any stage? Do we go through the thing of making a bargain with God?

NC: So many. We went to church fairly regularly. So, my plea-bargaining was way up there in terms of all the things that I was going to do, if we could have a miracle. But he was getting more and more sleepy.

So we went to see an amazing guy at Blackrock Hospice called Paul Gregan. He's perhaps the best palliative care specialist in Ireland. And Richard was so upset about going to the hospice. On the way in, in the wheelchair, he kept saying, "Please don't leave me here." And I said, "Look, we're just going in to talk to him." I have to tell you, the minute we walked in to Paul Gregan—he was the first person we had met who just sat back and said, "Tell me what happened to you, Richard." And for about two hours, he allowed Richard to speak. And it was so human. And he did prescribe him lots of new drugs, but actually what he gave him was so much more valuable than the drugs.

GB: You mean, just listening.

NC: He listened to him. Nobody had ever listened to him telling his story about what had happened to him.

So, we went into the hospice, Gay, and it was so beautiful. God, I remember: from the moment he arrived—felt at home. And he did go in there for respite, but within a few days he had developed pneumonia, and the nurses kept saying to me, "You know, your husband's very sick."

And I kept saying, "I know. Sure he has cancer in almost every major organ." But what they were trying to say to me was, "He's dying."

GB: You said he had a peaceful, a happy death . . .

NC: Ah, stop! Absolutely . . .

GB: What did you mean by that?

NC: Oh, I never understood the concept myself, given that I was a nurse. Everything happened right. Because he'd never had a chance to write a letter to Dara. He tried many times, and the chemo would make his brain fuzzy. He couldn't write properly. The doctor had said to me, this lovely man, Paul Gregan, "You know what I think? Dara might have some questions. Let's go and talk to him."

And Richard said, "I don't really want to talk with you and Dara."

So, myself and Dara went in to talk to him. And the doctor spent ages drawing a picture of Richard's body showing all the cancer. And he said to Dara, "Do you want to ask me a question?"

And Dara, straight away, said, "Yes. Is my dad dying?"

And he said, "Yeah, he is."

And he followed it with: "When is he going to die?"

And he said, "He's going to die in the next day or two." And I found out that Richard was dying that way.

And while I was with Dara, consoling him, Paul Gregan said, "I now have to go and see Richard, because I always go and see the patient after I've talked to the son and the wife."

Went in to see Richard, and Richard said, "Did Dara ask you the *hard* question?"

And Paul Gregan said, "He did."

And he said, "And what did you answer?"

And he said, "You are going to die in the next few days." And that's how Richard found out he was going to die.

And you know what? That was so important, because for the first time the three of us had an honest conversation. And he was able to tell Dara all the things that he had struggled to tell him. And Dara was able to talk to him honestly as well. We had one evening when we talked honestly and got all of the hugs and the love and everything you want to say.

GB: And then . . . ?

NC: What was so nice about that is that all his friends came to say goodbye . . . A wonderful friend, a priest, came and said the last rites.

And when they left, myself and Richard were together. Tracy, this lovely nurse, came and sat opposite me, and the two of us held his hand, and he died really peacefully and, I have to say, incredibly beautifully. And there was no big drama. I didn't feel the need to phone anybody. It was lovely to have quiet time.

GB: Go back now to what that did to your faith, if anything.

NC: I'll tell you one thing: the Catholic Church comes into its own, I think, when somebody dies so close to you like that, because all those rituals that happen after somebody dies, they carried me and Dara through what was a very, very difficult bereavement. Even family coming together, praying with him before he went to the coffin: the removal, the service—everything. And the Rosary became almost like meditation. We said so many decades of the Rosary. Almost like a mantra.

And there's something that is calming when you're standing together, collectively, and you don't know what to say to one another. And you're powerless and you're grief-stricken. Just repeating those familiar words over and over and over again—this tremendous peacefulness about it. And it helps you to get through those difficult moments.

We have a very good friend—a priest, Father Alan Hilliard—who did the service so beautifully. He spent a lot of time between Richard's death and the funeral talking to us about what we wanted. Nonetheless, if I'm being honest, I have had long conversations with God which I wouldn't repeat to you here.

GB: Pretty strong.

NC: Yeah, I was tremendously angry. And you do question, then, everything about your faith and spend a lot of time looking at people who you think are not worthy of spending another breath on the planet [laughs], wondering why your lovely husband, who didn't do a thing to anybody, could possibly have been taken so early, and allowing this old curmudgeon who you'd come across to stay alive . . . Which is terrible and not a good way to behave; but, nonetheless, I was tremendously angry. And the way I dealt with it was probably by *not* going to church for quite a period of time.

GB: As in, "That's it. I'm done."

NC: Yeah, pretty much, actually.

GB: And now, what is the state of your faith, one year later? What is the state of your mind about God and religion and faith and death and all of that jumbled-up thing?

NC: Funny: I actually think I'm coming much more around to chatting to Him again . . .

GB: Chatting to who again?

NC: God. It's like having a good friend that you've fallen out with, and you just have to tentatively start thinking about whether or not you can have a relationship again. Dara, on the other hand, has gone in the opposite direction. Dara has declared himself agnostic, and I'm hoping it'll be a temporary thing.

GB: He wouldn't be a normal young fella, if he didn't take time out.

NC: Yeah . . . He is the magic of my life. I look at him and I think there's that perfect combination of Richard and myself, through his DNA, through the values we've given him . . . He's changed enormously in the last year. I say to him all the time that sometimes, out of very bad things, good things happen. And he's a different child because of what's happened to him.

GB: Of course.

NC: He's turned into a wonderful boy. The meaning of my life is very much about him and passing on to him everything that I believe is important to him in his life.

GB: Last question. If, when your time comes, and you get to the pearly gates, everything that the Sisters of Charity taught you in Stanhope Street and everything that Richard learned in his conversion to Catholicism—suppose it's all true and you confront God. What will you say to Him?

NC: I'd be waiting to get Him out of the way so I meet my Richard, who would be inside, no doubt . . . But, yeah, the only thing I could reasonably ask of Him is to say, "Give Dara a happy and healthy life, and give him the joy of having children, because then Richard and I live on through Dara's children and grandchildren." And that's part of the magic and the meaning of life for me.

TOMMY TIERNAN

Divine Comedy

Very often, the *Meaning of Life* researchers have had to work quite hard to persuade potential guests to share their innermost thoughts and beliefs with the great Irish public. Coming under the banner of Religious Programmes, we do not have the resources to dangle any financial carrots in front of them. Our token fee is just that, and ours is not the sort of show where celebrities appear in order to promote their latest book, play, film or record. My focus is on the person, not the product.

All of which made it surprising when Tommy Tiernan made contact with us, via an intermediary, to let it be known that he wanted to do an interview.

Perhaps I should not have been surprised, since I have known for years that Tommy is very thoughtful, with real depth. I am also very fond of him. He is a one-off: a brilliant, quick mind and a mouth that somehow keeps pace with it. And unquantifiable charm and charisma. He will get people laughing at unthinkable and unspeakable things that from anyone else would simply be offensive.

Mind you, he doesn't always gauge his audience before he delivers a gag. To this day, I regret the slip-up that led us to book him for *The Late Late Show* to deliver material about the Crucifixion. That was our fault, not his. He was much younger then and did not have the experience to realise that material that might have them howling at a Vicar Street comedy night would fall dangerously flat in front of the *LLS*'s more mainstream audience. I should have known better, but it was an eye-off-ball moment.

Shortly before our *Meaning of Life* interview, however, an older, wiser Tommy Tiernan got into a scrape that was entirely of his own making when he made a joke about the Holocaust. That is just a basic no-no. There are some subjects about which some people will never see a funny side. Perhaps because there isn't one.

I know Tommy well enough to know that he is not remotely anti-Semitic. He's anti- lots of things—authority, rules, deference—but not Jews. But try telling that to the sponsors of his subsequent American tour, who came under irresistible pressure to cancel.

So what possessed him, if "possessed" is not an unfortunate choice of word? Our conversation started, as Maria von Trapp recommends, at the beginning.

GB: Was there religion in the family, Tommy?
TT: Not in the slightest.

GB: Nothing?
TT: Absent. Absent and unmissed. My parents never brought us to Mass. I sometimes think that you're attracted to things that your parents weren't, 'cause you need a sense of discovering something new yourself.

GB: Are you suggesting that your parents were aggressively hostile to religion . . . ?
TT: No, not even . . . It was like a channel on your television that you never switch on. It was there, but . . . My father would be a very wise man, now . . . I remember once telling him that I wanted to study philosophy, and he told me, "Tom, we're all philosophers."

GB: So, when on Sunday mornings you were let loose, as it were, out of the house, and you had the choice of going to Mass, did you . . . ?
TT: Oh, yeah, I did, and I remember going to Mass in Navan.

GB: And did you go to Mass because all your mates were going . . . ?
TT: Yeah, it would be the social thing. You'd go to see the girls, and it was where you'd hang out for a while.

GB: And then . . . why did you go to Ballinasloe?
TT: I was sent there, because I failed all my exams in Navan . . . We got a remark in one of my reports saying, "Tom has obviously decided that the Irish education system has nothing to offer him." [Laughs.] But I remember the day I came home from school and both my parents were sitting there, and they said, "You're being sent to a boarding school." And I said, "Great!" It was fantastic, and I worked for the first, I'd say, four or five months in school. And then I came 4th out of 84 in my exams at Christmastime. And in my summertime exams I came 84th out of 84.

I had hooked up with this priest, Father Dara Molloy, who ran a basic Christian community out in the Aran Islands. I was bored senseless in school, and I hated it, and so I hooked up with Father Dara, and I told all my friends, "I'm leaving school."

And they said, "What are you going to do?"

And I was seventeen at that stage, and I had all these naïve notions. I said, "I'm going to set up an organisation to help the world."

And they said, "Right." [Laughs.]

I says, "Well, I'm going to go around visiting schools, helping other young fellas who might not feel they fit in."

So that was the plan, right. And the exams came, and I sat and I didn't look at them. And then a letter arrived from the Principal of the school, who is now the Bishop of Clonfert, Bishop John Kirby, saying that "We have Tom's results. He got zero in everything. What's happening? We hear that he is leaving the school." And also there was a friend of mine that was going to do the same thing. And so my father said, "What's going on here?" And I told him, and he said, "Okay, you can leave, you can leave school" . . . And I chickened out.

GB: [Laughs.]

TT: I got scared. But the interesting thing was the Headmaster said that I had brainwashed this other guy, and I was only allowed back into the school on a trial basis, and one of the conditions was that I wasn't to talk about religion to any of the other students. Stunning!

GB: You were a danger?

TT: Well, it was daft. I mean, it was the daft trying to lead the daft. There was no wisdom in it, like.

GB: I'm trying to cope with this. You're a rare person, in my view, in Ireland, in that there was no religious background of any kind, good, bad or indifferent. Surely, in boarding school, the good, holy priests would have taught you the basics, the rudiments of the Christian faith . . . ?

TT: Yeah. I guess it was around then that I started to become interested in religion. So, you go into it gently, usually via music. So I would have started off with people like the band called the Waterboys, who had this kind of, erm, religious element to some of their music. And it went from there into, I guess, Catholicism, in a sense, listening to music from Taizé. I went through a phase where I got up before everybody else in the dormitory, and I went down . . . There was a Mass before everybody got up, at seven o'clock in the morning. I used to go down to that. There was a prayer room, and I used to go into that after everyone else had gone into bed. I became vegetarian . . . So, I was searching.

Then—and I can remember the moment, because I was uneducated and because there was nobody to guide me in it—it quickly became a very oppressive force in my life and very depressing and joyless. And I remember sitting in John Molloy's English class one time, and we were reading a poem called *The Collar* by George Herbert. And I read the first line, and it was: "I struck the board and cried, 'No more. I will abroad.'" And I just said, "That's it. I'm done with it, this oppressive force in my life. I don't need it."

Now, that was seventeen. It took me about four or five years for it to be washed out of my system. But I remember that moment. And I'm also very aware of how that poem ends, and it ends with the guy on his knees, saying, "Lord." So, it's a full-circle thing.

GB: And then the Aran Island experiences. What were they about?
TT: They were just the basic Christian community, a group of people who were trying to explore the Gospels in a Celtic sense, I suppose, and trying to be a self-sufficient community. And I went out there and, in a sense, I'm allergic to work, so. . .

GB: [Laughs.] I had a feeling this story was going to end in a disaster. So . . . ?
TT: They asked me to leave, more or less. They had a great regime. They'd get up early in the morning and they'd pray and they'd meditate and they'd go out into the field and they'd bring seaweed up. And I'm great socially, but, you know, they'd been up since six, and I would—probably, about half ten—I'd wander into the communal living area with my boxer shorts, scratching myself and looking for corn flakes, and it wasn't a marriage made in Heaven. But it was all part of the experience. And being out in Aran was great. And that's where I met Jamie, whom I was with for a long time, and we ended up having three children together. So, it was a great youthful thing to do, to cast off like that a little bit.

GB: And at what stage did the urge to join the Redemptorists come?
TT: That happened after Aran, actually. I went in, and I went on a couple of retreats with them, and I stayed with them, and they were all set for me to join. And the head Redemptorist visited my parents in Navan. And I was all up for it. And because I didn't do so well in my Leaving Cert, I didn't get into First Arts in Galway, and they wanted me to repeat my Leaving Cert. I said, "Ah, lads, come on . . . ! We'll leave it, so." And I left.

GB: [Laughs.] What was the attraction there, do you think?

TT: My father once called me a martyr without a cause . . . I guess it was the extremity of the life, in a sense. It was so simple. You know, it was you, some books, spirit. It was opposite in many ways to what I saw going on around me.

GB: It seems to me that you're still on a search of some kind, and I wonder how much of that is left in you?

TT: I don't know. There was a great man called John Moriarty, who I would listen to a lot, and I try and have a kind of a prayer routine like you're aware that Muslim people would have—a call to prayer two or three times a day. And recently I was going through one of the Glenstal Books of Prayer and it was language that I just wasn't comfortable with—a language of certainty, a language of answers. And I guess that's not the star that I would sail my ship by, but I would be somebody who is very drawn to Christianity and prayer . . . which, I am sure, is almost the opposite of my work.

But, you know, I used to say this saying to myself before I went on stage, a kind of a mantra to get me in the right frame of mind: "Please, Lord Jesus, let me do my work." And I'd say it a few times over and over, and the frame of mind that I took with me on stage was that, that my function here is to take nothing seriously. And that's my role. And I felt enriched and enlivened and energised by that kind of reckless irresponsibility.

And there's a particular breed of Zen monks and what they do is they travel around from monastery to monastery, and they piss in the holy bowls, and they'd shit on the scripture and stuff like that . . . And their philosophy would be: "Look, you can't take any of this seriously." So, I think, in a sense, there was an element of that on stage, the trickster figure: a kind of an amoral, profane, loose cannon is needed, and he's often despised. He's loved, but in trickster mythology, he's often the link between Earth and Heaven.

GB: Go back to those Zen guys. They were monks, and they were trying to make a point: "Take none of this seriously." Do you mean take none of this spirituality or religion seriously?

TT: Take none of the icons, the physical things, the bits of paper, the Ardagh Chalice. These are just things that people have. They're not holy in themselves. You don't need things to go to Heaven, to be in touch with Heaven, to talk to Heaven. The type of prayer that I'm very . . . silent prayer, a Christian meditation thing, where it's wordless. I guess it's based on the idea that your mind is the barrier between you and infinity.

GB: So, I guess you'd agree with Meister Eckhart that there is nothing so much resembles God as silence . . .
TT: There you go . . .

GB: So, when you say, "Lord Jesus, make me good . . ."
TT: "Please, Lord Jesus, help me do my work . . ."

GB: . . . which means "Lord Jesus, please make me funny . . ."
TT: Yeah, yeah.

GB: . . . what Jesus are you praying to?
TT: Oh, I don't know . . . I think that we are made in God's image, but it's not a literal image. He doesn't have eyes and, you know, hair . . . It's a soul thing, I think. That's the part that resembles God.

You know, a friend of mine died very recently, and I was at his removal, and I saw his body, and the body is such a shell. And I was thinking, "Okay, there's the human being that I knew, but it's packaging. And it would be shocking if that energy didn't go somewhere else— that life force that was in him, that spirit."

GB: Go back to John Moriarty. What did he do for you, and what was his outlook, as far as you're concerned?
TT: Well, I wouldn't dare to try and summarise his outlook, because he's beyond me in many senses, but part of John's thing was that we don't repress anything. He believes that Christianity hasn't caught up with Christ. I think Catholicism that we have now is quite repressive, and in many ways—this is going to sound crude—you should bring your balls to Mass. You know, a spirituality that encompasses all, as opposed to represses the body. Like, my mother told me, she was told by nuns when she was growing not to have a look at yourself when you're washing.

GB: Yeah, we all went through that stuff . . . What about the children? Are they being brought up as Catholics?
TT: No, but I think you pick up stuff unconsciously. They're aware that I meditate. They wouldn't participate in it or wouldn't refer to it very often, but they're aware that that happens.

GB: Do you do that every day?

TT: I try to do it twice a day, yeah.

GB: Right, go back again. When you talk about the spirit and the spirit of your dead friend and it must go somewhere . . . We're not just a random collection of cells . . . ?

TT: It would be bizarre. I don't believe in rationality. There's nothing about life that's rational. There's nothing. How could you be on a small spinning ball? It makes no logical sense. Life is irrational. I think one of the great journeys we've had is the journey through rationality. I don't think we're the far side of it yet, but we're still trying to deal with logic and how that resonates with our perceptions.

GB: And how do you cope with Dawkins and those chaps?

TT: I think that any spirituality, your Charles Darwin has to be there as well. Evolution is part of it, and I don't think we're done evolving . . . I'm fine with evolution. I've toured Mayo. I can see the road . . .

GB: [Laughs] So, what is your aim in life?

TT: Oh, not to die just yet. Death is going to come, and there's no bargaining, and there's no complaining or righteousness—but not yet, please. And I guess I want to spend more time in the beautiful company of my family, more time with friends and more time on stage. It's such a beautiful experience to be in a room like that, and there might be a thousand people there, and you're laughing . . . They are moments of joy. More of them, please!

When I'm in a room with people, it goes sometimes to this place where it's beyond intellect, in a sense . . . and nothing is taken seriously, and things are being said and people are laughing. It's almost like, if you can imagine, say, the moment after you pass away, and you're looking down at the world, and you've got eternity ahead of you, and you're going, "It was so funny. All that pain was so funny." There are moments like that where things are said, and you say something, and people's reaction isn't horror, it's "Oh, my God, that's hilarious!" And what happens—it's the times we're living in now—is that those sentences get stolen, and they get brought outside, and, on a Sunday morning, people are reading them in the newspapers, and they're going, "This young man needs to be shot!"

And you just think, "Why? Why did I say that? And you know that was mean and was cruel." And I get very distressed about that . . .

GB: Well, obviously . . . Since you brought it up, the offence that you caused with the Holocaust thing . . . Now, in the old days of comedy, comedians would no more have gone next, nigh or near that entire topic . . .

TT: Yeah . . .

GB: . . . So, what were the circumstances of that coming on? Because to me, you're a gentle person, and you don't intentionally set out to give offence to people.

TT: Uh-huh . . .

GB: And yet this particular topic is the worst . . . and yet you went straight into it. I'd love to know what that was born of.

TT: You come along to any show that I do and I might be on stage for ninety minutes, and you could easily pick eight or ten sentences and go, "No!" You know, if you go through, there's the Jews, the Travellers, people with Down's syndrome, immigrants, people from Offaly . . .

GB: [Laughs.]

TT: There is no logic to it. It's obviously not meant, you know?

GB: Were you upset by the severe criticism of Archbishop Martin about your comments . . . ?

TT: You know, the awful thing is—and maybe this goes back to my upbringing—I took no heed of it. It doesn't concern me, really . . . There are a lot of people who understand what happened.

GB: Do you mean you were quoted out of context in some way?

TT: Ah, no. The way I have of describing it is that there are certain sentences for certain situations . . . I'm a public figure now, and I take shots at people on stage. People want to take shots at me in the press, that's fair enough. I don't have a problem with it.

I very much enjoy being famous in Ireland. It's a gift. People come up to you shining, because you make them laugh, and people will see me in the street and just start laughing. And it's great.

GB: It is a great gift.

TT: Yeah, it is. Yeah.

GB: Who gave it to you?

TT: I think it's a way of being in the world. I think it's a way of coping. It's as natural to me as breathing. It's how I am.

GB: You know the basics of theology in Christianity and the Catholic Church. Suppose it were all true. How would you cope?

TT: And I was going up to be judged?

GB: Yes.

TT: I would say, "How dare you make me the way I am and not back me up!" You know, if I die and I'm judged, and He's there with the big book, and McQuaid is beside him, and he's going, "Him, him, he's Number 1 for Hell . . ."

"Supposing it is all true . . .?" But sure it is!

GB: Okay, what will you say to Him?

TT: I'll say [stretches and yawns], "What's next?"

GB: That'll do. Thank you.

FATHER SHAY CULLEN

Fisher of Men, Women and
Children

A hasty last-minute change of location. The three-times Nobel Peace Prize nominee and priest, Father Shay Cullen, had objected to the choice of a church as a location for our interview. "I don't want to be painted as some kind of holy Joe," he said, in the curious Speedy Gonzales accent of a man who has been living in the Philippines and speaking a foreign language for forty years.

He had a point. Our interviews are generally shot in people's homes or in hotel suites. Were we putting him in a church just because he is a priest?

Father Shay wears his priesthood lightly, almost to the point of unease. Almost. In fact you will struggle to find anyone more committed to living the Gospel values, but he sometimes seems uncomfortable with the company in which his vocation has placed him.

Vocation. It's an interesting word. What does it mean? A calling, sure, but in Shay's case not from a burning bush or a cloud. Actually the call came in the form of a telegram to the aptly named Grimsby, in the tough north-east of England, where he went to work in a fish factory after leaving school. He would possibly be there still, were it not for that summons from the Columban HQ in Dalgan Park, Navan. Compared with Grimsby fish-packing, the swashbuckling life of a Columban missionary sounded like an adventure, and his application had been accepted. He jumped on a ferry.

There were twenty-two in Shay's class who stayed the course to ordination, in 1969. God be with the days! I can only imagine how few are enrolling now. Shay nearly wasn't one of the new priests. A few years ago, he wrote about the last-minute pang of doubt which struck him on the big day. We have all felt them—those *"What am I doing here?"* butterflies. But Shay has carried them with him ever since. Clearly, he still asks himself, *"What am I doing here?"* And no bad thing. Doubt and faith are not always opposites, as Robert Browning once noted. They can be two colours on the same chess board; two instincts in the same head and heart.

If you fear that self-doubt might have paralysed Shay Cullen, however, don't worry. He is a man of action, whose PREDA Foundation tirelessly defends the rights and safety of the people he serves in Olongapo, in the Philippines—especially women and children, trafficked into the sex trade or lured into drugs; or the poor people displaced from their land by a combination of corrupt politicians and mining cartels. Sure, he has won international acclaim, but at some cost. Death threats remain a very real occupational hazard. Other missionaries in his region have been killed, and a Nobel nomination is not bullet-proof.

It is as if, in seminary, he drank in the Beatitudes—Jesus's Larkin-like call to action in the Sermon on the Mount—but paid scant attention to all the *post hoc* intellectualising of his theology classes. When I tried to pin him down on matters of belief, his response was, publicly, to toe the party line, but more significantly, to leave all that "religioso" stuff to other people, while he gets on with the business of loving his enemies and his neighbour as himself.

Shay knows he is part of the last chapter of the Irish missionary project. A young Irish man in Grimsby today would probably not respond to a telegram from Dalgan Park, even if he knew what it was.

Shay also knows that the leadership of the Church to which he committed his life has not always lived up to the vision of its founder. He is fond of quoting Jesus' uncharacteristically brutal words about what we should do to those who harm children. In a line worthy of *The Sopranos*, they involve a millstone round the neck and deep water.

And yet, for all the shortcomings of the institution and the life, he stays. Why?

Not just, I suspect, because the people he serves need him, but also because he needs them. Shay Cullen lives not just a meaningful life, but a fulfilled one, which is not something I could say of every person who sits in the chair opposite me.

∿

GB: Father Shay, do you ever regret the life you chose?
SC: No, not really. And I think *it* maybe chose *me,* rather than I choosing it. No, I'm very happy and content with the way everything worked out, despite all the ups and downs.

GB: Let's go back to your childhood and your parents and growing up.
SC: [Laughs.] Yeah, it's just very normal, out in Glasthule, in South County Dublin. Christian Brothers first, and then to Pres., Glasthule. And it was fairly normal for the '50s and '60s.

GB: And was your family very religious?
SC: Well, yes, my parents were traditional Catholic, going to church,

and my mother was very devoted and, as much as possible, a daily Mass-goer.

GB: At what stage did the vocation come, and was it a slow-growing thing or was it a flash of brilliant light?

SC: No. Maybe sixteen or seventeen. Everyone around was going off to England to work in the buildings or the factories and I did see the possibility of the missionary type of life, because we had visitors coming into the school. Father Michael Balfe gave this presentation one day. "Hey, that sounds exciting." You know, we're looking for adventure, not religious and pious type of thing. And you can be educated, and there's no payment. You know, it was now financially possible to get a higher education and at the same time do something worthwhile. "Hey, we'll give this a try."

GB: You paint a rather depressing picture of your ordination day, because, even as you were being ordained, you had terrible doubts about whether you were doing the right thing or not.

SC: Yeah, well, it was impressed upon us that this is the final decision. There is no way back. I wasn't racked with doubt. Simply, you're thinking of the future. You know, the big thing coming: I was going abroad. The anxiety would be what life would be when you get there and could you cope with that?

GB: So, paint me a picture of Olongapo when you arrived all those years ago.

SC: Well, Olongapo City, it's about 140 kilometres north-west of Manila . . . Big naval base. The United States had a long-time presence in the Philippines. The Vietnam War was going on at the time, so it was really quite a busy place and thousands of US Navy coming into the town and the sex industry growing up along the streets. Young people, their lives very much messed up. And the sex industry had a very negative impact on the whole city. So, that was quite a challenge, if you were in a parish and you're teaching young people.

GB: So, confronted with that situation and the exploitation of people, from babies up to prostitution and all of that kind of thing, and a lot of money floating around, you're stepping into dangerous ground now. Everybody is perfectly happy with the nice cosy set-up, and here's a guy beginning to meddle in this situation.

sc: Yeah, well, "meddling"—we might say "challenging the system," as we saw it. This is not a dignified way to live. This is destructive of human life. At the time, I was focused more on the young people, because my students, some of them, were being arrested. President Marcos had declared martial law. They were picked up and put in the prison and there was lots of executions. That's when the death squads began—young people were being shot and, of course, I have to respond to that as a human person.

GB: You have to?

sc: Well, not everybody would agree with that. They said, "That's not your business, that's politics. Just shut up and go and say your prayers."

GB: That's the point I was making: this guy is trouble; this guy is interfering.

sc: Okay, maybe that came later. But at the beginning, I'm just working in the parish. But we did see the terrible exploitation of women and children on the streets. I mean, I'd be walking on the streets, they think you're a sailor and they come and say, "Hi, Joe, you want a girl?" And they're offering children for sale at twelve years old. So, this is quite shocking and it does something to you.

GB: And what did you do?

sc: Well, I set up an organisation called PREDA Foundation . . . so that we could focus on human rights.

GB: What was the theology behind this? Could you have done it without being a priest?

sc: Of course. It's a human reaction . . . You don't sort of say, "I have this obligation to do this, because of this reading in the Scripture." It doesn't work like that. I think each one of us, being natural ourselves, will always have a response to human tragedy and to human suffering.

GB: But you wouldn't have done it, and you couldn't have done it, if you had been a lay person rather than a priest?

sc: Well, not so. But the opportunity arose . . . Many lay people in the Philippines joined me to do this work. Many lay organisations today are the more active people. And that is as it should be.

GB: Meanwhile you're a priest. What's your image of God?

sc: Yeah, well [laughs], certainly not the Michelangelo image. But I like to think in terms of the existence of eternal goodness or the power and force of love. God is love, but if all of us are caring and respecting each other and having this kind of willingness to sacrifice for another and bring about what Jesus described love as—as action for helping others . . . the Good Samaritan story—here God is. There is a power, a force, that is present; a spiritual force present somewhere that changes lives, that changes situations, and it drives people forward through this caring for each other. No greater love can anyone have than give their life for their friend . . . Call it God, but for me, it's that energy, presence, spiritual power. But it certainly kept us working and gave us great motivation to do all this stuff and take the risks that went with it, because we get death threats and opposition and all of the harassment that goes with this work.

GB: Come back to your priesthood and saying Mass. What do you believe you're doing when you're saying Mass?
SC: Well, I think the way we would celebrate the Eucharist is as the bonding force. I think we have to see it outside its bell, book and candle. You know, the rituals of the Mass, nowadays, and the ways it's performed is a little too *religioso*—a little bit remote and distant from what Jesus would have experienced.

This "Do this in memory of me." He knew, this guy, he's getting the death penalty in two or three days. It's inevitable. So, what's he doing here? He's bringing his Disciples together. These are his best friends. They're working for all these things, and he says we're gonna bond ourselves together and let's be strengthened by sharing together and remember what this is all about. That's the Eucharist for me.

You know, faith in anything, without action, is useless. I mean, that's what St James says. It's all very nice going for religious ceremonies, but if it remains a religious ceremony, what good is that? It's supposed to inspire, encourage and unite people for action to change the world in which we live, to make this a beautiful community, a way to live together, where people have no fear or they feel encouraged, they feel inspired.

GB: Do you believe that it becomes the body and blood of Jesus?
SC: Yes, in one way, yes.

GB: In one way?
SC: Yeah. Who can explain that? It's a mystery. So, we go along with that. As I was trying to say, it's a ceremony when people are re-creating

the presence of Jesus, right there, so as to carry on his mission, to carry on his work and to prolong his presence in the world as He wanted it and as He did it. That's the way I see it.

GB: Bishop Daly has recently come out in relation to clerical celibacy and has said that the Catholic Church has lost many a good priest because of the celibacy law. What's your reaction to that, Shay?
SC: I'd agree with him in many ways, with this guy. I mean, celibacy is just a rule of the Church. It's only a practice, mostly to keep property out of the hands of the married couples, I suppose. [Laughs.] It's more sort of a business-type of an arrangement, but all the other Christian Churches manage very well. They have a good system and married clergy. You can see that those many Anglicans who were married and had family and children, they came over to the Catholics. They were warmly accepted and now we have many married priests in the Catholic Church and it's working very good. So, why not?

GB: The ceiling hasn't fallen in as a result?
SC: It's only another step now to abolish this celibacy thing and get on with life.

GB: In these interviews, I ask people about the subject of evil and I quote the usual suspects: Hitler, Mussolini, Stalin, Mugabe and so on, and I do that because I think that most people do not encounter evil in any real way. But you *have* encountered evil. Would I be right in saying that?
SC: Yes, yes, absolutely . . . Nearly every day we have some new case of rape of a child or something coming in. It's terrible. Torture, abuse, human rights violations—I see that every day.

GB: And you have no hesitation in calling that evil?
SC: No problem. It's not good, anyway.

GB: So, do you believe that evil exists in the world, say in the form of the Devil, as we were all taught, way back in the school . . . that he is roaming the world seeking whom he may devour?
SC: No, not in that sort of way. I mean, evil is, of course, a very powerful negative force. It's the evil choice of individual people . . . and of evil groups of people that bring evil about.

GB: You're talking about paedophile rings and all of that sort of thing . . . ?
SC: Yes, that's part of it here, but I mean anywhere that people's lives are damaged, hurt and suffering is caused. I mean, you might say many of

the practices of the financial world are evil, because it causes so much hunger and starvation throughout the world—selfishness personified, that causes hunger and injustice.

GB: And whence does this evil come?
SC: From the free choice of human beings. That's the point. And if people want answers as to why, if there is a good, loving God, how come there's evil all around us, well, I mean, evil is the result of free choice of the people and everyone has free will, otherwise they wouldn't be human . . . We have reason and we have consciousness and we can have love or hate. So, when people choose to do evil and to hate, we have to see that and react to it.

GB: All right. Who and what was Jesus to you, Shay?
SC: Well, he was quite an inspirational figure, of course. Very few people really read the Gospel stories, you know, very slowly and think about what's behind it. And so Jesus, as a figure and a prophetic one, challenging everything, turning the world upside down: "Blessed are the poor, yours is the land?" No! "Those who are hungry now, you'll have your fill. There's gonna be a change. There's gonna be a revolution, if you change your lives, if you believe in what I'm telling you." I mean, Jesus was an agent of change. [Laughs.] A very dramatic revolutionary who got the death penalty for it. I mean, we tend to think of Jesus as meek and mild and sweet image, which is ridiculous.

GB: Was he divine?
SC: Well, he certainly claimed to be the Son of the Father. We can't really know that, because it's a matter of Faith. We believe it.

GB: You believe it?
SC: Well, yeah. But there's something of the Divinity in all of us. Work it out: if goodness dwells in us and if God is eternal goodness, then we're part of God and we are all part of the Divine. So, maybe we should give ourselves a little more credit for the fact that we do have an experience of trying to be good and trying to have the Divine living within us. And Jesus was full of it.

GB: Full of what, goodness?
SC: Full of the Divine and goodness and eternal love and God-is-love, as we say. So, if we're seeking God, I think we have to start looking at what is the meaning of love in the world and get away from

the corruption of the word and the corruption of the experience.

GB: You believe, of course, he was crucified and died. Do you believe he rose from the dead?

SC: Well, he lives on, certainly, in my experience . . .

GB: Oh, no, no, no . . . Physically, did he rise . . . ?

SC: Yeah, I mean we go with that.

GB: Would it matter if he hadn't risen? I mean, if somebody found a grave next week in Jerusalem and said, "This is the grave of Jesus." Would that affect your Faith?

SC: I don't think so. It wasn't really a physical resurrection. Nobody fully knows. But we can go with that too. It doesn't really affect our life . . . We've got to go beyond just this: physically, he's dead and in the grave and then he comes alive—and factually, it could have happened, a great event. But we've got to see that the whole thing he lived and believed in is alive, because if that idea dies, then what good is the resurrection of anybody? And if your whole concept, if all that you believe in, you work for and everything he gave his life for, if that had been forgotten, you know, that's it. But this lived on! And he, in this way, is present again with us, as of today, and we can choose to go with it or we can ignore it.

GB: You were suggesting to me that the Resurrection is metaphorical?

SC: Not really. I would more accept the traditional Resurrection as a physical act. There's good stories to support it . . . But that doesn't affect one's faith, because our faith is really in Jesus and in his beliefs and in his action.

He was gone, he was over. They had won. They'd wiped out all this goodness and this guy and his revolutionary thought. The rebel was dead. The movement was gone and they'd all scattered everywhere.

Then, they came back and said, "Hey, he's alive and he's alive with us. He's with us and we're still going. We're moving on." The point is that he is still alive and with us. It worked.

GB: Do you believe in Heaven?

SC: Well, I hope so . . . I believe that if our lives are pure and our spirit is strong enough, it can survive physical death.

GB: What does that mean?

SC: Consciousness: no-one knows what it means. I mean, how can you imagine a life after death? No-one has a clue. You just have to believe.

GB: Okay. The obverse then: for all these evil people that you've encountered in your life, is there a Hell?

sc: I don't think that evil-doing is going to give the strength for the spirit to overcome or to continue. That's the best I can figure out.

GB: So, what happens?

sc: No-one knows.

GB: Obliteration?

sc: That's a philosophical question, or theological, and I never think much about what happens to people after death. Doesn't bother me much. I'm quite focused on this life . . . [laughs] and to make this happier and better for as many people as possible.

GB: Were you ever attracted to any other religion, like Buddhism or Hinduism?

sc: Oh, yeah. Of course I was interested to know them. Christians are really a minority in the world. There's billions of people out there following their own path to Nirvana or to an after-life or whatever, so it's quite a good experience to be interested in other faiths and respect them all for all their good sides. But every religion has a downside too. And institutional religion may be very weak, because it doesn't always stay alive and burning with the spiritual faith that makes it meaningful.

GB: Come back to the Catholic Church . . . .

sc: I didn't leave it, by the way . . .

GB: [Laughter.] No, no, no . . . *I* want to come back to the Catholic Church . . .

sc: Well, God bless you. I hope you make it! [Laughter.]

GB: [Laughter.] Going through a battering at the moment, as never before. When you've given so much of your life to doing what you have done for forty years in the Philippines, what's your reaction to what's gone on in the Church over the last . . . whatever? The revelations . . . ?

sc: Oh, the very awful, terrible stuff going on . . .

GB: Including some Columbans . . .

sc: Yeah, maybe. But balance it all up, because I'm dealing with every kind of child sexual abuse. Very little of clergy, but we do have some and we deal with that. I have thirty-five cases going on in court now against abusers, most of them fathers of the children. Incest is the biggest problem we're facing, and the second one is the sexual abuse of minors in the sex industry. Mostly foreigners coming into the Philippines, abusing children and so on.

But in any institution you're going to find child-abusers. It's across the board. Every country has its quota. There is nothing extraordinary or unusual. It's the way it's being dealt with is the biggest problem.

GB: In the Church?

SC: Well, exactly, or in any institution. Tendency is that people will try to protect themselves, protect their institution, their profession, and they'll all cover up for one another. In the Church, they're going to cover up child abuse. Well, that's wrong, it's totally immoral and it's even criminal and it has to be dealt with and they just have to answer, and be accountable, for that.

GB: And what do you think went wrong, Shay?

SC: Well, I think it's an over-emphasis on the Church as a religious institution that has to be protected; and that people are over-identified with the institution rather than identifying themselves with Jesus and the Gospel and the mission that he has given to us. That's the problem: you put your faith, not in Jesus and in his mission, you put it in an institution. Hey, it can go wrong.

The one thing the Gospels tell us is we should not be afraid of anything. We are able to trust in our basic faith in what is true and right. But a lot of clergy feel insecure and they're afraid to speak out. They might be criticised or whatever.

GB: Do you ever doubt your vocation?

SC: No. Well, never doubt what I'm doing, or I've made a choice to do what I'm doing right now. I think it's the right thing to do and I'm doing it.

GB: You're sixty-eight. You're coming to a point when many fellas would be thinking of hanging up their boots and walking into the sunset. Any ideas to retire?

SC: Not now. There's no point. Why would you retire from doing good? And you may not do it the same way all the time or have the levels of energy to continue on at the same pace, but there's always people can continue doing good, trying to bring about a little more justice in the world.

GB: On the day that you were ordained, there were twenty-two fellas with you.

SC: Yeah, yeah.

GB: Vocations, as you well know, are really dropping away. Are you concerned about that?

SC: Not really, no.

GB: Why?

SC: The whole mission of the Christian Gospel, it's not depending on ordained, sacramental priests. In the early Church, everybody Christian was, were Disciples and they had to go out and evangelise and spread the Good Word and do good. So, that is a much more healthy community of people who believe in this Gospel. That's what Church is. Actually, in the early days of the Church, the priest had a very limited role. He wasn't really an important person like they build up on a pedestal now . . . and nobody can seemingly do any good, except *he* has to do it. I mean that's ridiculous.

They have to encourage the ordinary people and Christians to band together and implement in their communities these important values, the Gospel values. I think we have to get back to the basic Christianity of Jesus and of his early Church.

GB: Okay. Suppose it's all true and you get to the pearly gates and Jesus/God is waiting for you. What will you say to Him, Shay?

SC: Well, probably, "Hi, I'm here." [Laughs.] "Can we continue on the friendship that we established in life on this side?" Hopefully, it will continue on, because our relationship should be one of friendship and of unity, togetherness. A loving relationship in this world will continue into eternity.

That's the whole faith, but how it'll be, we can't tell. [Laughs.]

BERTIE AHERN

An Honest Account

First rule of interviewing: it's not about you. It's about the person in the chair opposite and the audience. Talk to the former, entertain and inform the latter. Period.

For over fifty years, my job has been to ask the question to which audiences would most like to hear an answer, in such a way that they are likely to get one. Antagonise a guest and they will clam up and hate you. We have all seen it happen, even to interviewing masters like Michael Parkinson and Terry Wogan. Equally, if you *don't* ask a guest the questions to which people want to know the answers, you will be accused of soft-soaping and complicity. Then, it's the audience that hates you.

As I prepared for this Bertie Ahern interview, I reminded myself, repeatedly, that this was *The Meaning of Life,* not the Mahon Tribunal. Many lawyers had spent many years and many millions of public money scrutinising the former Taoiseach's financial affairs. So far, at that stage, inconclusively. Thankfully, I was more interested in his values than his accounts, and surprisingly, he was willing to talk about them.

It must be strange to be Bertie: to have risen so high and achieved so much—peace in Northern Ireland, three successive election victories, a successful EU Presidency and an unprecedented period of economic growth—and then to be treated as a pariah, the source of all our equally unprecedented woes. No wonder, in the Middle Ages, they depicted Fortune as a wheel, which exalts the humble and puts down the mighty from their seat.

When I interviewed the former Taoiseach he was still a sitting TD. Actually he was a hobbling TD. His knee operation had left him hopping, sometimes literally, back and forth from his office on Setanta Street to the Dáil across the road, for votes. We had to interrupt our interview for one such.

The office had all the memorabilia of greatness—photos with Tony and Bill and significant keepsakes, flags and pennants alongside the family snaps—but, almost a year after his resignation, the man himself had a decidedly out-of-office demeanour. And that was even before the worst of the economic collapse and the unceremonious eviction of Fianna Fáil; and certainly way before the conclusion of the Mahon Tribunal.

Here is the shock, though, for all those now frantically writing history with the full benefit of twenty-twenty hindsight: the Bertie

Ahern I met that day in the spring of 2009 was a man of faith. He was also a man of experience: the unique experience of sitting in a room full of paramilitaries and being told he was the only one present who hadn't killed anyone; the amusing experience of taking Tony Blair to his own local pub, in England, at a time when the British Prime Minister no longer believed that that was an option; and the unlikely experience of trading prayers and religious insights with Ian Paisley.

This is his account.

~

GB: Your childhood and boyhood were steeped in religion and religious observance: Sunday Mass, confession, all of those things . . .

BA: Absolutely! Absolutely! I mean, both my father and mother . . . They didn't ram it down our throat, but there was no escaping it, coming from the community we lived in. Every day, I went to All Hallows with my dad. I remember going to Gardiner Street Church with my mother and father—you know, the Novena of Grace—and to Dominic Street to the Dominicans, because we were covered in the religious orders.

GB: Normally, at this stage, we meet somebody who is disaffected and has fallen away from the whole practice of religion and has no time for it . . . But you're exceptional, insofar as most of it has remained with you . . . or has it?

BA: Yes, it has. I've never changed. I mean, I'd still be close to the religious orders and I'd still, even to this day, when I want to get away from things, go for a walk in All Hallows College.

GB: So, you're a practising Catholic?

BA: Yes . . .

GB: You go to Mass regularly and—several things—you give up drink for November. Is that for the Holy Souls . . . ?

BA: The Holy Souls. We were brought up in a household that it was respectful to do something for Lent and to do something for November.

GB: And you also say that you do the Novena of Grace. You've done that every year from when you were very young?

BA: Yeah.

GB: Why is that?

BA: Well, when we were small, Gardiner Street was close and we got into the habit of going. Lots of my friends, who don't bother going to Mass on a regular basis, go Christmas and maybe go on Good Friday. But they go to the Novena of Grace. There's still huge numbers. It's the 4th to the 12th of March every year, and I still go and would really go out of my way to go.

GB: And what are you praying for there?

BA: Well, you know . . . You'd be praying for your daughters or you're praying for someone who's ill or somebody who's fallen on tough times.

GB: And it's not just comfort and tradition, as far as you're concerned?

BA: Yeah, I know some people would just go on auto-pilot. I try not to do that. I'm not able to go in and just sit in a church and go half asleep. If I can't actually listen to the speaker, I get quite irritated.

GB: When you go to Mass, what does it mean to you, what are you doing?

BA: For me, it's looking at the week past, thinking of the week ahead. You also think about people. I try to usually dedicate it to somebody. If I meet someone during the week and they tell me somebody is in for a big operation, that's all I can do. You're not a doctor, you can't help them any other way, but you can say a prayer for them.

GB: And do you believe in the Real Presence?

BA: I do. I mean, all these things take an act of faith. But I do believe it.

GB: You believe, whole and entire, that Jesus is there?

BA: I do, Gay. I believe that there is a God. I believe in the Trinity. I believe that there is a Jesus. I don't go in to question exactly where they are: are they up in Heaven or are they to the right or to the left?

Often, if you're doing a students' debate nowadays, people would throw you a question and it happened to me, quite recently, in Durham. An Irish student there asked me, do I believe in Heaven? I was after being asked questions about Northern Ireland, about the Irish economy, about property, about the ups and downs. And then, "Do you believe in Heaven . . . ?" [laughs] smack in the middle of it. But I said, "Listen, it's as simple as this with me: I believe that if you can live with yourself, if you've got peace of mind, then the rest will look after itself, and hopefully that'll be Heaven." And for me it's as simple as that. I do not believe that it all ends at the graveyard and I don't believe the ideologies that try to portray that.

GB: When you pray, who are you praying to, and what is the image in your mind?

BA: I pray to a God that is forgiving, a God who's caring, a God of love. And I think, through my political life, even when I came face to face, as I did time and time again, with the great Ian Paisley, that's one thing that we were able to share, which surprised him . . . The famous morning when we had the meeting, just one-to-one, in the Irish Embassy, when he was saying the prayer, and I joined in with him: that had a sound impact on him. And it started a whole new relationship with Ian Paisley. And I often wonder, if I hadn't been able to join in on that prayer, or if I hadn't have known the words, 'cause he was coming from his Presbyterian religion, would we have got on as well?

GB: What prayer was it?

BA: He was saying one of the ones like our Confiteor, slightly different in words, but I knew enough of it. Then, I started discussing with him what rules do you live by and the values that he had, 'cause he said, "You're a Christian." He knew my father was an old IRA man, but I think he didn't know too much else. But I started saying, "Well, I live by, kind of, three sets of rules: I live by the Commandments, as best I can . . . and didn't perfectly manage to get through them all. And I said I understood the Beatitudes, and he's discussed the Beatitudes. He was surprised that I would know about the Beatitudes at all. And then, I said, by my own conscience. But I told him that I couldn't be informed just by make-it-up-on-the-hoof, that I had to be informed by things. So we had quite a long serious discussion. Afterwards the officials said, "What the hell were you talking about for so long?" [Laughs.]

And that's where we hit it off. Because up to that, he wouldn't shake hands with me, he wouldn't have much time for me. I hadn't much time for him either. But it did change from that day. We made the famous handshake, which, to me, was a handshake that went all over the world. But I had deep respect for him. And I keep in touch with him, keep in touch with his son and keep in touch with Eileen.

GB: When you're confronted by the Richard Dawkinses of the world, who say that the whole thing is a lot of baloney, how do you react to that?

BA: Yeah, I resent it, because I just don't think that adds up. I mean, everyone is entitled to their own beliefs, but sometimes people just try to make the rest of us cynical, and they give glib answers. And I do often pick up and read some of this stuff, just to annoy myself maybe.

But the religion of my parents and my grandparents was their whole life. Medical practices weren't great, they often had to suffer unfairly and life was tough. But they had enormous beliefs. They had enormous respect for the dead and they had enormous respect for their ancestors. And they prayed to the people. And the question is, can you pray, believing that there's some spiritual thing there that you can actually connect back to people? And if you don't believe that, you think that's all a lot of baloney, it'd be very hard to pray.

I actually believe that you *can* pray to people, that you can make contact with people and that, if you are in a spot, that they will think of you, or if you do some good deed for somebody, it can help you along the way.

GB: Do you believe the prayers are answered?

BA: I certainly do sometimes, and when they're not, you know the old thing my mother would say is, "That's God's will." I'm not too sure it *is* God's will. I mean, whenever I ever went to a young person's funeral, I'd say to myself, "No, that couldn't be God's will. God is crying as well," because I couldn't believe that God could be heartless. It's a God of love, not a God that wants to see a ten-year-old die with some terrible disease . . .

GB: So, how do you account for that?

BA: I account for it, Gay, by saying that God cannot influence every single thing. I do not think that, in seven days, God built the world. I think we know from our geology that that's not the case. What I do believe is that it is a God of love, a God of forgiveness and a God that's just.

GB: Would you pray during an election or a by-election? Would you have prayed during your Presidency of Europe? During the Mahon Tribunal?

BA: Yeah, I would . . .

GB: You would pray when your back is against the wall?

BA: Yeah, I'd pray, just to get through it. I wouldn't pray that He'd influence it . . . If you're travelling around Europe, as I did during the

Presidency, when you had to go three times round, in eighteen months, the twenty-seven countries ... that you just get safely through it, when you've that many air-miles.

GB: It strikes me, from reading about you, that you were well treated by the Christian Brothers.

BA: Yeah. I mean, I have no argument with the Christian Brothers. They were tough: I was in school for the days when you still got hit by a leather for not being able to spell some word with sixteen letters. I still have the view that it didn't actually do me any harm either and they gave us all fairly cheap education. You know, God help us, if we *hadn't* had them ... I never saw a case of abuse or anything else in the place ...

GB: Do you think that you were too trusting of the Religious Orders when you were there dealing with the Ferns, the Ryan and now, God knows what's in the Archdiocese?

BA: Well, it ended up a bit the other way. I mean, if I had been following my own prejudices, I wouldn't have set up any of these things. But when Christine Buckley came to me, in opposition, and outlined to me what had happened in Inchicore, with the Sisters of Mercy—and I'd worked for the Sisters of Mercy, in the Mater Hospital—I said, "It just can't be let go." Because I came to the conclusion that these people were telling the total truth. So, as soon as I was in Government in '99, I gave the apology on behalf of the state and then proceeded to set up all the other tribunals.

I realised I was opening up a huge can of worms. And once I moved, then there was no ending this . . . And that was very hard on the Church. But the other side of that, when the report came out recently, the last report, I was invited along by Christine Buckley. And all the people who'd suffered were there and they really, really appreciated that I walked that road with them. So I left with a happy heart, saying, "You did the right thing."

GB: So, what do you think went wrong ...?

BA: I think the Church made a few basic mistakes. They were working under rule of canon law. I remember, as a politician, even as Taoiseach, when they tried to put up the defence of canon law, I went back to some of my ministerial colleagues . . . They just looked at the sky and said, "You're joking." Unfortunately, they weren't joking. They made bad mistakes, when somebody clearly had a problem. They transferred the person to another institution who were dealing with children. Was that just stupidity? Was it lack of understanding? Was it not being able to face up to the responsibilities, or what? I just don't know. Unfortunately, they paid a big price for it. And it's right that it's out and it's right that it's put right.

The only thing, I hope it doesn't do damage to the present generation of priests and nuns, because they weren't responsible for a lot of this. I notice more and more people taking sabbaticals, at the very time that they desperately need them.

GB: Have you ever had a crisis of faith?

BA: Not really. I mean, naturally, when somebody dies or you see your friend going down the hill slowly, you do say to yourself, "What's all this about?" But I mean, even Sister Teresa of Calcutta—and we know from her diaries afterwards—she had doubts. But as far as a crisis, I didn't . . . I believe that life comes from God. I believe that it's dedicated to God and your fulfilment is in God.

GB: What do you mean, "your fulfilment is in God"?

BA: That whatever happens afterwards, Heaven, to me, is the deeds you do in your life. If I've spent most of my life—I *hope*—working for other people, I think Heaven is a cosmos of looking back and seeing what did I do in my life. Heaven mirrors that.

I have a difficulty about Hell. I mean, is that the God of forgiveness and love? Is that the God that said to the poor woman who was being stoned . . .

GB: "Let he who is amongst you . . ."

BA: " . . . send the stone. Has nobody condemned you?" And she said, "No, my Lord." And the Lord said, "Well, neither do I." And so, it doesn't match up that you're judged in a way that you're going to be sent to a torment of fire.

GB: That suggests, then, that Hitler and Stalin and Saddam Hussein and all those guys get away with it?

BA: Well, do they? None of those people could have lived with themselves in peace and felt that they had a fulfilment that was in God. They couldn't have had. So, what happens to them precisely? Who knows?

GB: I think of the parallels between yourself and Tony Blair, and Alastair Campbell saying, "We don't do God," when, in your book, you make it quite clear that you find it perfectly okay that your private faith and religion should be in the public sphere, since you are a public person.

BA: I do. I don't think you can live it any other way. You believe it or you don't. You can't hide the fact you believe in something. I'll give you the example, when I used to wear the ashes . . . And then the guy from the *Daily Mail* rang up to see what happened to the Taoiseach. "Did he get a belt on the head last night?" That was true. The poor fella just didn't understand it.

You'd be almost slagged over that. It didn't matter to me, but because I was being slagged, others stopped, actually. But I think that's kind of almost intimidation the other way.

GB: So, what part does your faith play in your politics, then?

BA: I don't think, in my politics, it does . . . Obviously, I'd like to see the Catholic Church doing well, because I'd like to see the Catholic Church be strong and continue, but that didn't influence my decisions when I was sitting at the Cabinet table.

GB: Bill Clinton, during the Middle East negotiations, said, "You don't make peace with your friends but with your enemies," and during that whole Northern Ireland situation, you were dealing with Paisley, as you've talked about earlier on, and Trimble and guys who are hard-line . . . who had nothing in common with you . . . probably had a bit of contempt, would you say . . . ?

BA: A lot of them would have . . .

GB: And then the hard-line Republicans on the other side. Talk to me about that a little bit, about how you handled it.

BA: Well, I had formed a judgement that most of them—I wasn't sure about Paisley—most of them wanted to find a solution. Most of them did not want to pass on the killing and the mayhem to their children, to the next generation. And that was the one thing I could see in them all. So, when the negotiations started, in 1997, I worked very hard to get inside all of the individuals. And there were easy days and hard days.

I remember a day going in—I won't name the individuals now, but it was a very private, confidential session, mainly of people at leadership level, so, you know, all the usual names. And one of the Loyalists said to me, "As far as we know, Taoiseach, you're the only one in this room that isn't a murderer, because the rest of us are." And that was the opening of the discussion, so it was kind of chilling. But you couldn't blink an eyelid, even if you did inside.

It was to get to know them, get to understand them, and then see where we could find ways forward . . . to try and get people to work together and to get people around the table. And while the Good Friday Agreement was a great success, the success, to me, was when Ian Paisley accepted the St Andrews Amendment, in 2006. And he always promised me, from the time we started dealing with each other one-to-one, he promised me that, if he did sign up, he'd totally sign up and that he'd carry it through.

GB: And he did?

BA: And he did. He honoured his word. And I think people should be extremely grateful, because without him tied in, we would not have brought a total end to the Troubles.

GB: In the midst of the final throes of it, your mother died, Lord rest her . . . Was there any sign of sympathy from the people around you for that?

BA: There was, incredible sympathy. You know, John Taylor, who wasn't my best friend at the time, he went out of his way to come over and to be helpful.

I had to leave the graveside and come straight back to the negotiations, and negotiations were going horribly wrong and there were, you know, 2,500 journalists accredited to the final negotiations of the Good Friday Agreement. I don't know how many hundreds were on the plinth when I arrived back in the helicopter and landed. Eamonn O'Malley had asked them all to put down their cameras, in respect of that fact that I came back, and everybody did. So much so, I never got a photograph of the event, which would have been a nice one to recall. So, I mean, there was huge sympathy. But once we got back in, we got on with it.

GB: Do you think you'll see your mum and dad again?

BA: I don't know if I'll see them again, but I do believe that their spirits still exist. I do believe that, in some way—God knows what way—that you can connect with them and that when you do try to talk to them, or you do ask them for something, that they know you're there.

GB: Do you think of death, and are you afraid of it?

BA: I think everybody would be afraid of it. But you know, ultimately, when you have to face it, you have to face it . . . You would fear death far more if you don't believe there is anything after it. And I believe there *is* something.

GB: I do not want to go into the intricacies of the Mahon Tribunal, but are you waiting for the final come-uppance from the Mahon Tribunal with trepidation or with confidence . . . ?

BA: With confidence, because the one issue that I have to answer is the issue I know the answer to . . . that I received money from Mr O'Callaghan to, in some way, down or bury or damage Mr Gilmartin. That's the only substantive issue. All the rest is very messy and stupid affairs, but that's the allegation, which is a very serious one. And I'm not guilty of that. So, you know, I'm confident that that's what will happen. And if that isn't what happens, they've got it wrong.

GB: You're very much a man of the people . . . How disconcerting is it for you to realise that in a survey, seventy-eight per cent of the Irish people didn't think you were being fully honest and straightforward about all your dealings?

BA: Yeah, I have no difficulty about that, Gay, because what happens is, when you're up against a group of clever lawyers, who had the luxury of a few hundred staff—I don't resent them for that—of course, they plotted out on their grounds, not on your ground. So, you know, they take something small and then turn it into something big . . . So, you're kicked around the place. But listen, that's life.

GB: Did you get depressed about it?

BA: I lost some sleep over it. Probably lost more sleep than I lost over most things, because I thought it was downright unfair. But, you know, I'm a realist as well and you have to go through it.

GB: Okay . . . When, after you split up with Miriam, your partner was Celia, with that kind of background that you have and your faith and your commitment to the Church and all of that, was there any sense, to you, that you were "living in sin," as your mother would have said . . . ?

BA: Whether I had the sense or not, I got letters . . . !

GB: And Archbishop Connell had a go as well . . .

BA: He did. But in fairness, Archbishop Connell and I were good friends . . . and the man was just saying how he saw it, and I had no difficulty with him.

GB: With regard to yourself, though, and your own feelings, with the background, that you were doing something immoral . . . ?

BA: Yeah, I didn't really feel it was immoral, but it was certainly different, and it didn't fit in with the stereotype of what your parents would like you to do. I certainly was very conscious of that . . .

GB: So, how did you get around that?

BA: Just got on with it. And because I was a church-goer, people have a right go at you and we would get lovely letters . . . well written . . .

GB: [Laughs.]

BA: . . . giving you every rule that was in it and even telling you you shouldn't be going to Communion. So, it made life a bit awkward, but not impossible. And you just have to reconcile yourself to your God. You couldn't get everything right. But I didn't have difficulty in that, because I'd read enough books . . . the Apostles and the kind of lives that they had. But anyway, it didn't cause me too much problem. It did upset other people, because we got a fair hate-mail for a long time.

GB: I'll bet! On your last day you quoted Father John O'Sullivan, the Jesuit: "Be always beginning. Let the past go now. Let me do whatever I have the power to do." Is that part of your philosophy?

BA: Yeah. You've this life to live and I don't believe this thing, you can make it all up in the next life. I think you have to make it up today. I have to have peace of mind, and if I have peace of mind and enjoy life, you know, then I'm happy.

GABRIEL BYRNE

Namesakes

In February 2007, my namesake, the Golden Globe-winning actor, Gabriel Byrne, flew all the way from America especially to present me with an IFTA Lifetime Achievement Award. I was terribly touched, not only by the gesture, but by the very kind words which accompanied it. Needless to say, I am a fan.

Given that lifetime achievement awards are generally given, like Extreme Unction, to people whose working life is generally assumed to be nearing an end, Gabriel was probably surprised to discover that I was not only still alive, but still working, when he received our interview request in 2010. Nonetheless, he graciously accepted.

Which is how the two Gabriel Byrnes—each of us the Christian Brothers-educated son of a Dublin Guinness worker—came to be sitting in a hotel suite, discussing the experiences, the values and the loves that have given his life meaning.

He is a man of many talents and hidden depths. Actually, his depths are not that hidden. You can sense them within moments of sitting down with him. He is decidedly his own man, as the Irish Government discovered when, having fêted him for a year as Ireland's cultural ambassador in the USA, they had to listen to him accusing them of turning *The Gathering, 2013*, into "a shake-down" of our friends and rellies overseas.

The quiet intensity Gabriel Byrne brings to his performances on screen is also in evidence in his conversation. Less expected is the humour and the passion. Perhaps several seasons playing a shrink in *In Treatment* brought out the confessional element in him. Or was that his period in junior seminary, in England, when, with the support of his family, he pursued what he thought was a vocation to the Catholic priesthood?

There is no reason why a *bona fide* "Hollywood A-lister" like Gabriel Byrne should feel obliged to discuss such private matters as his experiences of sexual abuse or his battles with depression; or the intimate details of his relationships with the late Áine O'Connor and Ellen Barkin. In another programme, questions on that terrain might have seemed simply intrusive. However, he understood that, since those people and those experiences have played a huge role in shaping his sense of what makes a life meaningful, it would have been odd if I had left them out of our conversation. So, with his usual mixture of generosity, candour, eloquence and humour, *the other Mr Gabriel Byrne* gamely answered whatever questions I put his way.

૨

GAY BYRNE: Were your parents religious?

GABRIEL BYRNE: I certainly did not know anybody, growing up, who *wasn't* of a religious persuasion. Mostly, we were surrounded by Catholics. And my mother was a religious woman. My father went to Mass every morning, before he would go into Guinness's. He would get up at half past five. He would bring my mother up tea in the bed. And then he would come in and he would put the sign of the cross on our foreheads. Then he would go down the stairs and there'd be silence in the house and you knew that my father was on his way to Mass.

GAY BYRNE: School. Christian Brothers: systematic, persistent indoctrination, which worked; and physical and sexual abuse. I would have to preface my question by saying that I saw nothing of sexual abuse with the Christian Brothers at all. Physical abuse, certainly . . . What was your experience?

GABRIEL BYRNE: The world that I lived in, from an educational point of view, was full of fear. I feared being beaten and I was beaten very regularly and, like everybody else that I knew, it *did* affect my sense of myself. And unnecessary corporal punishment for something that you didn't even understand. Like maths was my bogey. To this day, I can't understand maths. I used to do these problems: "If it takes four men to dig a hole in three days, how many inches to the square mile is the Bishop of Cork?"

GAY BYRNE: [Laughs.]

GABRIEL BYRNE: I had no idea. So you'd be beaten for that. I would never contemplate beating a child. I have two children myself. I've never laid a finger on them, because I do know that with physical punishment comes humiliation and with humiliation comes loss of belief in oneself and loss of confidence and dignity and so forth. Unfortunately, I experienced some sexual abuse . . .

GAY BYRNE: With the Christian Brothers?

GABRIEL BYRNE: Yes.

GAY BYRNE: Tell me.

GABRIEL BYRNE: It was a known and admitted fact of life amongst us that there was this particular man and that you didn't want to be left in a dressing-room with him. And I *didn't* know . . . Certainly, boundaries, sexual boundaries, were crossed. And it was mixed up with fear and ultimately with shame. And I didn't feel that I suffered, at the time, from it. I just felt it was the way of the world. And of course, many children internalise it and I think I internalised it and it took me many years to come to terms with it and to forgive those incidents that I felt had deeply hurt me. And I still don't know if I have, 'cause I don't know if you can possibly truly, truly, in the depths of one's soul, forgive.

And I had the misfortune that when I went to England, the seminary, that there was another incidence of it and I had to face it again. So, I was unlucky in that way.

GAY BYRNE: Come back to me about going to the seminary at eleven, twelve years of age. Even for that time, that seems extraordinary to me . . .

GABRIEL BYRNE: It is extraordinary. But again, at the time, not strange at all. I guess, I was brought up in an atmosphere where religion was tremendously important. The ethos of the time was that a priest in the family was a great blessing and a great call.

GAY BYRNE: Sure. But not at twelve?

GABRIEL BYRNE: I was an altar boy and my response to the Catholic religion at the time was very much emotional. It was the very simple faith of a child. But it didn't feel like religion to me. It felt like a deep sense of connection to another world.

The Catholic Church at that time had such power! They went from school to school and they presented the notion of the priesthood in a way that connected to a fairytale world of adventure and fantasy. So, when they put slides on and I saw pictures of men in Africa with straw hats, and then he said, "How many boys would like to do that?" I thought, "Wow, that seems like a great thing to do."

I found myself on the mail boat, at eleven, going from Ireland to England, having been kitted out by the St Joseph's Priests' Society, which helped not-so-well-off families to get the money together to go to the seminary. And I remember being loaded down with money from neighbours and thinking, "I've made it. My pockets are full of money and I'm off and I can afford Pepsi Cola."

What I went to, essentially, was what they called a junior seminary. It was run on the model of an English public school, and I have to say that in many ways, it opened my intellectual curiosity.

GAY BYRNE: There was more abuse there?
GABRIEL BYRNE: Yeah.

GAY BYRNE: The same kind of abuse? Worse?
GABRIEL BYRNE: It would have been more intense there. Now, it didn't go on over a prolonged period, but it happened at a very, very vulnerable moment. You know the nature of the sexual predator is that it takes advantage of the innocence and the limited perspective of a child. When you are sent to the room of a priest to be told the facts of life, which is what happened—and I was told the facts of life *as* this happened—you kind of knew that there was something that wasn't right about this, but you didn't know what it was, because you had absolute trust in the person that was doing it. So, again, I didn't think that it had severely impacted me at the time, but I suppose, when I think about my later life and how I had difficulties with certain issues . . . I'm not saying that they *were* attributable to that, but there's the real possibility that they *could* have been.

GAY BYRNE: Well, the Murphy Report, Ryan Report, would seem to indicate that there was rampant sexual abuse going on in the Church in Ireland. To what do you think you can attribute that?
GABRIEL BYRNE: I think that the Church itself, in terms of what it regards as moral rectitude and the moral way of life, contravenes what I would regard as the law of God and denies the most basic human right, which is the right to love, by making people become celibate and not leaving it a choice. It's fine if somebody *wants* to be celibate, but to impose obligatory celibacy on men and women seems to me to be a crime against the human soul. It's a man-made law. Certainly, it's nothing Christ ever said. I think the Catholic Church has become a vast and powerful corporation and it's moved further and further away from the simple notion of Christianity which is contained in the Sermon on the Mount.

GAY BYRNE: So how long did you last in the seminary then?

GABRIEL BYRNE: Four and a half years.

GAY BYRNE: And at what stage did you think, No, this is not for me?

GABRIEL BYRNE: Well, to me it was a very Joycean Sandymount Beach moment. I went down to London during a break and we got on the bus and I walked up the stairs behind two girls in mini-skirts and that was the end of it for me. That was it.

GAY BYRNE: [Laughs.]

GABRIEL BYRNE: Think about it: when you're seventeen or eighteen . . .

GAY BYRNE: Of course, of course. Did you lose your faith as well?

GABRIEL BYRNE: No, I didn't lose my faith at that time. Just lost the vocation, and just knew that I wanted to be around girls.

GAY BYRNE: So, you come back to Dublin. Did you come back in disgrace?

GABRIEL BYRNE: There was silence. I was "a failed priest."

GAY BYRNE: Failed priest . . . did you feel that?

GABRIEL BYRNE: Silence spoke thunderous volumes, that you had somehow pulled the wool over people's eyes. And I remembered the pockets of money. Maybe I should give it back . . .

GAY BYRNE: So you're back now and Da wants you to get a trade, earn your living. So, what did you go into?

GABRIEL BYRNE: I eventually got my Leaving Cert and I got a scholarship to university to study archaeology and languages. And I was teaching for about six or seven years, teaching Leaving Cert students Irish. And *they* asked me, would I form a drama group with them, 'cause I used to take them to the theatre and the movies. And then we started writing and directing our own kind of little plays, and so forth.

And I decided I should join an amateur drama group, because there were girls there. And it was the most exciting thing. And I remember the first review I ever got. It was in an Irish newspaper and it said, "Tá Gabriel Byrne ar ceann de na haisteoirí is fearr sa chathair," which means "Gabriel Byrne is one of the best actors in the city." Well, I was absolutely floored, and I thought, "My God!" The uninhibited joy of finding what it was that you wanted to do and feeling that it was absolutely right for you to do.

GAY BYRNE: For some actors, it's getting away from themselves; for some actors, it's hiding behind the character; for some actors, it's hiding their deficiencies. What is it for you?

GABRIEL BYRNE: I think it has changed. What I've come to believe now is that it is about revealing the deepest part of yourself.

GAY BYRNE: In every character?

GABRIEL BYRNE: Yes.

GAY BYRNE: How do you do that?

GABRIEL BYRNE: I believe that we all share a common humanity, and I believe that we are all capable of either empathising or identifying with, or recognising, the darkest parts of each other or the greatest parts of each other . . . You cannot become somebody else. The way that I've found to express myself is this other way, which is about trying to find the deepest emotions in me that are hidden and apply them to the character.

GAY BYRNE: Now, I want to talk to you about Áine O'Connor. And only say what you want to say about this . . . You had this twelve-year relationship with Áine.

GABRIEL BYRNE: She was a huge influence on my life. And I suppose, if that French expression *coup de foudre,* which literally means "a blow to the heart," has any significance, I felt it, when I met her. It just felt like *bang.* This beautiful woman . . . And I fell in love with her.

And she was responsible for opening the doors of perception for me. Her whole attitude was always "Question everything: question authority, question everybody who tells you this is the way it has to be." And she said, "What do you *really* want to do with your life? That's what you *have* to do." So I gave up teaching and I became a full-time actor at the Project and, after a very successful term at the Project, breaking into Irish television and *The Riordans,* which was my father's favourite programme. And I remember going up to his house to watch my first episode of *The Riordans,* in black and white with the family in the dining-room, and there I was. And he looked at the television, and then he looked at me and he said, "Isn't television a wonderful thing, all the same? There you are and there you are." He couldn't believe that I was in the room with the television and that his son was in this thing. Nor could I believe it.

GAY BYRNE: Are you suggesting to me that Áine propelled you forward?

GABRIEL BYRNE: Yeah. And she had utter faith.

GAY BYRNE: Why didn't you marry?

GABRIEL BYRNE: It never came up. She had been married once before herself, and she didn't have any desire, or any sense that marriage was terribly important. The real thing was being together. And she was the one who said to me, "You've done really well in Dublin. I think you could do well in London, so why don't we go to London? I'll give up my job in RTÉ and we'll go to London." So, because of her, I went to London, and because of her, my career changed. I don't know that I would have left for London. By now, I would be a retired Irish-teacher. Probably in a mental home, but a retired Irish-teacher. [Laughs.]

GAY BYRNE: Okay, a lot of people judge actors by the amount of money they have in the bank, by the amount of hardware they have on the mantelpiece. What's your measure of success?

GABRIEL BYRNE: I think it has to do with challenging oneself to do things that one is afraid of, so that you push yourself beyond certain limitations that you have about yourself. It's a journey inward. My ambition now, at the end of my life, is to know who I am, *really* who I am, deep down. And I don't know if I've reached that stage yet.

GAY BYRNE: Okay, in view of what you said about Áine, when you met Ellen Barkin then, in 1988, on the set of *Siesta*, was that *wham*? Did you fall in love straight away again?

GABRIEL BYRNE: Yes, that was another instantaneous *coup de foudre*, and I was helpless in the face of it, just as I was helpless in the face of Áine. That meeting changed my life too . . . for ever.

GAY BYRNE: When you fell for her, the fact of her Jewishness, was that difficult for an ex-seminarian, good Catholic boy . . . ?

GABRIEL BYRNE: No, by that time I wasn't a practising Catholic. I was what Brendan Behan used to call "a daylight atheist." When it was daylight, I was fine. There was no God. But once it started getting dark, or you were on an aeroplane, there *could* be a God . . .

GAY BYRNE: Is that the way it is now?

GABRIEL BYRNE: I'd say I'm between agnosticism and atheism. I would love to believe that there is something after, but I think, if there is something after, it's like Shakespeare said: "That undiscovered country, from whose bourn no traveller has returned."

GAY BYRNE: Do you pray?

GABRIEL BYRNE: I have a spiritual world that I can tap into. I don't know what that is, but I know that it is very much part of me. It has nothing to do with organised religion. But I find that, when I am in connection with the spiritual part of myself, I am a happier and more contented person.

GAY BYRNE: Let me try you on this: what do you think the Old Testament is?

GABRIEL BYRNE: In my opinion, the Old Testament fulfilled the same function as the old Irish myths. I think that the Old Testament is a mythological guide to living for the community and sometimes for the individual.

GAY BYRNE: Allegorical, then?

GABRIEL BYRNE: Yeah.

GAY BYRNE: What do you think the New Testament is, then? Matthew, Mark, Luke and John?

GABRIEL BYRNE: The New Testament seems to me to be the writing of the message of Christ. And the fact that Matthew, Mark, Luke and John differ in their interpretations wouldn't be a cause for concern for me, if that was something that I was following as a way of life, because any guard will tell you that if somebody falls off their bike and six people see it, they'll have six different versions of what happened. But at the core of the New Testament is the message of Christ, which is about the love of one's neighbour, the Ten Commandments and the Sermon on the Mount, which is not that terribly different in context or in essence from the philosophy of Marxism.

GAY BYRNE: What do you think Jesus was?

GABRIEL BYRNE: I think he was one of the greatest revolutionaries of all, because he revolted against everything that had gone before and his message was about love and it was about peace and it was about resurrection. It was about the notion of being able to resurrect *oneself*. And he was crucified, because he was a revolutionary and he was dangerous. The Roman Empire was about conquest and power, and Jesus Christ was against power and conquest and threw all those guys out of the

Temple. He was against the acquisition of wealth. He was against the exploitation of poor people. He was against the idea of conquest. He was a direct threat, so they had to kill him.

GAY BYRNE: Do you think he was divine?

GABRIEL BYRNE: If you mean "Did he come down from Heaven and assume the form of a man, and was he born of a mother who didn't have sex with another man?" I find that hard to believe. He lived and died as a man, and I don't know that there was anything really, truly divine.

GAY BYRNE: Do you believe he rose on the third day?

GABRIEL BYRNE: I think that's allegorical too. I think there is a message of inspiration and hope for people, that there is something to move toward, that we will all one day be resurrected. I don't know that I believe in that.

GAY BYRNE: In the physical Resurrection . . . ?

GABRIEL BYRNE: Somebody said to me once about the pursuit of an answer: "You know, it's enough that there's a garden. There don't have to be fairies at the end of it. The journey of life is what it's about. It's not about how we demand a second and eternal life, when what we've been given now is the great gift of this one." That's what they said to me. And I kind of believe in that. But our spirits may in some way continue.

GAY BYRNE: This is a trite one, but your own experience of therapy surely contributed to helping you to play Paul Weston in the award-winning series *In Treatment*.

GABRIEL BYRNE: No, it didn't, because I hadn't gone to therapy when I started that series. I had one friend who was a therapist, but I thought he was kind of bonkers. After the programme went out, they all started coming up to me and saying that they thought it was a very accurate portrayal of what they did. I was amazed. But for me, it's acting, and it was also going into who I am myself.

GAY BYRNE: When you went to take therapy yourself, though, did you have to get over that old Irish notion that your parents would have had, that this is self-indulgence of some kind . . . ?

GABRIEL BYRNE: Yeah. I think that's something that was deeply rooted in me, the notion that expressing feelings of any kind, or talking about who you are intimately, is something that, you know, "Would you go 'way out of that!" and "You're paying money for that? What kind of an eejit are you?"

To go to therapy I had to get rid of that thinking and just say, "This will be a better thing for you. It will make you feel better."

GAY BYRNE: And did it work, in your opinion?

GABRIEL BYRNE: Any time you open yourself up to another human being, honestly, I think it can do nothing but help. When a detached, objective observer is listening to that and perhaps comments on it and probes it a bit more, you probe deeper into yourself and you come to an understanding. And when you come to an understanding, you come to an acceptance. And when you come to an acceptance, you come to a forgiveness, not just of other people, but of yourself. Let go the things that you didn't succeed at, just let them be. You did the best you could. You are who you are now. Just live life.

I have to say, I am not an unhappy person. I'm a contented person for the most part. That's not to say that there aren't days when I don't feel so great, but generally speaking, if I hadn't dealt with these things in my life, I don't think I would have been anywhere as content as I am now.

GAY BYRNE: And what do you say to people who would say, "Hey, you are a star, you're a wonderful actor, you earn good money, you've realised your ambition, you're doing what you've always wanted to do from the time you were very young. How could *you* be depressed?"

GABRIEL BYRNE: I think that's a very simplistic perspective, because one of the things that I *don't* believe in is the obsession with celebrity.

GAY BYRNE: Fame.

GABRIEL BYRNE: Fame is actually a delusion. It doesn't help you go to sleep at night and it doesn't help you to get up in the morning. It doesn't help you in your interaction with other people; it doesn't help your sense of self. It doesn't lead to contentment or happiness *per se,* just like money doesn't lead to contentment *per se.*

If you believe in the notion that fame is something that is tremendously important to your life, or that money is, you're on a course for unhappiness.

GAY BYRNE: I know you've become associated now with the Hospice Movement . . . Is that from a sense that you've been given this talent and you have won this measure of success, therefore you have a responsibility or an obligation to do something for other people?

GABRIEL BYRNE: I think we *all* have a responsibility to give back in some way. I work with people in New York, I work with people here. The Irish Hospice is a tremendously important organisation, because it's about the notion of living, and dying, well.

We try to understand how we live, but how do we die? I mean, it's the one inescapable fact of life. How do we approach that, and what dignity do we give it? And if you go into certain hospitals, you find that the last thing that's there is dignity and the humanity that the sick and the dying should be afforded. And I think that just working towards something as simple as a place where there is a single room for people to be ill in and to be with their families seems to me like an achievable objective.

GAY BYRNE: Is there any question that you think about death regularly?
GABRIEL BYRNE: Yeah.

GAY BYRNE: Afraid of death?
GABRIEL BYRNE: Ah, no. I might be slightly afraid of suffering *before* death and hope that I can manage to be brave enough to get through suffering. But I don't think I'm afraid of it, no. But I think about it quite a lot.

GAY BYRNE: Why?
GABRIEL BYRNE: Because the fact of death is one thing that we cannot ignore, and the more we are aware of death, paradoxically, I think the better the life we can live. That's not to say that it doesn't give me the shivers. It does give me the shivers, at times. But I must say that, for the most part, I'm not afraid.

GAY BYRNE: And in the heel of the hunt, will you expect to see your loved ones again afterwards?
GABRIEL BYRNE: I wish that I could say that I will, but I don't think so. And if I don't, at least in this life, I have known the beauty of being connected to them.

GAY BYRNE: All right, suppose it's all true, Gabriel, everything that you were taught by the Christian Brothers and that your dad and mum believed in and that they were teaching you in the seminary, when you pop your clogs and you meet Him at the pearly gates, God, what do you think you'll say to him?

GABRIEL BYRNE: Well, *if* that happens, I think *He'll* have some explaining to do. I mean, He'll be the one who'll have to say something to me. I would ask Him why He did it. "Why? Why did you put us through all this? For what? Why did you make us such tormented, complex, mortal, longing, yearning creatures?"

But I'd be very happy, I must say. I just can't see that happening.

BRENDA FRICKER

Don't Ask. Don't Tell.

Brenda Fricker is a national treasure. I hope she knows that. Moreover, I hope she wakes up every morning and looks herself in the mirror and tells herself that: "I am a national treasure." You can't always count on the nation to tell you. And, Lord knows, we treasures need to be told.

There are some people who have been around so long, you think you know them. And I'm not just talking about the famous. The same can go for family members. And then, suddenly, they say or do something which makes you totally reassess them. That happened, one afternoon, in 2009, in a Ballsbridge hotel suite, when I interviewed Brenda Fricker.

I knew that she was prone to depression. I had no idea why. Before our interview, I had vague notions about getting her to share with me what depression feels like, not having experienced it myself, thank God. Instead I stumbled, unawares, into a deeply confessional exchange, which reminded me of the duty of care we have to the people who sit in that highly exposed chair opposite.

Unexpectedly, in the process of answering a series of questions about the meaning of life, an internationally renowned Oscar-winning actress found herself speaking publicly, for the first time, about her deeply scarring experience of sexual abuse, over forty years earlier.

By law, sexual abuse victims are entitled to anonymity. Given that Brenda almost certainly did not come to the interview intending to reveal that experience, and given that, for a high-profile figure, once something like that is out, it haunts every subsequent cutting and interview, everybody in the room realised that Brenda should be immediately offered the chance to retract what she had said or to ask us to omit it from the programme. Instead, she thanked me for the interview, which had clearly unburdened her.

I hope so. She deserves to be lifted, not burdened.

∾

GB: Take us on a quick trip first of all through your childhood and family and upbringing and school.

BF: I had very little schooling. I've no education at all. I went to national school and got my exams there and then I went to Stephen's Green to the nuns. And then I had the car crash, which kept me in hospital for two years. Then I got TB, which kept me in hospital for a year, so I missed out on a huge amount of schooling. And I never quite understood why my mother, who was a teacher, my father, who was a journalist, didn't arrange some kind of education for me in hospital to keep me going, because I never did my Inter, I never did my Leaving, I never did anything. So, I'm completely uneducated.

GB: Okay, go back to the car smash—what was that?

BF: I was on a bicycle and I was passing somebody out and a car was coming the other way and I went through the front windscreen and went out the back windscreen and broke every bone in my body and was in hospital for two years.

GB: For two years?

BF: It was dreadful. And then TB, which was almost predictable, because my mother was dying of it when I was born; and I had been vaccinated and everything, but I still got it.

GB: And you never went back to school after that?

BF: No. And I never understood my parents not doing that.

GB: And where was your mother a teacher?

BF: In Stratford College, the Jewish college in Rathgar. A roaring Catholic teaching in the Jewish school. [Laughs.] They all loved her!

GB: And what happened to you then when you sort of gave up school?

BF: I got a job in the *Irish Times* . . . Nepotism, pure nepotism . . . ! [Laughs.] Ken Gray said to me, "You're Des Fricker's daughter. We'll give you a job. Come on in." I was kind of a cub reporter, spending most of my time in the Flowing Tide or the Fleet Bar, across the road, getting drunk. And then Jim Fitzgerald said, "We're starting a programme in Telefís Éireann—and we're calling it *Tolka Row*, and we'd love you to come out and do a couple of episodes." And here I am.

GB: So, tell me about your mother and father. Did you get on? Did you love your mother?

BF: Not really, no. I had a bad relationship with my mother. I'm sixty-four years of age now, and I'm learning to forgive her. Because she was bipolar, she was manic-depressive, and she had nobody to turn to and nobody to help. So, she took it out on me and she was very violent. I mean *extremely* violent.

GB: Physically violent?

BF: Oh, dreadful. Whereas my father was the complete opposite. He was the most gentle man you could meet.

GB: But hold on, you said the students in Stratford College loved your mother . . .

BF: They adored her. She was wonderful with them. She couldn't handle *her* children at all. Couldn't handle my sister. Gráinne, who died recently, God rest her soul, had a worse time than me, even.

GB: Isn't that extraordinary? . . . And your father?

BF: My father was a bit detached. He did his job, he did his fishing, he did a bit of writing, and I'll never know, Gay, till the day I die, whether he knew. I mean, I was covered in scars and stuff from the beatings, and she used to say it was hockey in school. Now, whether or not he did believe her, I feel he should have done something.

GB: But she never chastised you while he was there?

BF: No, never, never, never, never, never. Never!

GB: Did she drink?

BF: No, never.

GB: Was she religious?

BF: Madly. She'd walk six miles to Mount Argus to get six o'clock Mass, then she'd walk back to Dundrum to get eight o'clock Mass. And then, when evening Mass came in, she was over the moon. She had another one to go to in the evening. And my father was an atheist, so I had the two influences. So, naturally, I was inclined to lean towards the more peaceful one.

GB: But did they love each other, Brenda?

BF: I think they did at some point. When I was born, my mother was dying of TB, and she was told not to have any more children. And in those days, contraceptive wasn't available, so I think they moved into separate bedrooms, and I think that's when the marriage broke up.

GB: Did it break up?

BF: There was no sexual relationship between them. He stayed in the house, but they had no relationship.

GB: So, she'd beat you up regularly . . .

BF: And then she'd be sorry.

GB: Oh!

BF: When she was in good form, she would apologise. But I mean, she was in pain. And I see that now. But you don't, when you're three and four and you're being beaten to death with a Hoover.

GB: And you say, at sixty-four, you're just learning to forgive her?

BF: Yeah.

GB: Have you carried this baggage all your life?

BF: I have, yeah . . . But I mean, I am understanding it, because I myself, as you know, suffer from depression, and she was definitely a manic depressive. I forgive her . . . I will forgive her.

GB: And for the small amount of time you were in Loreto? Did you like Loreto?

BF: No, I hated it.

GB: Oh? Why?

BF: I hated the nuns. They were awful.

GB: [Laughs.]

BF: Didn't like priests or nuns. I was terrified of them.

GB: And we have this situation where your father is a complete atheist and your mother is going to three Masses every day. It seems extra-ordinary.

BF: Yeah. I don't know if I've ever spoken about this before. I can remember testing the Church: the things that we had been told that we would die if we did, like if we bit on the Communion, the blood would pour forth from your mouth . . . So, I did that. I bit the Communion one day . . . And nothing happened. And I thought, "Interesting."

And I remember this moment—this moment stays with me for ever—of taking a little picture of the Infant of Prague and taking a scissors and cutting up the little fat hands and cutting the little fat arms. And I was waiting to die, to be killed. I was waiting for God to strike me dead, you know. He didn't. So I began slowly just disbelieving in it. And I began to look for God in people. And I found a belief there.

GB: But can you remember about what age you said, "Nothing in this for me. I'm leaving this behind, once and for all"?
BF: Sixteen, maybe.

GB: And you had no regrets? You didn't feel that you'd lost an old friend or a consolation of some kind?
BF: No. I never had the faith. And I wish I had, 'cause I have friends who have it and I see the comfort they get from it.

GB: So what do you believe now?
BF: Depends on what day you ask me. If you ask me on Monday, I might believe in God; if you ask me on Tuesday, I'd say, "Oh, no, it's all rubbish." You see a new-born baby, you think, "God, there must be something wonderful up there to make this." You hear of Stephen Gately dying at the age of thirty-three or something and you think, "What the hell is gone wrong? What's he doing this for?" So, I fluctuate.

I believe in goodness. I believe in Christianity, if you like, and honesty. And just trying to be good.

GB: Were you ever attracted to any other faith, apart from Catholicism?
BF: No. I did investigate a couple of things, like Buddhism and Islam, in my early twenties. Didn't find anything to clutch to there either. It's like, I remember saying to my father once, "What's God? And what's all this about God and different religions and everything else?" And he said, "Look. Take a map of Ireland, and you have Dublin and you have twenty people who want to get to Dublin and they all come from different roads. They come from Donegal, they come from Mayo. They would all come from different roads: the A50, the M50, the M1, but they get to Dublin. So, they get to God, if that's what you want to call it. There are huge ways of getting it, huge and different, but if that's what they want, that's the way they do it." And that kind of made sense to me.

GB: So, in fact, you're saying one religion is as good as another.
BF: Absolutely. Or as bad as another . . . !

GB: Or as bad as another! Would you subscribe to the idea that religion has been responsible for much evil and badness and violence in the world?
BF: I mean, what's going on recently? I was a child at the Father Mathew Feis. The priests were putting their hands up my skirt. I mean, it was

going on *then.* You know, it's dreadful, it's appalling, and the covering up and the denying and the moving people to other parishes . . . it's absolutely dreadful.

GB: The priests were at you . . . ?
BF: Oh, yeah . . . from an early age.

GB: And how did you react to that?
BF: Well, I'd kind of giggle and tell them to go away, because you wouldn't understand what they were doing.

GB: It didn't leave a lifelong mark on you or anything like that?
BF: No, but I remember thinking, "They shouldn't be doing that."

GB: I don't see any sort of resentment of the Church in you, or is there?
BF: No, no, there isn't. It's something that I'm not involved in.

GB: So, do you think Jesus existed on this earth?
BF: I think he probably did, yes.

GB: And what do you think he was?
BF: A prophet, probably; a good person. I mean, he died for us. I believe that. I think he went all the way and did that. Just a fantastically good person, who got followed by millions of people, you know.

GB: And you don't think he was the Son of God? Or do you . . . ?
BF: No . . . And I do scream his name regularly . . . Anything happens, it's "Oh, Jesus, help me!" [Laughs.]

GB: [Laughs.]
BF: And I've started, since my sister dying, I've decided not to call it "praying," I've decided to call it "meditating" in the morning. And I hope that she's in a happy and beautiful place, but I don't know if there is an after-life, so I don't know where she's gone.

GB: You were close?
BF: I adored her. She was as bright as a button. She was funny. She was lovely. And I miss her terribly . . . She died of a heart attack in her sleep. Lovely death. Smile on her face and her arm around the dog!

GB: That we should all go so easy . . .
BF: Oh, that we should all go so easy!

GB: And do you think you'll see Gráinne again?
BF: That's a tough one. I don't know. I hope I will.

GB: What do you think happens when you die?
BF: I haven't a clue.

GB: What do you *think* happens?
BF: I think I'll just die and that's just the end of it, that I'll just be gone and that there's nothing else. But it's when you love . . . love is quite spiritual. When people you love die, you want them to be in a happy place. I don't particularly love myself, so I don't care what happens to me. [Laughs.] But if you do love somebody, like my husband when he died, I want him to be happy and somewhere beautiful, that maybe we could meet again. But I don't know, Gay.

GB: All right, since you mentioned your husband, tell me about him—Barry.
BF: Barry was a darling, but he had a drink problem.

GB: And where and when did you meet him?
BF: I met him at an interview in the Gresham for a play for Granada. And it was love across the desk! He was the Director.

GB: Right.
BF: And we eventually got married, but he began drinking, very heavily . . .

GB: Hold on, now, you're skipping a lot. You went for this interview in the Gresham, and there was Barry Davies and *zing*, straight away . . .
BF: Yeah! And he even kept the notes that he wrote down about me when I came in: "Girl with the chin . . ." [Laughs.]

GB: I wouldn't have thought you had a big chin!
BF: And then I met him that evening, bumped into him in a pub somewhere, in the Flowing Tide.

GB: That must have been fate . . .
BF: Yeah, fate.

GB: Or God . . . ?
BF: Or God, I don't know. [Laughs.] And then we fell in love, and then we courted for a while, and his divorce was just going through and we waited for that to finish, and then we got married . . . And then he started drinking, quite heavily.

GB: Why?
BF: I don't know.

GB: But you loved him?

BF: Adored him.

GB: And he you?

BF: Me, yeah. When things were good, it was really good. And then the drinking got so bad, Gay, that I couldn't take it any more, and I said, "I'm getting a divorce. I can't handle this any more."

So, I got a divorce and that frightened the life out of him. So he started, then, to talk sense and he said, "I may be an alcoholic," and he started to approach the subject, and I thought, "That's fine," and we started seeing each other again. And we were still in love. You don't just fall out of love just like that . . . And he fell down the stairs and died.

GB: . . . Drunk, presumably?

BF: Drunk.

GB: God love him! And would you have married him again, do you think?

BF: Oh, I would, yeah. And again and again and again.

GB: And was there any sense of blame towards God?

BF: No, I didn't feel that at all. I blamed *him* for being drunk and falling down the stairs.

GB: And you hope to see him again?

BF: I pray/meditate to him . . . I actually make the sign of the cross, which I feel a little bit hypocritical about doing, and I just talk to the people who are gone that I love in the morning and ask them to help me and hope that they're well, and pray for people who are sick.

GB: Well, that's prayer.

BF: Yeah, it's a kind of spirituality.

GB: And was there never anybody else in your life?

BF: Never. No, no . . . Never in love again, no.

GB: Never fancied anybody again?

BF: Well, fancy is a different thing . . . I mean, I'm a healthy woman. I'd do that . . . But I don't think I could marry again. I don't trust anybody.

GB: You see, I think you're a loveable woman . . .

BF: Thank you.

GB: . . . and always were, and therefore I think that you were much loved by so many people, but you don't seem to be aware of this.

BF: You're very sharp, now, to spot that one. And it's because I don't love myself.

GB: Why don't you love yourself?
BF: I don't know. Don't ask me that . . . I think life is very difficult. I find *life* very difficult.

GB: Why? How?
BF: I think because of depression, which I hate talking about, really . . .

GB: Well, please talk to *me* about it. I'd like to know the effect of it.
BF: I find huge spirituality in kindness. I mean, your wife, Kathleen, once, when I was in the depths of depression, took me out to your house in Howth and gave me lunch and cheered me up. And that's loving and that's kindness and that's spiritual. And I think if you get that, then you can keep going.

GB: And you remember that morning?
BF: Oh, God, it meant the world to me. She got me out of hell, you know. Whereas other people would put you into it. They just laugh at your depression. They just kind of mock it, you know.

GB: You see, I don't understand that, because I don't think I've ever been depressed . . .
BF: Well, lucky man!

GB: . . . I've been cast down, I've been sad . . .
BF: Yes . . .

GB: . . . I've been sombre, I've been in a bad mood, but when I've talked to people who suffer from depression, I realise that I've never been depressed.
BF: Well, you're very lucky. God bless you, and I hope you never get it.

GB: And you don't even pray about that?
BF: You don't do anything when you're depressed. You just look at the wall . . . You just don't go out and you just cry and you think you're no good and you've no hope. And then it passes, it passes. The clinical depression passes and then you're fine and you're out again and you're okay. But it's tough. And particularly when you're on your own, which I am now.

GB: Except for Juno.
BF: Except for my darling Juno.

GB: How old is Juno now?

BF: Juno is thirteen—look at her! My soulmate. She has a little heart condition; she is borderline diabetic, just like her owner ...

GB: What do you mean when you say that you don't love yourself?

BF: I just mean that. I know there are people who love me, and I'm so lucky.

GB: Absolutely!

BF: I'm really lucky to have such good friends. Really, really good friends ... and I can't understand why they love me.

GB: Now, that wouldn't be a sort of an *actressy* false modesty ...?

BF: Ah, no, I'm not falsely modest, and I'm not making it up. That is genuinely true. Because being told all my life by my mother that I was useless and rubbish and all the rest of it, it goes in, you know.

GB: That would do it ... But Gráinne loved you?

BF: Gráinne loved me towards the end, yeah. She did love me towards the end.

GB: You never had a baby?

BF: No. I had a lot of miscarriages.

GB: Ah.

BF: So the body wouldn't do it. Unfortunately. Yeah, I wish now it had. I really do.

GB: Do you think you would have been a good mother?

BF: Oh, I haven't a clue ... I would hope I would have been a good mother, yeah. We were going to try and adopt a baby, and then Barry died. And he was getting old, and he was drinking and things. But I would like to have had children, 'cause I think that's what it's all about.

GB: It's extraordinary to me that you divorced Barry, and then later on you were on the tip of marrying him again ...

BF: Absolutely.

GB: That leads me into, do you think that there is one man for every woman, one woman for every man?

BF: Not necessarily, no. He was just the one that I adored. And my father, who died in the same week, I just adored the two of them. They were the two men in my life. Never met anybody since that came close.

GB: And can you explain why you loved them . . . ?

BF: Barry—I loved his talent, his intelligence, his humour, his loving me, his patience with my fear of sexuality, which he was wonderful about. I just loved everything about him. He was great. Funny, funny, funny man.

GB: What was the fear of sexuality? What was that about?

BF: Well, I was abused as a child by a family acquaintance, and that gave me . . . I've never talked about this, ever—it made me very frightened of sex. And he, he handled that. He was wonderful. It was a year before we made love after we got married. And he was so wonderful. I could never thank him enough.

GB: And is that taken care of now?

BF: I think so. I think so, yeah . . .

GB: . . . You won your Oscar for *My Left Foot* and then you did *The Field* and you were in *Casualty* and the lovely piece in the RTÉ drama *No Tears* . . . You've played some wonderful roles and you have met some outstanding people in show business. What are your thoughts about show business, overall?

BF: I'm very cool about show business. I regard it as a job, as a craft. I love *doing* it. I hate the crap around it. I remember an interview with Julia Roberts with Barry Norman and she was the first actress to get paid twenty million for a film. And he was questioning her, saying, "Do you think you're worth it?" And she said, "I do the acting for free. I get paid twenty million for the shit that I have to handle around it." And that's the way I feel about it.

GB: And when you're playing a part, first day on set, are you off-put by being in the presence of big names . . . ?

BF: No, not at all. I do a lot of homework and I'd go with my case fully packed . . . And I'm not impressed by stardom. And if you're prepared, you'd be okay . . . If you go in with an empty suitcase, you're going to be in trouble. And you'll find that the good actors come with a *very* packed suitcase.

GB: When you won your Oscar, what did that mean to you?

BF: Well, it was very nice to get a present from your peers for being good at something.

GB: It's more than that, Brenda . . . !

BF: But we didn't really know about Oscars in Ireland then . . . When I first heard that I was nominated for an Oscar—and this is absolutely true—I thought it was something to do with Oscar Wilde. I was completely ignorant. And then the whole din just started, miles away, and got louder and louder and louder. But it was lovely to win it.

GB: And what does it mean, in realistic terms, in a career?

BF: Well, it means, as I say, you jump the queue. People suddenly know your name who would never know your name, so you get to work in America, you get to work in Australia, you get to work in Thailand . . .

GB: Is acting a vocation for you?

BF: Gosh, that's a good word . . . "Vocation" has religious implications. I just love doing it, Gay. You know, I never think I get it right. Somebody is going to find me out, someone is going to catch me . . . I just like doing it. It's the only thing I know how to do that I get paid for.

GB: Do you think acting can be taught?

BF: [Laughs.] No. No. That's a tough one, but I don't think it can. There is a moment when . . . it's like high-diving, when your feet leave the board and you're going towards the water, that between that moment there is complete freedom. And that's what I feel when I'm acting. That's what I get from acting, and it's beautiful.

GB: You've lost yourself . . . ?

BF: Yeah. When you get into it, you love it.

GB: And when will you stop doing it, do you think?

BF: When I die and go to . . .

GB: Where?

BF: Where?

GB: . . . Suppose it's all true, Brenda, what your mother believed in . . .

BF: Well, then I'm in a shambles really, aren't I? Or maybe He'd be full of forgiveness. Maybe He'll forgive me all my doubts and say, "Come on into Heaven." I don't know.

GB: But you don't think you've ever done anything so bad in your life that He would say, "Down you go . . ."?

BF: No, I don't think that. I don't think I've ever done anything really bad in my life. Little things, but I mean, I try very hard to be decent.

GB: So, if you met God, you'd say…?

BF: I'd ask Him was He real? [Laughs.] I'd say, "Do you exist? Are you real? Why did you allow the tsunami to happen? Why do you do cruel things? Why do you cause wars?" I'd have a lot of questions for Him.

GB: Do you mean "cause" or "allow"?

BF: Cause. If He's God, He's causing it … That's a good question. Cause or allow? … Both! … You've set my head a-thinking!

Just as a postscript, Brenda's lovely dog Juno—our silent companion during that interview and her soulmate—died soon afterwards. I'm pleased to report she has since bought two more dogs. I sense she could do with some unconditional love.

NEIL JORDAN

When "Don't Know" Is the
Right Answer

"Why are we here, Gay?"

I thought it was my job to ask the big questions, but as the Oscar-winning writer and director Neil Jordan sat down in his beautiful mid-Victorian living-room, overlooking Killiney Bay, it was he who posed this one. I don't think he was thinking existentially.

"I'm not at all religious, so this could be a very short conversation," he elaborated, as his wonderful Canadian wife, Brenda, served us tea and delicious home-made Christmas cake.

However, as Neil Jordan knows all too well, not having *certified* answers to "the big questions" is a very different thing from having *no* answers. For one thing, whom would we trust, these days, to stamp the certificates?

Religion is one area where you can have your Christmas cake and eat it, if only because, when it comes to matters of belief, we all seem to be selecting our cakes *à la carte* these days.

In fact, Neil Jordan is probably more typically Irish than he would like to admit: solid, Catholic upbringing and schooling; rebel period of ceremoniously kicking over those traces; and then, a career which includes, guess what, a huge series on the Papacy, *The Borgias*. Not, by any means, a return to the faith of our fathers, but certainly a return to fascination with it.

All that was a twinkle in his eye, back in early 2010 when we met. His new movie then was *Ondine*, and he had managed to ensnare no less than our Golden Globe-winning divo, Colin Farrell, in his fisherman's nets. But I wanted to talk about his life, not his work.

❧

GB: Tell me about your upbringing and your childhood.
NJ: My father was a teacher and my mother was a painter . . . I went to St Paul's College in Raheny, grew up there, went to UCD . . .

GB: Was it a very Catholic upbringing?
NJ: Totally, yeah. 'Course, it was . . . Everybody was Catholic, it seemed to me, except people who were Protestants . . . who you didn't meet . . .

and one or two people who were Jewish . . . My mother used to go to Mass every day, and my father was very religious. I was an altar boy for a bit and I remember that the different orders came around to the school giving out these leaflets. I went to my mother and I said, "Look, I want to be a priest," and she very wisely said, "No, don't do that." [Laughs.] But it was like I couldn't separate Catholicism from the grass.

GB: When did you begin to fall away from your belief in the Catholic Church, if, indeed, you ever did believe in the Catholic Church?

NJ: Oh, no, I did. I mean, frankly speaking, the things that you're told when you do your Communion and your Confirmation, there's a terrible, shocking beauty to them, isn't there? And you're told that they're actually as much part of the fabric of everyday life as the food you consume and the bus you take to school . . . You end up living in a world where the real world is not as important as the imaginary world. I suppose I always connected with the imagination in some way, and I was quite religious up to the age of about twenty. And then it just all went—*bang!* It just vanished, and without any sense of trauma or anything like that. I just kind of lost interest in it. I didn't say, "I don't believe in God now," or "I don't believe in the Communion of Saints and the forgiveness of sins or all those wonderful Catholic concepts . . ." I just got interested in other things, I suppose.

GB: Do you believe in God?

NJ: I don't know, really. That's the truth . . . It's not to do with an abstract yes or no—this is true or not. It's a different kind of question, I think . . . I mean, in terms of the proof of the existence of God, the one I like best is St Anselm, where he said, "How can he have an idea of that which does not exist, because to have an idea of it is to bring it into some form of existence?" That seems, to me, to be the most logical one. And the most beautiful one, actually, in a way . . . So, I would kind of believe in everything, really.

GB: What do you mean, you believe in *everything*?

NJ: I don't know. I mean, all religions are absurd, aren't they? You know the idea that God made the world and the Garden of Eden in six days and Adam was expelled and all that. Of course, that's not factually true. But there is something incredibly powerful about the sense of being excluded from a remembered paradise, in the sense of one's life in the world is an experience of abandonment. There is no other way of expressing certain conditions of being in the world than a religious way of expressing those conditions. And there's a whole series of questions that there are no explanation to. And to me, religion provides answers.

GB: But yet they're absurd?
NJ: They're absurd, absolutely absurd, yeah.

GB: So, when you encounter people who pray, what's your reaction?
NJ: Well, it's an incredibly powerful thing. I mean, you've read the Richard Dawkins books, haven't you, on atheism? And to me, those books are absurd, because you can't stop human beings believing in things. Even if they are irrational, they'll still believe in them, so why do you try and convince them their natural instincts are irrational or somehow wrong?

GB: If you were in the fox-hole, would you pray?
NJ: Yeah, probably.

GB: To whom or what?
NJ: I don't know, really. You mean, if I was about to die?

GB: If you were in danger.
NJ: Every time I'm in a plane and it's hit by lightning, I bless myself. But that's more superstition, isn't it?

GB: I don't know. And if you were really under pressure . . . ?
NJ: Well, I wouldn't find any particular satisfaction out of leading a worshipful life. Could I put it that way? Because I'm not religious and I don't practise any particular religion, I don't feel any absence in my life.

GB: Are the children being brought up Catholic?
NJ: Well, that's a very interesting question . . . I have five children—I have been married before—so, we have two children, Daniel and Dashiel, and they're both being brought up Catholic. Now, I was brought up a Catholic, and Brenda, my wife, she's from Canada and she was actually brought up in some strange Mennonite tradition.

GB: Mennonite?
NJ: Yeah, and actually, when the New Year of 2000 came along, she and her brothers fully expected not to be in the world any more. They fully believed the world would end—yeah . . .

GB: In 2000?

NJ: In 2000. There was no point in planning beyond it. I mean, people's beliefs are absurd . . .

GB: What was their reaction, incidentally, when it didn't end in 2000?

NJ: Well, it's the reaction religious people always have. They say they got the date wrong. Seriously! [Laughs.] Calculations must have been wrong.

GB: So, has the date been shifted now?

NJ: I don't know. I haven't followed that one.

GB: Do you think you might return to your faith on your deathbed?

NJ: I really don't know. If, at the hour of death, you want to return to see your childhood, yeah, I definitely would probably do that.

GB: If a Catholic priest turned up and wanted to give you the last rites, would you push him away?

NJ: I might, actually, yes.

GB: Why?

NJ: Well, I *might,* because I don't believe in that kind of certainty. That kind of "yes or no" certainty is what I don't like about the Catholic Church. If this does not happen, you should go to Hell. I would not subscribe to that belief. I believe, if my soul is lost, it will be through actions of my own.

GB: You have enormous talent. Do you ever think of where that talent came from? . . . Or do you ever think that you have an obligation to use it in a particular way?

NJ: Yeah, in a way . . . One doesn't know where it comes from, in a way. When you sit down at your desk to write something, if it is good, it comes from some place that you cannot explain, and one invites that. But I think, in terms of using your talent well or for ill, the job of an artist or a writer actually is to cleanse, to make sure the language expresses whatever things are coming through as cleanly and as honestly as possible. That's the way I think of what I do.

GB: Do you think there is a Day of Reckoning?

NJ: Oh, yeah, absolutely. Well, I mean, you've only got so long, don't you? And have you spent your time well enough? Have you been dishonest? Have you robbed people? Have you lied and cheated and stuff like that?

GB: Are we talking about the judgement seat of Christ, as you were taught in St Paul's, Raheny, or some other Day of Judgement?

NJ: [Laughs.] I don't know, really. I suppose, in terms of what I do myself, the judgement will be people who look at your work when you aren't around and say, "Why did you mess around with this stupid thing, when you could have been doing that other great thing?"

GB: You think that's the judgement?

NJ: I do, yeah.

GB: What about reincarnation?

NJ: Would I like to be reincarnated? Oh, yeah, I'd love to . . .

GB: All right, let's join in the fun . . . What would you like to come back as?

NJ: I'd like to come back exactly the same, just better. [Laughs.] When my father died, he used to always tell me ghost stories and he used to terrify the life out of me with them. And when he died, I thought, "Okay, fulfil the promise of these ghost stories. Come back and haunt me." And the haunting never happened. I was kind of disappointed, really, because there was no contact; there was no voice from beyond that grave. And that went on for about four or five years.

And then, suddenly, I began to feel this presence. Gradually, you know. Now, it was very odd. Actually, it was on a plane going from Los Angeles to Dublin and there was ferocious turbulence, you know, bouncing around the sky. And I woke up and there was this man standing in the aisle wearing a cardigan. Dark hair. And it was my father. And I said, "Okay, this is *really* strange," 'cause the last place you expect a ghost to appear is on an aisle of a 747 coming back from Los Angeles to Dublin. And it was very bizarre. I don't know whether it's my imagination or whether, when you're dead, you go through five years of absolute stunned silence, because you cannot believe that you have no existence any more . . . and gradually you find a way to make yourself manifest.

GB: Did he speak?

NJ: No, just stood there.

GB: Reassuringly?

NJ: Kind of looking lost, actually. You know, I probably was dreaming, but it was an experience of dreaming, of waking, actually . . . It's probably to do with my psyche or my need . . . But there was a period where there was just absolute silence, which was shocking to me, actually, 'cause I was not the believer. The dead one was the believer.

GB: He believed he was going to come back to you?

NJ: Oh, absolutely. He believed in all that stuff: reincarnation and Catholicism and Buddhism and, you know, everything that employs an after-life, my father believed in. Everything.

GB: Are you stubbornly refusing to accept that they might be there, your parents or your loved ones . . . ?

NJ: Well, it's almost as if the departed go into some awful silence, isn't it? And then, after some kind of gap of dead silence, some other whispering starts . . .

GB: Well, do you think that's going to happen to you . . . ?

NJ: I really don't know. I really haven't got a clue . . . I'm not afraid of dying, at all. Well, I wouldn't *like* to die, but I'm not afraid of it. Sometimes the thought seems very comforting. I mean, if you live to the age of seventy, the thought of leaving this life, particularly if your kids were in good shape and your family were in good shape, it's not the most appalling thing in the world, is it, to vanish from life?

GB: Speak for yourself! I'm over seventy and I have no such thoughts . . .

NJ: Sorry . . . It's just, we are born, we die, don't we? That's what happens, isn't it?

GB: If, by any chance, God is there when you get there, what do you think you'd say to him?

NJ: I'd say, "Was it worth it?" [Laughs.] If I have to believe in what I was taught when I grew up, every form of sexual activity was extremely punishable, so in that case I would have to say, "I'm sorry." Do I think I'll meet a God . . . ? Probably not, maybe a white light . . .

GB: But if you do . . . ?

NJ: I will say, "I'm sorry. I have no language with which to address you. Please give me that language, because, in life, I didn't have it."

SIR MICHAEL PARKINSON

Questions and Answers

Michael and Gabriel. Two archangels. The great warrior and the divine messenger. Hmmm. Here on earth, Mike Parkinson and I first crossed paths in the early 1960s, at Granada Television, when he joined their producer training scheme. I was presenting a show for them called *People and Places* and was trying to get used to the experience of being recognised in the street as "that bloke off the telly." Mike was new to television, but was already well established as a print journalist in London. He knew how to ask a question. He still does. He was a handsome devil too, so, within a matter of weeks, he had been asked to present a summer filler series about cinema.

The rest, as they say, is his story.

Michael came from—and sounded like he came from—Barnsley, in Yorkshire, at a time when regional accents had suddenly become fashionable. Sidney Bernstein, the boss of Granada, took his cues from the angry young men, who were turning over the tables in theatre and cinema. Bernstein wanted the commercial "third channel" to challenge the BBC's received wisdom and pronunciation, which demanded that every presenter stifled their own accent and spoke like a latter-day Eliza Doolittle: *"The rain in Spain stays mainly in the plain."* Bernstein was a businessman and knew that his customers—the viewers—spoke with all kinds of accents. He created a channel where they could hear people like themselves, and, not surprisingly, they liked it.

Which is how a blow-in Dub and a young lad from Barnsley came to be rubbing shoulders and signing occasional autographs on the Granada lot.

We talked about jazz rather than religion back then, so I wasn't at all sure whether Michael would have much to say about "the big questions", when he accepted my request to appear on *The Meaning of Life*. It wasn't exactly reassuring when his publicist blithely told our researcher that, as far as she knew, he hadn't a religious bone in his body.

And yet Barnsley is chapel country—there's a Nonconformist prayer hall standing at the end of practically every back-to-back terrace. *Onward, Christian Soldiers* was written down the road, in Wakefield. I had a hunch that, even if he had subsequently kicked over the traces, he would have grown up surrounded by Sabbath observance and hymn-singing miners. And what about his Irish wife, Mary Heneghan?

Surely, a Catholic, at least to start with? Would some of that have rubbed off?

I was right. Michael quickly told me something that even his son, Mike Junior, had never heard before: that he had been a teenage Sunday school teacher, albeit that he was more inspired by devotion to another of the young, female teachers than to the Almighty.

Of course, the other great Yorkshire religion is cricket, and the young Parky's idols were nearly all of the sporting kind. They still are. It is what made his interviews with Muhammad Ali and George Best so compelling in the 1970s and 80s. He had been a good sportsman himself—good enough to know that he lacked that touch of god-like genius which marks out "the greatest." That said, whenever he was allowed to sit in the presence of this greatness, he was never so over-awed that he forgot his journalistic duty. If his idols had feet of clay, you could trust him to reveal them.

After I moved back to RTÉ and Dublin, in 1962, we continued to meet from time to time, but the Irish Sea put paid to any serious close-ness. That said, I like and admire him a lot, and so, as we sat down, I was looking forward to turning the tables on one of the world's great interviewers and finding out what has given meaning to a life lived largely in parallel with my own.

༄

MP: My father was a miner, more often out of work than in work, and my mother was a housewife superstar and didn't much like being a miner's wife . . . She was the engine of my ambition, but she actually made me want to leave as much as she did. I inherited my need to get out of that background from her. And from my father too, who took me down the pit when I was about eleven, twelve, and showed me the reality of working there.

GB: I see no record of you all shuffling off to church regularly. I thought that in the north of England there was a robust reformist tradition of hymn-singing and Sunday school and biblical studies and scripture.

MP: Very much so. My parents weren't regular church-goers, but insisted I should take my Communion and go and be confirmed and all that stuff. But I never found much interest or much need for religion. Except to say, you're quite right about the Nonconformists:

there were six Methodist chapels in the village where I lived and we had a continual running of *The Messiah,* right the way through the year, and I was very much engaged by the music I heard. I love *The Messiah* to this day . . . Didn't convince me about the existence of a God, but convinced me that something that could inspire me like that could not be all bad.

GB: Did you actually go to services?

MP: Well, I had to, to be confirmed, and then I fell in love with a Sunday school teacher. I fancied her like mad, so I became a Sunday school teacher . . . and I was probably not a very good Sunday school teacher, but at least I made contact with the girl of my dreams, who rejected me totally out of hand.

GB: But you actually taught young children?

MP: I did. I taught them the ways of God, without really being convincing at all, I'm sure. I never really bought in to it. It seemed to be a wonderful story, but I never bought in to the idea of there being a divinity.

GB: Move on to Barnsley School, which was not a happy occasion for young Michael.

MP: No, it was horrible. I was bullied at school, not by pupils, by teachers, by a German teacher particularly, who had the great gall, when I became famous, to write to me and say, would I attend his farewell ceremony? Anyway, I knew what I wanted to be, a journalist, and I went.

GB: At some stage, you thought: "Television. I want to get in there." What prompted that?

MP: Necessity. I was working in Fleet Street and I had a row with the editor of the *Daily Express* . . .

GB: [Laughs.] And you came north . . .

MP: . . . So, I landed myself in the middle of this wonderful conglomeration of talented people and I embarked upon the happiest bit of my life.

GB: And outside, somewhere, they were making *Coronation Street,* and when the Beatles first came on our show, Paul McCartney asked you for an autograph.

MP: He did, for his mum. Still my greatest moment.

GB: And he asked me to take on the job as manager, which I turned down for some reason.

MP: That is a *real* career choice . . . But it was possible, wasn't it, Gay?

GB: Anything was possible, and Granada was a fine company . . . Now, you have a special affinity with sporting people, you love them and get on so well with them and you're a fan and an admirer. Do you ever— I'm getting back to the spiritual end of things now—do you ever consider where outstanding people get that gift from?

MP: It's a good question. I think that if I analyse what intrigues me about people, it's where the gift comes from. Why, for instance, can Pavarotti sing and I can't sing like him? Why can Astaire dance like he does and I can't dance like Astaire? There are people who are special and I've made a lifetime's career, I suppose, as you have too, talking to those people. The only conclusion I've ever come to is that you can't explain the inexplicable, that genius has its own genetic code, but the one thing you do understand about those people is that none of them took what they had for granted. The difference, often, between the *greatly* gifted and the *merely* gifted was that the *greatly* gifted worked harder at *being* greatly gifted. I don't believe they are touched by a divine thing at all. You can say that they're touched by God or whoever it might be, created differently, there's a pattern and a purpose to it, and that's as unarguable as my belief that it's not . . . Who knows the answer? I don't. I'm in a state of perpetual confusion.

GB: Now, let us come to Mary.

MP: Yes, let us.

GB: Where did we first come across Mary? And the impression I have is that it was—*"bingo!"* first time, goose cooked . . .

MP: Absolutely. On top of a bus. I was going to a council meeting in a mining village called Tick Hill, near Doncaster, and she was a young teacher, trying to earn an extra bob at a keep-fit class. I saw her, she was wearing a red duffel coat and she had this golden-red hair. She's Irish. And I thought, "I've never seen anything like this in all my life." And we came out of the council meeting and she was taking this class and she persuaded myself and a friend to go and do a bit of dancing. I was very shy, so I got my friend to call her. It's pathetic really, but she was engaged and I was engaged, but eventually anyway, within about a year, we got married, and we've been fifty-one years now, which is a fairly long time.

The alternatives have been there, the possibility of leaving each other have been there, but, thank God, neither of us ever thought any more of it and continued in this imperfect state of bliss, basically, which is what long marriage is about. I got as far as the front gate once. She got about two miles down the road in a car and turned around and came back ...

GB: Are you serious about that? The front gate, and two miles down the road?

MP: 'Course. And then "I don't know, I've got nowhere to sleep." No, it wasn't like that, but these things happen in marriages and we overcame an awful lot ... We don't sit down and analyse why it did work, we just thank God it did. And we thank God for those moments when it could have gone upside down and it didn't.

GB: You had an innings with booze ...
MP: I did.

GB: ... and you were drinking a lot ...
MP: We all were—apart from you.

GB: What pulled you back from the brink? Because you talk about Richard Burton in your book, a horrifying description of the gradual progression into drinking, drinking, drinking; and of course Georgie Best and God knows how many others ...

MP: I was drinking heavily, because I was unhappy, I suppose. I enjoyed drinking and I enjoyed the company of fellow-drinkers and, as you know, in the Granada days and certainly in the BBC, in the seventies, there was a huge drinking culture. And Fleet Street, you *had* to go to the pub at night, because if you didn't they'd think there was something wrong with you. So I grew up in that and I had a capacity to drink as well ... And before you know where you are, you've got a problem.

Mary was the first to say to me, "Look, can I say something to you?" Wives know men's vulnerable points and she picked on mine. She said, "Do you know your problem when you get drunk—the worst part?" I said, "No, I don't." She said, "You're ugly."

GB: Ugly?

MP: And I thought, "Oh, my God!" And that vanity thing really, really upset me. Falling down I could have dealt with; stupid I could have dealt with; ugly ... ? And in that moment I just thought, "God, if she's right, this is not bright, must do something about that." So, I did. And I stopped for a year or so.

Now, I drink very moderately when I'm working. I don't drink if I'm doing a show; and I only drink *very* good wine. See, we made that a rule: what you do is you prohibitively exclude the possibility of drinking too much, because there are certain wines, as you know, Gay, that cost an *awful* lot a bottle. And I could do a bottle or two in my time. Nowadays, it's about a glass, because I'm mean, basically!

GB: You never had recourse to AA or twelve steps or any of that . . . ?
MP: No.

GB: You see, you, several times in this interview, have said "Thank God" and referred to the Divine and all of that sort of thing. And you had that religion in your childhood. And Mary Heneghan must have been Catholic . . .
MP: Oh, she's a Catholic. Yeah, of course she is, and all my children became Catholics. None of them are practising Catholics, but that was the deal I did with the Catholic Church.

I took instruction from a very young priest in Doncaster, who said to me—and this is absolutely true—he said, "I suppose it all started with Adam and Eve." And I said, "Look, how long have we got here? 'Cause I really don't have the time. I've got a council meeting . . ." I did it because Mary wanted it, because her parents were devout Catholics, coming as they did from Galway. Mary herself could not have existed in her family situation without the help and nurturing of the Catholic Church, because she went to a Catholic convent and they looked after her and she got her tuition for free, because she didn't have parents. So, they cared for her and looked after her and she owes them a huge debt. And I understand all of that, and so I went along with the notion of the kids being . . . because I take the view, I don't care what people believe in, they make their own minds up in the end. And they did. Mary remains . . .

GB: A practising Catholic . . . ?
MP: Yes. She's not devout in the sense that she goes to church every week, but at root, at her core, she is a believer and it affects her life and her judgements on things.

GB: And do you believe she prays regularly?
MP: *I* do. *I* do.

GB: *You* do?

MP: 'Course I do.

GB: You said you don't believe in God . . .

MP: A dog turns round in a circle to make a hole in the grass without explanation. Men do exactly the same . . . I used to pray before every show. I wasn't praying to—I have my own notion of who I'm praying to, but it's not some deity. It's something else. It's me saying to myself, "Come on, get a grip on yourself." But I think anybody who was brought up as we were with the Church, no matter how frail it looks now, that relationship, it's still there. There is still a kind of mystical, umbilical link between.

GB: But that's the brainwashing . . .

MP: Well, maybe. And I don't make any judgement about people who are devout . . . I wish I could be as certain as Mary is that we're going to meet again. See, I'm not. She is. That is a great comfort. If I could believe that, I'd be a lot happier than I am.

GB: You're a year younger than I am.

MP: Is that right?

GB: Do you think about death?

MP: As little as possible! I can't be bothered thinking about something which is inevitable. But I do know that I don't want to die like my mother died: confused and baffled by the world and living in a dream, a nightmare really. I observed that happen and it was the worst thing that has ever happened to me. She didn't know anybody. I became her brother, Tom. She brought my father back: she'd been a widow for thirty-five years and she brought him back and she had him down the pub every night—he rarely drank, my father—but she had him down this pub. She'd go down and give the landlord a bollocking about not sending him home . . .

But there were moments when farce took over—farce and tragedy, the twin faces. And there was one marvellous moment where she said to me, "You know he's down the pub again drinking." I'd just had enough. I said, "Mum, I've got to tell you, love, Dad's dead." "He's what?" "He's dead." "When did he die?" I said, "He died thirty years ago." She said, "Nobody told me." I was nearly crying with tears of laughter and also sadness. She said, "All right, Mr Clever Clogs . . ." —she used to call me when I was arguing with her. "If your father died thirty years ago, answer me this question: who did I climb over to get out of bed this morning?" I had to go away. There were tears streaming down my face.

GB: So, this arose out of my question about death. You don't fear it, but you don't want to die in agony?
MP: No, no, I don't want to die like that . . . I want a pill.

GB: Death. Light goes out. Gone, finished, done.
MP: I think that's it, really. We turn into manure, basically.

By way of postscript, in July 2013, it emerged that Michael had, for some months, been battling cancer. I was not surprised to see how he handled that revelation. Without so much as a whiff of self-pity or self-indulgence, he turned the news into an opportunity to raise vigilance in relation to men's health issues, before readying his bat confidently for whatever the future may throw at him.

You can take the boy out of Yorkshire, but you can't take Yorkshire out of the boy. And neither should you try. I know that that courage, clear-sightedness and doggedness will serve him well and the love of his family and the many, many people he has entertained down the years will be an even more dependable support. He certainly has mine.

ABBOT MARK PATRICK HEDERMAN

An Asset to the Abbey

There is a certain irony in the fact that someone who speaks as slowly as the Abbot of Glenstal has the initials MPH. His manner definitely seems "Built for comfort, not for speed," as the Willie Dixon classic has it.

Mark Patrick Hederman was wryly amused that our Director had chosen to record this interview in a Jesuit chapel, in Dublin's Milltown Institute. Was his own beautiful Benedictine abbey not good enough for us, or was it simply too far from D4? Actually, we would all, I am sure, have been very happy to go to Glenstal, but, in penny-pinching times, with the crew promised to another production that afternoon, we were confined to Dublin.

Mark Patrick has become something of a star, since his election as Abbot. In fact, he was already headed that way before. The matinée-idol good looks of his youth may have become slightly greyer and more jowly, but he has the kind of voice that makes you want to pull in at the side of the road to listen. Moreover, he says interesting things with it. Even in print, his "voice" is unmistakably resonant.

At a time when many people are sceptical about much of the leadership of the Catholic Church in Ireland, he has somehow managed to escape the general tarring brush and is consulted, like an oracle, by all the leading *chatterati*. He seldom disappoints.

By all accounts, he was a surprise choice as Abbot—to nobody more than himself. Be careful what you don't wish for. He hadn't wished to be a priest—brotherhood is a much more comfortable role than father-hood, to his way of thinking—and yet there he was, having to be ordained as one, as the role of Abbot demands. Even brothers need a father.

That role also carries responsibilities. The greater the authority, the less the freedom, it seems, in Catholic circles these days, which is why I was intrigued to know whether, and how, someone who has made an art form out of unorthodoxy now toes the line. We have all seen how Rome deals with its more turbulent Irish priests of late, so can he still speak his mind?

Thankfully, yes. At least, so far. Not least because, I suspect, that mind has a good deal more intelligence and subtlety than those who "cough in ink" and scrutinise his words for heresy. I admit his answers are occasionally maddeningly lacking in straightness, but that is usually more a matter of mental agility than "mental reservation." How do you catch a cloud and pin it down?

No, Mark Patrick Hederman is very definitely an asset to the abbey.

❧

GB: Take me back to your boyhood. It would occur to many people that you had a fairly posh upbringing.

MPH: I had the most idyllic childhood, living in Co. Limerick on a large farm. My mother was American, my father was a stud farmer. We lived in the most extraordinary beautiful country setting.

GB: Your parents, were they religious?

MPH: Well, my mother was very religious and my father wasn't religious at all. In fact he was very disappointed when I said I was going to join the monastery. He thought that was a terrible waste and he thought it was also a waste of all the money he had spent on my education. She was very interested in the intellectual life; he wasn't the slightest bit. My father felt that the only time you read a book was when you were in bed sick.

GB: The vision I have of you, then, as a boy is having wonderful freedom and being educated by your mother, and not a particularly religious or pious household?

MPH: No, but . . . I remember distinctly, by the age of nine, that I was in connection with God and that that was a kind of regular occurrence, all the time. I was trying to find out why God was so ineffective in the running of the universe at the time.

GB: But what do you mean then by being "in connection with God"?

MPH: I have distinct recollections of places where I would stop on the avenue going into our house, for instance, and know that I was actually in connection with God and that God was telling me something and I was responding to that.

GB: And it was altogether a happy experience, was it?

MPH: Oh, yes. I mean it was kind of, you know, when you're a certain age you have to make a big decision as to whether either *you* are God, or there's another one. So, therefore, you say, "Okay, well, there's another one. So, I'm going to make sure that I'm in contact with whoever is running this universe."

GB: And this connection, did it consist of a voice speaking to you?

MPH: No, no, never was that. It was a presence. It's that kind of connection which is really sensing people rather than directly speaking to them.

GB: Now, the decision was made to send you off to boarding school at a fairly young age . . .

MPH: Yes . . .

GB: Glenstal. Boarding school. All of that. When did you decide that you wanted to be a brother, a monk?

MPH: Well, first of all, at Glenstal, at that time, the school was meant to be a place where they fed the monastery. So, there was no secret about it at all: all the monks would surround anybody who was in any way eligible to join the monastery. They said, "Okay, well, we've been discussing with people up in Heaven and they think you'd be a wonderful monk." So, half of you is kind of flattered, you know. You say, "Oh, goodness me, to think that they are talking about me up there." And then the other half of you is horrified, you know: "I could end up like this crowd here!"

GB: There was a certain amount of recruitment. Would you go so far as to say that?

MPH: I would call it kidnapping.

GB: Kidnapping . . . !

MPH: It wasn't just recruitment. It was absolutely clear that they were saying, "This is what we have a school for."

GB: And then did it become a gradually growing conviction?

MPH: Well, really, for me, the first thing was I wanted to remain in connection with God and I wanted to find a place where that was possible. So, I never had any difficulty about it. It was a very good place to achieve the main goal of my life, which was to be in constant connection with God. Now, it wasn't as if I were without selfish motivation. I wanted to be as close to where the action is, as close to wherever, whoever was guiding the planet, in whatever direction it was meant to go. I wanted to be as near to, I suppose, the cockpit as possible.

GB: In that, did it occur to you that you had developed this sense of God to a greater extent than most people around you?

MPH: No, I didn't know that. It took me a long time to recognise that people were completely different and that I was odd, you know.

GB: Odd!

MPH: Yes, definitely.

GB: And did anybody suggest to you that you might be hallucinating, even?

MPH: Oh, well, I mean, that would have come later. When you meet psychiatrists and people who do tests: they'd be laughing, you know. And there is no point in discussing things with people who are absolutely convinced that you are a lunatic.

GB: It strikes me that you never wavered in your faith. Or did you?

MPH: No. I never had any occasion to, I suppose, question it or to prove to myself that what I have always believed was true.

GB: And during the time when they sent you to Paris as a young monk and you were studying there, it was during the student revolution, wasn't it? They were out on the streets and so on. Were you, even at that time, as a young man, ever distracted by the good life or by girls or "I could have this . . ." or "If I left the monastery I could do what all these guys are doing," and so on? Did that ever come up?

MPH: Yes, of course. Well, first of all going to Paris, in 1968, was a major revelation to me, because what happened was that the whole of the city of Paris was taken over by the students, and the students drove the trains.

Now, it did actually come home to me that you could destroy the whole of a society, that it's very fragile, that it's actually like a greenhouse. And if you start throwing rocks through it, it can disappear. So, that was a very, I suppose, for me, wonderful thought: that we could change everything about the world we're living in by just making a few decisions.

I think that the present Pope [Benedict xvi]—he was a professor at this time, you see, I was a student—and I think it had exactly the opposite effect on him: that he was terrified and horrified by the fragility of everything and the possibilities that students could actually destroy a whole structure. And I *felt* there was nothing in the way we live or the way we conduct ourselves that wasn't open to negotiation and we're going to change everything and that we can do it overnight. So, that was an amazing thing.

About "..." [sexual relationships] I've always felt that I would not be able to spend the rest of my life with another human being. I don't, I wouldn't, want to actually restrict myself to that. Now, obviously, I'm very attracted to people, and you can fall in love with people, but I wouldn't want, and couldn't imagine, another human being that I'd want to wake up every morning and be with. And in bed, I prefer to have my bed to myself.

GB: There are people who would say that this is tinged with selfishness.
MPH: I would say not just tinged. I'd say it's *entirely* selfish!

GB: [Laughs.] Now, you wrote a book called *Walkabout,* and you went walking about, in order to find the Holy Spirit.
MPH: Well, I'll put it another way. I didn't write that book: that's my view. I was the secretary for that book. I was certain that if I gave myself to this task of finding out where the Holy Spirit is working in the world, that I would be led to those places by the Holy Spirit.

GB: Yes, but what did you find then about the Holy Spirit?
MPH: Well, I mean, everybody in my own community would tell me that I was as mad as a hatter and that I found whatever I wanted to find.

GB: Quite!
MPH: As one monk said to me, "The trouble with you is, every time you have a cup of tea, you think the Holy Spirit has poured it out for you."

GB: [Laughs.]
MPH: But all the time in my life, I'm following these hints or suggestions that come in tangent to your ordinary life. You see, God has to find a way to communicate with us which doesn't damage our freedom. That's the game, as it were. So, we have to be able to connect. These are the kind of opportunities that God is providing us with, if we are listening. And that's what I feel is the hope for the universe: that there are enough people listening. If we are actually interested in what God wants for the planet, well, then, we have to, with very bad radio equipment, allow ourselves to get in contact with headquarters. That's basically what I find contemplation means.

GB: How does the God that you first encountered all those years ago compare with the God which is taught to us in our theology and by the Christian churches in general, not just the Roman Catholic Church?

MPH: Well, I'll take one example. I was told when I was a child that I shouldn't bother having any friends who were Protestants, because I'd never see them again once I died: that they were going to Hell and we were all going to Heaven, so, it was a waste of energy. You see, why would you waste your friendship on somebody who wasn't going to survive? So, I mean, the most appalling things, the most terrible libels and detractions against God have been perpetrated. We were told that somebody who died by suicide couldn't be buried. I mean, it was just anti-Christian, dreadful stuff.

So, I don't really hold much hope for most people, especially in Ireland, who were taught, when they were young, the most dreadful untruths. And God came out of it very badly, you know. I mean, God has tried for two thousand years in Christianity, and before that for four thousand years, in every way that was possible, to explain to us that God is love. That was the message all the time. Well, we have turned that around to the opposite of that.

GB: I don't know how you feel about this, but we in our generation may have been taught our theology and our religion very, very badly, but at least we were given a grounding of what our theology was, however badly it was explained. It seems to me nowadays that they're not taught anything at all.

MPH: Well, it depends. I think mothers and families teach children and I think that the education at primary level is really good. I really think that there has been a change which is very positive.

So, I don't accept for one minute that our generation were given a theology. I think they were given a package, which was dangerous for many of them, because they thought then that they had all the equipment necessary to persecute the rest of us. And they will tell you—and they'll tell me—that you're not explaining properly to people what "transubstantiation" means. You're not saying Mass in the right way, because you're not using this and the other. You know, there's a whole way in which it becomes a power chase and "I know what should be done and I know the rules and I know all the protocols." So, I have no time whatever for the Catechisms. That's not religion. That's a safeguard.

The actual experience is in Worship or Liturgy or how we connect with God, which, basically speaking, for us, in terms of our tradition, is to do with the Eucharist. And that's something which I do regret that people don't actually understand: the mystery of how God communicated to us the energy, the divine energy, through this extraordinary medium which is the Eucharist. So, I mean, that's my take on it, because I happen to be a Christian, but there are other ways of connection with God, obviously, too.

GB: Well, now that you are an ordained priest of the Holy Roman Catholic Church, what aspects of the doctrine are you troubled by?

MPH: Well, I became a priest and an Abbot three years ago. I couldn't be Abbot of Glenstal without being a priest. So I felt, therefore, that this had been the work of the Holy Spirit, and so I was prepared to do whatever was required. And the book I'm writing at the moment is called *Dancing with Dinosaurs*. And that, I presume, is because I became part of the dinosaur which is the Church.

You see, every multinational, to survive more than ten years, has to become a dinosaur. And that's true of the Church as well. It took on all the trappings of the Roman Empire. And everything about it became Roman Empire. But in order to reach the point where we're at now after two thousand years, that was necessary.

And the trick is to *dance* with the dinosaur—not to allow it to be an all-consuming force. So, I don't take any of the Roman Catholic dinosaur's beliefs, as it were, unless they have been written down and pronounced as being dogmas. And if you read into it, there's very few of them. And when you actually examine each one of them, they're very nuanced.

So, I don't allow myself to be taken in at all by the thoughts and the writings of very human people. We have to be extremely discerning about what we accept as being the truths that have been revealed to us by God and the ones that have been made up, put up into a lovely package for us by human people, all through human people.

GB: Now that you are a priest, what is the difference in the Mass, for you, now, as compared with when you were just a brother?

MPH: I do find it a great change, as it were, to be the celebrant, to be the person who voices the actual words. But that's all. You're just a channel for that, yeah.

GB: Do you think you're constrained in any way by becoming a priest?

MPH: Yes, definitely. Now that I am a priest, I recognise that I am part of an institution.

GB: And are you a believer in the Real Presence, that you change this host into the body and blood of Jesus Christ?
MPH: Yes, definitely.

GB: Whole and entire?
MPH: Yeah.

GB: Then, why were you talking about the bad teaching of transubstantiation?
MPH: I'm saying we don't need that word. We have the reality. So, if you translate that into one word which is called "transubstantiation," that is a word that nobody on this planet understands at this moment. It becomes a shibboleth. And not only that, but it becomes a barrier between us and the various other denominations who have fought this out. And if that word is an anathema to certain people, take it away. Jesus Christ never used the word "transubstantiation," ever.

GB: In *Symbolism* and then the book—what was it called?—*Kissing the Dark,* you make the point that one of the great tricks which is being perpetrated on people is that, in order to understand the relationship between God and humankind, there is imposed this band of middle-men called priests, who have gone to the trouble of studying meta-physics and all of that and can interpret all of that very difficult stuff to understand for ordinary people, and that that was somehow one of the great con tricks perpetrated on people.
MPH: Absolutely, yes. The Holy Spirit never depended on the priest-hood or the hierarchy. The Holy Spirit can inspire any person at any time, and we have direct connection with God from our earliest childhood, without any mediation, without any necessity for a third person, and that's our privilege. So, the priesthood, the hierarchy, are there to help that connection, but the idea that they are *necessary,* or that you *have to* go through them, or that there's a third person between my connection with God, is an evil that should never have been perpetrated.

GB: You're promoting your own redundancy now, Father!
MPH: Well, absolutely. But I mean, the Church is redundant always. I mean, the Church is the dinosaur that exists on this world. It disappears completely when we go to Heaven. "Nothing lasts, except one thing," as St Paul says. And he says, "Faith, Hope, and Love, and the greatest of

these is Love." So, we will be judged, if we are to be judged, on only *one* thing: how have we *loved*?

And that's something which I think many of the hierarchy and many of those who are in the priesthood will find a much more testing examination than mothers of six children, teachers, nurses, people who have had a direct connection with people in difficulty. And I would imagine that we're in for a big shock when we eventually discover what God is really like, when we get to the other side.

GB: And when the monks in Glenstal gather together and sing plainchant and pray, do you think there is special power or an influence in that prayer, as a community?

MPH: Well, I mean, prayer is when the three persons of the Trinity are talking to one another in your heart. That's what prayer is. And this is very important for the whole world, as it were: that there are a group of people who are living at a different register. God is showing us how to connect with God and that that's done by certain rituals and by silence. You see, silence is really the idiom where we connect with God. And we're so afraid of it and we're so unused to it. Especially, I think, nowadays where everybody has got noise going all the time. So, it's a reservoir of connection, which is important for our society generally, I would think.

GB: Okay. Let me ask you this: why did Jesus come?

MPH: Well, I suppose, Jesus came for, I'd have thought, two reasons. I mean obviously—this is me being all-knowing about it!—the first thing was to show us, and himself, what a beautiful thing to be human. And secondly, to show what God is like. Jesus Christ came on earth as the revelation of what God is actually like. And that's the only thing that we should take our theology from, we *have* taken our theology from.

And that means that, therefore, if you want to find out what Christianity means today, you have to meet people who have used that as their inspiration for life. It's all to do with the way people live their lives. And if you believe in this, and if you live your life by direct inspiration of the Holy Spirit, well, then, you're a different kind of person and you have a different way of being on the planet.

And that's what Nietzsche, who was the great adversary of Christianity, said. He said, "If you want me to believe in your Redeemer, you'd want to look that little bit more redeemed yourselves." And that's the truth.

GB: Do you believe in the Resurrection?
MPH: Yes, yes.

GB: The bodily Resurrection?
MPH: Yes, yes, yes. And in fact, I believe in it *now*. I believe that what I am asked, and what every Christian is asked, is to *live* the Resurrection. That's what I think is the energy that we get from the Eucharist: it's Resurrection. That's what it boils down to. It's divine energy.

GB: And do you believe in what we call Heaven, an after-life of joy and bliss?
MPH: Yes, whatever that means, "joy and bliss."

GB: And connection with God?
MPH: Yes, that's exactly it. I mean, "joy and bliss," I don't know what that is or could be, but I know that being with God for all eternity is what I experience, *even from now.*

GB: And do you believe there is a Hell, and if so, what would it be?
MPH: I don't believe, for one minute, that Hell will be as it has been depicted by all these people who seem to have the architectural plans for it. But I do believe that it is possible for us to refuse to love and that that means that you could be for ever a prisoner to your own sweating self. And I'm sure that's true.

GB: Did you ever pine about any other faith or religion or mode of life?
MPH: Well, I never pined about any religion, because they're all pretty human. So, I don't find that any of them are more attractive than the other. I just feel that the religion I belong to has got, if you examine it very carefully and are very discerning, all that you need in order to have a very fulfilling relationship with God during this life, and then Resurrection for the rest of your eternity.

GB: The programme is called "The Meaning of Life".
MPH: Yes.

GB: Have you summarised the meaning of life for us?—You have?
MPH: Well, I would think that there are six-and-a-half billion people on the planet. There are six-and-a-half billion ways of connecting with God. But the meaning of life is making that connection. And if you do make it, there's a wonderful life out there.

SEÁN GALLAGHER

"The Two Best Presidents You'll Never Have . . ."

In the autumn of 2011, I found myself briefly, inadvertently, the favourite to succeed Mary McAleese as President of Ireland. I am still not sure how it happened. What I do know is that, while the current Mrs Byrne—who, incidentally, has a much stronger sense of civic responsibility than I—encouraged me to think carefully about the real possibility of responding to Ireland's call, I, myself, was generally horrified by the idea of spending the next seven years of my very enjoyable life on ceremonial duty.

I decided that the only reason why anyone should ever run for the highest office in the land was if they really, really wanted the role. I don't. And so, without ever really throwing my Donegal tweed cap into the ring, I put it back on the hat-stand in the hall and went back to the day job.

At which point, Seán Gallagher's fedora came sailing over the ropes and on to the canvas.

I had only come across him once before, in person, at a fund-raising event for Crumlin Children's Hospital. I came away mightily impressed. A fella I had previously clocked only vaguely as one of the "Dragons" in RTÉ's business den turned out to have hidden depths. He spoke that day about the eye condition which had rendered him nearly blind at birth and the operations—crude by today's standards—which had transformed his world by restoring, at least, partial sight. He then talked about how he had been determined, ever since, to turn this disadvantage into a strength. He now not only had sight, it seemed: he had vision.

I therefore listened all the more carefully when he declared that he had a vision for Ireland, as well as himself.

We won't go into what happened next. Suffice to say that when the *Meaning of Life* team contacted him, through a third party, in the autumn of 2012, a year after his electoral defeat, to ask if he would be willing to record an interview, the intermediary's first response was, I'm told, a guffaw. What on earth might lead us to think that Seán Gallagher would want to give his first broadcast interview since the election débâcle to RTÉ?

Except Seán Gallagher is subtle and smart enough to know that RTÉ is a hydra-headed animal. *The Meaning of Life* is quite separate and quite different from those programmes where his presidential aspirations came so dramatically unstuck. In fact, Seán himself responded to our invitation pretty quickly, and with no preconditions: he would do the interview.

Which is how the two best presidents Ireland will never have came to be sitting opposite one another in a suite at the Four Seasons, Ballsbridge.

∽

GB: Now, I have a pretty good idea where *I've* been since that fandango last year. But what have *you* been doing?

SG: Well, it's almost a year this week since the campaign ended and Trish and I had a period where we took some time off and got to know each other again, quietly. Initially, after the campaign ended, we took a week's retreat in the lovely Carmelite monastery in Sligo and we meditated and prayed and went for walks and slowed the whole thing down to the pace of nature and got back in touch with ourselves . . . and discussed everything that had happened and then planned for the future.

GB: So, what are you doing now?

SG: Well, I'm now back looking at business and working with a number of projects that are involved in the biotech and IT sectors . . . And the other news we've had . . . we're going to start a family.

GB: Oh.

SG: So, Trish is pregnant.

GB: And when is the big day?

SG: End of March 2013.

GB: Your life is certainly going to change.

SG: I think it will. And you know, I guess things come to you when you're ready for them. We have a wonderful relationship, and I'm truly blessed to have met a wonderful woman like Trish, and I think this is just going to be the cherry on the cake.

GB: Well done. Congratulations to you and Patricia for that.

In fact, said cherry—Robert James Gallagher—was born on the 29th March—Good Friday, 2013. Mother, baby and slightly bemused father are all reportedly doing well.

GB: Now, you and I were at a fund-raiser for the Children's Hospital in Crumlin and you spoke about your sight and the operation which was carried out on you at a very young age.

SG: Yeah, I was born with what's called congenital cataract, and many people are familiar with older people who get cataracts. It's a filament across your eye that stops you from seeing properly. Nowadays, it would be a simple operation to remove that, but when I was born that surgery just didn't exist. And so when I was three or four I had a different type of surgery which left the cataract in place but cut my pupil to allow me to see on the periphery of the lens. And so my sight was challenged, but I often say that I'm more grateful for the limited sight that I have now than most people are for their perfect sight. And I say it every single morning: I spend the first twenty minutes of my day in gratitude for the fact that I can see and hear and walk and talk.

GB: But you were pretty well blind, then, were you?

SG: Well, yeah, very, very poor sight. I mean, it's almost impossible to see through a thick cataract, so I don't see as well as most people, but it hasn't stopped me. And there's certain things I can't do—I mean, I'll never be a pilot. Where the real challenge for me was when I was in school, I could never see the blackboard, no matter how close I sat to it, and I could never read small print. And so when I read, I read one word at a time, slowly and awkwardly, and I think most teachers thought that I was the slower learner. And so that's where it had a real profound effect on me and on my confidence and self-esteem. That's why I spend so much time working with young people now, because you feel different.

GB: Go back to the school for a moment. Did you make a special effort to read things or did you compensate in some way? Somebody said to me that you have a great memory.

SG: Absolutely. So, if you can't see what's been written on the board or in a copybook, you begin to memorise what's there, and so I developed a great memory. When somebody was talking to me, I would understand it and file it away, so I could draw on it again, without having to read it. I learned by asking questions. I was good at history, I was good at geography. I wasn't good at science or algebra, because I couldn't see any of the symbols on the board. And so I had to give up. And I never told anyone that, ever.

GB: That was your secret.

SG: That was my secret, yeah. But I found other ways of doing things. And I often say that most people, when they're born, can do ten thousand things. I can do nine thousand. So, I'm going to have my life defined by the nine thousand things I *can* do and not the one thousand things I can't.

GB: Now, let's go back to your father and mother. How many of you were there, and what did he do for a living, and was there money?

SG: Well, my father grew up in Donegal, in a very small farm holding and, like many, he barely finished primary school, and he went off to Scotland to work with others in the mountains and on the railways. He never forgot that. He would often tell us at night time, occasionally with a few drinks in him, when he was feeling a bit melancholy, about the time he was hired out, at the hiring fair. Like, we would know about marts and animals being sent to the mart. Same happened back then.

My mother came from Tullamore, and they met because my father got a job eventually in the Department of Agriculture, based in Tullamore. They moved to Monaghan, where I was born. After a couple of years, we then moved to Cavan to a small village, Ballyhaise.

GB: So, overall it was a happy childhood?

SG: We had a relatively happy home. I think my parents grew to understand they were different. My father was more the old school, didn't do a lot of praising. My mother was more caring and sensitive and, while we know that both of them loved us dearly, there wasn't a lot of sort of praise and recognition. In my early teens, I always filled the position of being the fixer, of trying to mend things, and that became a weight on my shoulders and became a pattern that, when I saw difficulty, I had some innate drive in me to go in and fix it and to make it all better.

GB: Was it a religious household?

SG: Well, my mother had a very strong faith and there were lots of pictures of the Sacred Heart. She had a strong devotion to St Anthony and there were novenas all over the place. Her greatest tribute to us was that, every time we travelled, she lit a candle every day for us. And I just thought that was wonderful and loving. I guess there was lots of religion around us, but we weren't very religious.

GB: Mass every Sunday?

SG: Mass . . . and I was a good altar boy. And then I went to St Pat's in Cavan, which was an old seminary, so I guess there was lots of religion in our community.

GB: Did you, in your young life, ever get the idea that you might go that way . . . ?

SG: I didn't see myself ever as being a diocesan priest. I had a calling at one stage, I felt, for a more contemplative life. And I had a great affinity to St Francis, partly because of my love of nature and animals. And I did go on many retreats to Franciscan monasteries, to test that out, and in the end I felt a draw to do other things.

GB: You liked the contemplative nature of that whole thing, did you?

SG: I did. You know, I'm not a great believer in the fact that priests shouldn't be married. I think they should be in the community and have that right, and I think that would bring the Church closer to the people. But for me, there's always been what I call a structure of tension: the monastery or the market-place. And I think it's easier, if you just focus on being a monk, where your responsibility is to be contemplative and to pray and to do good acts. And it's easy to be in the market-place, where you just focus on the simple thing of making money. The challenge is to live in the middle and hold on to both: to be able to earn a living and hold on to the values and find balance.

GB: And have you found that balance?

SG: I believe I have, Gay. In the mornings, I do my gratitude. I walk in nature. That's what brings me to the pace that I believe is my spirit. And I always have to go back to that. And even after the campaign, it is about going back inside to say, "Who am I and what am I really about?" Because, while I'm driven to do lots of things, I want to be authentic; I don't want to be led by the ego. I want to do what's right. And it's never about having and getting. It's usually about *being* and *becoming* the best that I can do.

GB: The epiphany which you experienced after seeing the Pope in Galway, in '79 . . . On the way home you all seemed to be suddenly propelled into enthusiasm . . .

SG: Evangelists!

GB: What happened there, and was that the beginning of Foróige?

SG: Yeah. It was the beginning of Foróige, and my whole involvement in youth work. About fifty of us had gone from my local area to visit the Pope, the time he was at the Ballybrit Racecourse—the Youth Mass of almost a million people. And we were so enthused, on the way home we said, "Gosh, we should meet more regularly." We set up a youth club and we joined Foróige. And I say now that I put down most of the success in my life to joining Foróige—the leaders who came in and spent time with us developing our confidence, our speaking ability.

But the most important was the first day of the training that I ever did with Foróige. Somebody brought a sheet out and gave it to every single young person and said, "Write all the things that you would like to do with your life." I thought that was profound. And so I wrote down, I wanted to be a farmer; I wanted to be a youth worker and work particularly with young people who had disabilities, just like I had; I wanted to be an entrepreneur; I wanted to be a politician; and I wanted to be in sport and martial arts. That's what I thought I was going to do.

GB: But then, at what stage did you go into Maynooth?

SG: I went to study youth work. I was working in the local agriculture co-op and I was working in the bar at night, and life was going swimmingly. And then I had a car crash one morning. Somebody hit me coming on the wrong side of the road. And so, I was knocked up for almost twelve months.

GB: What happened to you?

SG: Well, usual whiplash—but I pulled muscles in my back and discs . . . But I was so grateful to be alive, after I came through the whole thing, and I started to develop and get fit. Some youth project that was in Cavan at the time, a Youthreach project, was working with young people who had fallen through the educational system, who had left school early. And they asked me if I would come in and give some talks to the young people, because of my interest in Foróige and youth work.

And then I was talking to these young people and I was so down-hearted and despairing of what I saw as their lack of expectations for their life. And so I said, "I wish I could do more, but I need to train more to be able to be a real service." And so I went to Maynooth and I went on the first two-year course to become a professional youth and community worker.

GB: So, now you're a guy who has a reputation of being a fixer, a good organiser, a good leader of people and a guy who can get people to do things, which they wouldn't have imagined doing before. Is that fair?

SG: That's fair, yeah.

GB: Was there a scent at all, at any stage, of going for election to the Dáil?

SG: I had thought about it way back, way back in the early eighties and mid-eighties, but you know, I never saw that it was me. And I had spent time with young offenders in Finglas and I was very committed to that area. And I was on a platform one day, speaking about the need to create a proper youth service for young people and to fund it, and Dr Rory O'Hanlon was there and he was Minister for Health at the time. And he asked me to become his political secretary. And so I spent two years doing that. And at that stage, I thought, "Well, could I become a politician and effect real change?" But I looked at it from the inside and I didn't think the system worked well. And I think most politicians spend time trying to continue in power and to get re-elected and the system takes over.

GB: The system beats them.

SG: Ironically, only they can change the system, but this is the challenge. And so, I felt that I would be frustrated in the process. With politicians, as indeed with the Church, it shouldn't be about the institution. It needs to be about serving the needs of the flock, not about protecting the institution. And I think sometimes, we forget that. We need to go back into our core: what are we really here for?

GB: Okay. Let's move on to the business end of things, and you're now well up and going with the wiring company and with Smart Homes and all of that. And you were helped with grants from Enterprise Development Boards and all of that sort of thing. You *were* that Celtic tiger at that time . . . ?

SG: Well, when I take it back to 1995, when I left all the politics and decided to take control of my own destiny, I went back and did my MBA in college and I started a business with a very good friend, Derek Reilly, putting cables into houses, and in year 1, we really worked hard. I think we put cables into about fifty homes. By 2007, we were wiring 2,700 houses a year. We were employing seventy or eighty people and we were driving really hard.

Sometimes people think that business is all about making profit, and in the first couple of years, we took no salary. For us, it was never about making tons of money. It was about setting up a business and growing it.

My own period of nil employment in the eighties had such a profound effect on me that it almost broke me. And so, I was absolutely committed to making sure that I could support the creation of jobs, that I would have a job myself.

GB: Arising out of the car crash, you started to rehabilitate yourself physically with judo and karate . . .

SG: I started, because I'd heard that judo was very good, and so I took it up and I made a decision on the first day that I landed on the judo mat that I would get a black belt and become an instructor. And so, five years later I did. And then I moved to Dublin shortly after that and I took up karate. I'd always wanted to study karate, and the first time I stood in my bare feet on the karate floor, I said, "I'm going to become a black belt karate instructor." And five years later, I did. So, in a strange way, that accident led me to my judo career, my karate career, my fitness career.

GB: And then arising out of that study and the Eastern mysticism generally, you learned about Buddhism and Taoism and all of that. So, where are you now, Seán?

SG: I believe that most religions, at the core, are the same. I grew up in Cavan. My family were Catholics. I'm a Catholic. I'm a Christian. If I grew up in India I'd probably be Hindu or Buddhist. But when I studied all the religions, I noticed that they all came down to three things primarily. I call it soul. S-O-U-L. S for Self, O for Others, and U for the Universe. So, if you look even at the Ten Commandments, it comes: "Love your neighbour as yourself, and love God." So, it didn't say love your neighbour *more than* yourself. You love your neighbour *as* yourself. And if you do that, then you won't pick bad and abusive relationships; you won't do work that you don't enjoy; you won't get involved in alcohol and drug and other problems. But once you have learned to develop yourself, then it's about having your relationship with others and caring for others, being of service.

But even when you get those two elements, they're not enough, because you will die and you will get sick and those around you will die and you have to make sense of it. And so, it is about respecting and loving the universe in which we're in. The ground that gives us food; the environment, sustainability. But also, we know that there is something bigger, even if we don't know what that is.

GB: Is it fair to say, then, that you've left behind the Catholic Church?

SG: No, I haven't left it. I still go to Mass—not as regularly as I used to—because it is about me taking time to pray, to reflect, be part of the community. And whether my God wears a white beard or is a spirit or whatever, or is a source or an energy, whatever, it doesn't matter. Because I don't think any of us know.

And I've always found that religions who try and tell you what the answer is, automatically, you're off-side, because nobody knows. And whatever it is, is beyond us. It is most likely not within our human comprehension.

And I think you don't have to be a theologian, you don't have to have degrees in religion. Most of the spiritual people I know, some of them are farmers out in a field, who see a calf being born and wonder at the beauty of nature. But let's honour that there is a higher power. Let's respect each other. Sustain the world, and let's love ourselves as a starting point for it all, and respect ourselves.

GB: Well, then, who do you think Jesus was?

SG: It's a challenge, if somebody is born a Catholic, to think that Jesus *wasn't* the Son of God. I don't know. I believe he was a very wise man and a poet, a sage, a mystic. He could well be the Son of God. I've no idea. But I respect him and understand the values that he was teaching . . . So, Jesus talking about loving each other, about being compassionate to sinners, about being supportive to those who are in prison . . . that's the way, and I'm happy to follow the way. I'm way too small and insignificant and humble to ever think that I know who Jesus was, or who God is.

GB: The Buddhists reckon that when you die you come back as something else, and the Christians say that when you die you either go up or you go down. What is your belief about what happens to us when we, when we die?

SG: We have to be more than our body, because everything is there, but you die. Ten minutes later, what's missing? It's a spark, it's an energy. I think our soul leaves, our energy, our spirit, and that, if I understand energy right, you can't destroy it. It just changes form. And that spirit goes to a higher land and maybe higher spirits.

GB: And do you think there's a Day of Reckoning?

SG: I just don't know. And so I'm not taking any chances. So, I'm gonna live the best life I can and at the end, who knows?

GB: Arising out of that, when you address this other person, this higher power, when you're meditating, who are you addressing, and what image is in your head?

SG: Again, it's a combination. So, am I speaking to myself and my inner self or am I speaking to the universe? Am I speaking to a higher spirit? I think I'm doing all of that. I think, once I name it, I've put a box and a label on it. And so, I don't know. I put it out there to a force that's greater than mine. Because somebody is directing all this traffic down here and I don't know who it is.

GB: You think there is somebody directing the traffic?

SG: Absolutely. There's some higher power, yeah. I don't know what it's called. But I absolutely believe that. There has to be something that's co-ordinating it, because it's way too co-ordinated.

GB: You entered the presidential race and, without going into all the details of the unfortunate happenings, from this vantage point now, are you sorry you did that or do you write it off as part of life's experience?

SG: I don't regret it for a moment, because I don't consider it a failure.

GB: What possessed you to enter the race and leave the lovely secluded anonymity and peace of your existence, to take this on?

SG: I really wanted to do for enterprise and jobs what Mary McAleese had done for the peace process. So, people would have been electing somebody who had been unemployed, who had created jobs; who was passionate about enterprise and supporting more of them; who had a disability and wanted to say, "There's nothing wrong with having a disability. People with disabilities are not outside ourselves. They're part of who we are. Let's offer support and encouragement, and let's work together. One community at a time."

I think, to have had the desire to stand, to have wanted to make a difference and not to have had the courage to stand, that would have been the failure. I had a wonderful experience. I met some of the most amazing people.

GB: Most people would think that you were mauled. Well, it's a question: are you not astonished at how well you did, in spite of being mauled?

SG: Yeah. And I got to head the polls a few days out from the election. And so, I think it was a great success, albeit the last week didn't come the way we would have wanted it.

GB: Would you go again?

SG: Who knows? Six years is a long way off, and who knows where any of us are? My focus is now on Trish and starting a family, being a good father, being a good husband, being a good parent, and getting back in and earning, but still holding on to the balance of being of service to people in every way I can.

GB: Is that now your meaning of life?

SG: That's my meaning of life.

GB: And suppose you finally make it to the golden gate and it's all true and you meet God, face to face, what will you say to Him, Her or It?

SG: I will say, "I did my best. I hope I passed the test, whatever the test is." My core tells me that I won't be in a human form and I will be a spirit, and if two spirits can just nod that we now know what it's all about, I will just probably nod and it will be like going back to the source, back to the well from which I came.

GB: Peace.

SG: Peace.

There is one little footnote to that interview, which offers a little insight into the way public figures like Seán Gallagher are treated by the press, even after they have left public life. As you saw, he revealed to me that he and his darling wife, Trish, were expecting their first baby. Since this was not public knowledge at the time, my producer asked if it would suit them to keep it that way until the night of our programme—a little scoop for the series. Seán kindly agreed, and he and Trish studiously avoided telling even friends and family members their news. We also kept that detail out of the programme's press release.

Which made it all the more galling—not least for Seán and Trish—when, on the day before transmission, they started getting calls from friends and families, congratulating them on their good news, but asking why they had not told them in person, before announcing it in the national press. I can only guess that listings and preview writers, who are frequently sent a DVD in advance, had simply passed on their copies to their celebrity-watching colleagues, who, without so much as a phone call to the couple themselves, ran the story.

And that is yet one more reason why I know that both Seán Gallagher and I are better off out of the goldfish-bowl life that is the presidency.

PADDY MOLONEY

Grace Notes

I couldn't swear to it, but as Paddy Moloney sat down for our interview, I got the distinct impression that he was nervous. Fancy that! He has played on all the world's great stages and with all the world's great musicians; he has played for royalty and for presidents. But talking is different. And talking personally about the things, people and beliefs that give your life meaning is very different indeed.

My suspicion was confirmed when he told me, rather touchingly, how his wife, Rita, had reassured him, just before he set off for the interview: *"Don't be worried about this. It will be all right."*

Rita was right. It was all right.

The Chieftains are among Ireland's greatest cultural ambassadors and Paddy is the Chieftains' Chieftain. His vision, creativity and talent have kept them at the top for decades, always willing to experiment with new collaborations and genres, but remaining masters of their own.

We still use that very biblical word "talent" for artistic ability, as if it is, literally, currency, loaned to us for safe-keeping. We will be judged on how well we use it: will we bury our coin or invest it and return a profit to our "Master"? Paddy was undoubtedly given a very great talent—and he is perfectly comfortable applying that religious terminology to it—but through hard work and dedication, he has repaid that talent with interest.

He is quietly religious: not a theologian, not a Holy Joe, but certainly someone whose Catholic faith has always been an important handrail. His childhood, like many at the time, was steeped in family Rosaries and regular Mass and he can still recite elements of the Catechism he learned by rote. He talks about "the Lord" with a mixture of deference and love that borders on the quaint. Jesus is his "saviour" and he knows his redeemer liveth, as the old phrase has it.

Part of this very comforting theology is a firm belief in Heaven and the Communion of Saints—that supportive group of "those who have gone before us, marked with the sign of faith," who, Catholics believe, are cheering and steering us from on high. For Paddy, this club includes not only his parents and his big sister, but a brother he never knew, John, who was killed in a road accident before Paddy was born, casting a long shadow across the family home.

To a person with Paddy's sort of humble, but confident, Christian faith, death is more a gateway than a final curtain. Occasionally, we may even get glimpses of what lies on the other side. He recounted to me a ghostly experience he had in New York, when he played a lament at Ground Zero, after 9/11. I won't spoil the story by telling it for him, but clearly, the experience had shaken and moved him and was as real as day.

∽

GB: 1938. Douglas Hyde became the first President of our country. We were still one year away from the outbreak of World War II and Paddy Moloney was born in Donnycarney in Dublin. What are your earliest childhood memories?

PM: Gosh. It was a great childhood, but the early childhood memories would be the old steam radio, just listening to that, and people getting up and dancing to the various céilí bands.

GB: Were there musical evenings in your house?

PM: There was musical evenings in Donnycarney. Leo Rowsome, who taught me the pipes, he lived up in Belton Park. Dan Dowd, he was on Malahide Road, and Peadar Flynn, piper, they'd come to our house. But we'd have ramblers: relations, non-relations and people would come to the house, mostly at the weekends, and my mother did play the accordion and my grandfather played the flute.

GB: Now, when did you become aware that there was a boy who died, who was born before you?

PM: Probably when I was about four or five years of age. They used to talk, and there was a photograph of his First Communion. That was my brother, John. And it was a terrible tragedy. It was the first motorbike with a sidecar that came to Ireland. It was the army who had them. It was just the one and only, and it would be coming down Malahide Road and he was walking up to the shops. He was only eight. And they went out of control and ran up on the path. He lived for a few days, but it almost killed my poor mother.

GB: How do you mean?

PM: Well, the story was that she turned grey after the tragedy.

GB: And was he a constant presence in your house then?

PM: Always remembered in the Rosary. The Rosary was said every evening and he was always talked about—a delightful little fella he was. And that photograph is still there, you know.

GB: Yes, was it a religious household?
PB: It was religious. You know, it wasn't over the top. Never miss a Mass on a Sunday or a holy day. And on Christmas morning, you went to two Masses . . . They were great memories that are still with me.

GB: How many of you were there?
PM: There was four of us: three sisters and myself.

GB: And you're telling me you weren't spoiled with a mammy and daddy and three sisters and just you . . . ?
PM: [Laughs.] Destroyed! I mean, my sister, Esther, God love her, she used to give out to my mother: "That fella, he won't do anything. He won't even pick up his clothes." I was totally spoiled.

GB: Now, what's your earliest memory of you playing music? The tin whistle, was that it . . . ?
PM: My mother went into Bolger's, on a Christmas Eve, and she bought this tin whistle for one shilling and ninepence . . . and I remember bringing it home and teaching myself how to play. Then, I went on to the uilleann pipes, and it was Leo Rowsome . . .

GB: And then what about in school? Did you play with your mates in the Christian Brothers?
PM: Yes, down in Marino. There was a Brother McCaffrey there, who was absolutely brilliant, Séamus McCaffrey, and he saw this talent in me and he had me doing all sorts of funny things . . .

GB: He encouraged you?
PM: He encouraged me. But also, this Christian Brother, McCaffrey, taught me singing, every day. It was one *whole* hour, and he'd write up the notes, you know, *do, re, mi, fa, so, la, ti*—tonic sol-fa—and I became very learned in tonic sol-fa. Even to this day, I still have sick bags from aeroplanes where I write out tunes—*do, re, mi, fa, so, la, ti, do.* I got that gift from him.

GB: Going back to the talent, do you reckon it's a gift that you got, or is it hard work, or what?
PM: To me it was a gift and still is. It's a God-given gift.

GB: A God-given gift.

PM: Yeah. I mean, where else would you get it? These visions of music . . . When I try to write a tune, or if I hear it, I see it first and it's sort of like a vision that comes to me.

GB: As long as you have the technique, you don't have to think about it?

PM: Precisely, yeah, exactly. It just flows out of you. I don't know where, how . . .

GB: You get the thought, and the fingers do it . . . ?

PM: That's exactly right. And the heart is there . . .

GB: Do you give thanks for this talent?

PM: I do give *great* thanks for it.

GB: Go back to your mum . . . For a while now, she was very keen on you being musical, of course, and earning your living off music, but first of all a nine-to-five job . . . So where did you go to work?

PM: Yeah. Well, I never did my Leaving, to be honest. And I got a job in Baxendale's of Capel Street, the number 2 builders' providers in the country at the time. And I went in there as an office boy and I earned 36 shillings a week. 30 shillings I gave to my mother [laughs] and the other six bob was for myself.

GB: And was it in Baxendale's you met Rita?

PM: Ah, the plague of my life! [Laughs.] No, the love of my life! I was in charge of this pool of typists and girls in the office, thirty or forty of them. I sort of worked myself up to that. But one day, in 1958 I think it was, in came this whippersnapper, proud as punch, the long, beautiful hair flowing down and wearing these moccasins like the Indian, criss-crossed, and a green skirt, you know. And she was sixteen at the time.

GB: And you were—?

PM: I was twenty, twenty-one. But I knew, you know, something clicked: this is trouble . . . !

GB: Pretty much straight away.

PM: Straight away. *Bang. Bang.*

GB: So, how long did ye court, as they say?

PM: For about four years . . . And I went in to my boss on a Saturday morning and I said, "Can I get off at twelve o'clock? I'm taking somebody out to lunch. I'm getting engaged." He took off his glasses—"What?

Getting engaged? Who is it?" He never copped on. I said, "It's Rita!" So, I took her out to Portmarnock, the Portmarnock Hotel out there, and we had a great lunch and a swim afterwards. Always remember that.

GB: Wonderful . . . Now, the Chieftains . . . Why did you call them the Chieftains, by the way?

PM: Well, yes, it was a band that I was, at one stage, to call the Quare Fellows . . .

GB: No!

PM: [Laughs] . . . because Brendan Behan, I knew Brendan very well. But Gareth Brown from Claddagh Records gave us the opportunity to make an album. And John Montague, the poet, he was part of Claddagh's company at the time, and John said, "Why don't you call it the Chieftains, after my book *Death of a Chieftain?*" And strangely enough, after thirty-five years, I got John to record himself reading his own poetry. It happened two years ago. He's eighty-three years of age now. And I put music to it and I just finished it yesterday, would you believe. Tin whistle and pipes. So, that's Chieftains and how that came about.

GB: Before I forget it, were you a member of the Legion of Mary?

PM: Believe it or not, I was. My sister was a member and I went along with her at one time, went to one of the presidiums. And I used to enjoy it, sitting there talking, praying and things. And another thing about that too, you were meant to go out and visit, but what you could do was bring some of the Catholic papers with you. And I built up a huge, you know, people-love . . . I just got this thing, going off talking and telling stories with them. And at first, it was just at the front door. Eventually I was invited in, and I used to love that.

GB: Come back to the Chieftains again. I know the personnel changes from time to time. Nonetheless, as a group, they continue to function as a coherent whole. How is that done? For example, it doesn't seem to me that drink and drugs ever became part of your lifestyle . . .

PM: No. That's right, it wasn't . . . We do have a golden rule: no drink before a concert. [Laughs.]

GB: Never.

PM: I could never go on and deliver a concert if I was indulging in alcohol. It would be nice to have a glass of wine afterwards or something like that.

GB: But a group of people, living in close proximity over so many years, all with their own little idiosyncrasies and little bad habits. How do you cope with that?

PM: It's horrific! We all have to have window seats in the aeroplane when we fly. Everybody has a window seat. They're not sitting together . . . And we even have different floors in hotels, in case somebody wanted to practise. You wouldn't be getting on their nerves. Because sometimes they'd bunch you all together.

GB: And do you eat together?

PM: Sometimes. Now Derek Bell, or the late Ding Dong Bell, as I call him, and I . . . we used to go together, and Matt and Seán. But we try to avoid that. As a matter of fact, people couldn't believe it: we'd come down in the morning for breakfast and you'd have Seán over here, Matt in that corner, Kevin here and I'm here. [Laughter.] We wouldn't have breakfast together. And that's a little rule. It's just space, and it works.

GB: And apart from alcohol, the other thing doesn't enter into it?

PM: Never did, no. The music is our drug. You get on stage, and after all the harshness of getting there and the terrible time with travel and security, get on to that stage and you start to play for an audience . . . that's when the magic happens.

GB: The 27th of January this year, in New York, Paddy Moloney Day . . .

PM: Oh, yeah.

GB: That's not bad, is it, that recognition . . . ?

PM: Yeah. The National Arts Club. It's a very prestigious place, you know, Whoopi Goldberg and De Niro—everyone has been honoured. But for me to get this big lump of a gold medal was incredible, and the key to the City of New York . . . and something from the White House and something from the Capitol Building. And the Mayor of Harlem came and spoke and Mayor Dinkin spoke and it was a great night. And all organised by my darling little daughter, Aedín, who is an actress.

GB: Well done . . . Were you strict Catholic parents?

PM: Not over the top. Definitely, we went to Mass every Sunday and we used always love to go to Clarendon Street to listen to the choir there at eleven o'clock Mass. Still do, to this day. My parish now is Glendalough, because I have the house down in Annamoe. There's a priest down there who is great, Father Crotty. But we're just the old, traditional Catholic people. We don't go overboard about it.

I wrote a Mass, one time, by the way. It was performed in Glendalough ten years ago, the first Mass in Glendalough, on the ruins, since 1849, a Eurovision Mass for Choir and Chieftains.

GB: Who is Jesus Christ to you?

PM: Jesus Christ? Well, growing up, of course, you had your Catechism and you were told the stories, and the nuns told you the story of Christmas, the story of Easter . . .

GB: And you believed him to be what?

PM: I believed him to be the Saviour, and to this day it's somebody I'm going to meet up with one of these days and account for everything that happened. [Laughs.] I hope he'll be kind . . . You go to the Lord when something goes wrong or . . . when your father died and when your mother died. And you know he's around here. You would love to put your hand out and shake hands, you know.

GB: And why do you think he was crucified?

PM: Yeah. If he was God, why *did* he go through that? I think he wanted to come down to our size and say, "This can happen to you; it *will* happen to you." And it *has* happened: you think of the Famine and you think, to this day, the famine that's going on in the world . . .

GB: Do you pray?

PM: Now and again, yeah, and in times of trouble.

GB: And what do you pray to, Paddy?

PM: I can see the Lord, you know.

GB: And how do you see the Lord?

PM: I see the Lord through young people, friends, the love of people. I just love people. This is what I think religion is all about, and being kind to people . . . And that to me is what life is all about, you know.

GB: Clearly, money was never your goal?

PM: I was always looking out, and even to this day I'm always that bit worried, with the ways things are at the moment; I'm going to have to work twice as hard to keep things going. [Laughs.]

GB: The insecurity of the self-employed man . . .

PM: Exactly. Exactly. You know, to give up the job in Baxendale's, in

1968, a pensionable job, after being put on the management staff—you know, big noise, your own key to the private jacks. [Laughs.]

GB: Do you have doubts about God at all?
PM: Sometimes. I often did, and then I said to myself, "Snap out of it, for Heaven's sake." I'm convinced now that I still have God up there.

GB: You've travelled the four corners of the globe. Is there anywhere that you would rather be, over anywhere else? I think you're going to say Annamoe . . .
PM: I love Annamoe. I mean, that's my little place, and the tranquillity there . . . Just to go upstairs and look out over the valley . . . and listening to the birds. There's blackbirds and larks and everything and I do repeat what they sing. I'd actually whistle back and I'd copy what they'd do, driving them mad, the poor things. [Laughs.]

GB: And do you fear death? You think about it?
PM: Oh, I do . . . You know I'm at that stage. I definitely do.

GB: Do you fear it?
PM: I don't fear it too much. I just would be very disappointed. That man above there, you know, he's after giving me this gift and I want to pass it on a little more than what I've done. I'm still doing it, but I still have a lot to do.

GB: Tell me about that 9/11 moment that you had.
PM: Yeah. Conor O'Clery was the man. He witnessed the whole thing from his penthouse, only five blocks away.

GB: He did.
PM: It must have been terrifying for the man. But he rang me up and he said, "Would you like to come down?"

GB: To Ground Zero?
PM: Ground Zero. Just felt that I would like to maybe perform a little tune, which I did. It was about two weeks after and, you know, it was all the girders and that frame of the building was still there. And the fumes! The smell was terrible. And they said, "Just do two minutes."

So, I walked out and I started to play a little lament. And as I played, I closed my eyes and this vision came that sort of I couldn't believe it. I was thinking of Carnegie Hall down the road, but over to the left there was four shadows in a box, you know, at a concert. Just shadows, no faces. Further down in the auditorium, there was this red-haired person, very Irish-looking, sort of whitish face and smiling. And I can see his white teeth. And so that remained with me, that vision, to this minute.

GB: These were ghostly visions while you played?
PM: Ghostly visions while I played. And after I played, people were crying around me and even some of the staff or the rescue team came over and said, "Oh, my God, that was amazing." They were moved by what I'd done. Sort of electrifying, it was. The old shivers went up the back.

GB: So, do you believe then that you will see your parents again and your dead brother and Derek and all of those people, you'll meet them again?
PM: I do, yeah, yeah. Ronnie Drew, the whole gang. [Laughs.] I do believe that will happen and even to this day, my sister, dear sister, who passed away very early in life, she was always kind of minding me, you know, and I often have little visions of her: dreams about her long, curly hair—beautiful.

GB: And do you believe that they are up there at certain critical times in your life, to give you a little help and a little guiding hand?
PM: I do indeed, yeah.

GB: I presume you think you'll make Heaven?
PM: I'm hoping! You know what I mean . . . ?

GB: Well, let's go the other way. Do you believe in Hell?
PM: I don't believe in Hell. I don't believe in this fiery business. I think it'll be just so depressing that you didn't make it, you know. But I have a funny feeling, the Lord being so forgiving . . .

GB: And when you come to the pearly gates will you be judged in some way? Is there a ledger . . . ?
PM: [Laughs.] There will be an account, yes. I definitely won't be a shoo-in anyway. [Laughs.] But I'd say it'll be a situation where . . . "Ah, he wasn't a bad lad . . . I think we'll let him in."

GB: You'll scrape in?
PM: I'll scrape in, yeah.

GB: And suppose it's all true, Paddy, and you get up there and He's waiting for you, what will you say to Him?

PM: "Well, there you are. It's yourself." [Laughs.] That's what I say to everybody who comes on the telephone, so I think that would be my greeting to Him, in a pure, good Irish way. I think He's going to be smiling, you know . . .

MAEVE BINCHY

Light a Penny Candle

D ear, wonderful Maeve. Is there anyone who didn't love her? Anyone sane, that is.

Her brilliance as a writer was that she not only had an ear for people, but a heart for them. She could reproduce characters and conversations we all recognised, mainly because, like her, we've all overheard them on the bus or at our own kitchen tables. She told me life became much more boring when the telecommunications industry in this country was sorted out and you no longer got crossed lines. They had been a gold-mine for the aural magpie, Maeve.

What was always intriguing about her was to discover such radicalism cloaked in such cuddly conventionality. Because she talked the talk and looked the look of the Dalkey middle-class Irish Catholic, she could get away with a whole host of wild *isms*—feminism, careerism, atheism, etc.—which, from a more threatening figure, would, in their day, have provoked turbulence or terror in some quarters. Instead they provoked, at least, affection and, at times, admiration.

Nowhere was this clearer than at her funeral, when a packed church heard the clergy doing battle with her atheist feminist friends to claim her as their own, notwithstanding the fact that, on *The Meaning of Life*, she had explained, unequivocally, exactly how, when and why she became a non-believer. Never mind that she had given generously to the local parish church. Maeve gave generously to all sorts of people. And anyway, she had the discernment to see that a parish church performs a valuable service to the community, whether you believe in its deity or not.

She told me that the first time she discussed her atheism on air she was inundated with letters, trying to reclaim her immortal soul from the eternal fire. But it was kindly meant, so she replied courteously to them all. They wanted her in their club, because they all wanted to be in hers. That's quite an art. In fact, it's probably more than an art: it is a talent or a grace and Maeve certainly had both.

The same grace and talent was in evidence, as you will see, when she told her father about her loss of faith. He asked her not to upset her mother by revealing something that would have distressed her enormously. And Maeve kindly and considerately obliged until, after her mother's death, her father gave her permission to drop the charade. It is hard to disrespect any form of belief or unbelief when it comes hand-in-hand with such kindness and consideration.

Our interview was recorded on a snowy day, in Polly Villa, the punningly named home she shared with her beloved husband, Gordon Snell. He's a very accomplished writer himself, but, as was brilliantly captured in Maeve's portrait in the National Gallery, he was content to be banished regularly from his own living-room while people like me descended on the house to drink in his wife's reflections on life, the universe and everything. Perhaps, knowing that Maeve had stalked him across the Irish Sea was solace enough for a thousand such petty humiliations, although I think we also bought him lunch at the pub next door.

Gordon is an important, if barely acknowledged, element in Maeve's story. "Thy firmness makes my circle just," John Donne famously wrote in his metaphorical description of marriage as a pair of compasses. Unless the centre holds still, the drawn circle cannot be wide-ranging and true.

Yes, wide-ranging. It's an irony that Maeve, who started her adult career as an almost recklessly adventurous traveller—hitch-hiking on ships to the Middle East in her schoolteacher holidays—should have ended up so confined by ill-health to her Dalkey home. And yet, as she so often proved, it is imagination, not travel, which really sets us free. "I could be bounded in a nutshell and count myself the king of infinite space," as Hamlet says. Or bounded in Polly Villa and be the Queen of People's Hearts, as Maeve might secretly have hoped.

God rest her, whether she believed in him or not.

∼

GB: Maeve, start at the beginnings: what sort of childhood did you have? Describe it to me.

MB: Well, I was very lucky and I had a very happy childhood, and very often when you see so many stories written by Irish people about miserable childhoods, you almost feel, to have had a happy childhood was a poor start. But it was wonderful. I was the eldest of four children and my mother and father thought all their geese were swans and they thought we were wonderful. It could have made us absolutely unbearable, but I don't think it did. I think it made us feel very secure.

GB: Was it a Catholic house?

MB: Oh, indeed, it was a Catholic house. You'd as soon go out without your clothes as to miss Mass. We all went to Mass every Sunday and we went to Confession every week when I was a child; and we said the Rosary at night and we always said three Hail Marys for the conversion of Russia—which I'm glad to see worked. And we had statues around the house and we knelt down, listening to the Pope on Christmas Day, when the Pope's message *Urbi et Orbi* came on. So, it was a normal Catholic household of the forties and fifties, but it was a simpler and a more straightforward time. And nobody questioned any of it.

GB: Nobody questioned any of it?

MB: We just thought we were lucky that we had found the one true faith.

GB: And do you remember any feeling of that being restricting to your life at the time?

MB: I didn't think it restricted me at all, no, because, first of all I regarded God as a pleasant Irishman—you know, what else?—and I regarded St Patrick as somebody very high up, a senior member of the Cabinet up in Heaven. So, what was restrictive about that? It was lovely. I didn't do much sin when I was young, really, I think, and so it wasn't a question, when I was fifteen, sixteen or anything like that, of saying, "Oh, if only I wasn't a Catholic, I could do anything I like. I could have affairs; I could do this and that." Such things were absolutely so far from your life, like going to Mars.

GB: I get no sense that you rebelled in any way against your parents.

MB: No, I was never a rebellious person, because they were too nice. They had given up too much for us. Everything they had was put to our education and our good and they were so interested in us. It would have been terrible to throw it all back in their faces, so, no, it never crossed my mind to rebel.

GB: For a young woman at that time, it seems to me you did a fair bit of travelling, which was kind of unusual?

MB: Well, I was very anxious to see the whole world and I said once to my mother, "I'm really terrified I might die before I see the *whole* world." And I saw an awful lot of it and it was very good, because you went off to a different country and you saw people behaving in a completely different way. And of course it was good for you. The best Chinese proverb I ever heard is "If you love your child, send him or her on a journey." And that is so true, because when you come back from a journey, first of all you're so delighted to be home that you behave like an angel. And secondly, it has broadened your mind.

GB: So, where did you go?

MB: Well, I went to France first of all, to learn French. Then I went to Greece, and then I went to Israel, sleeping on the deck of a boat. I taught in a Jewish school in Dublin, in Zion School in Bloomfield Avenue, and the parents very kindly gave me a present of a ticket to Israel. And when I went to Israel, I worked in a kibbutz, plucking oranges and plucking chickens as well. It was a great and very strange time in my life, but it was also useful to me.

GB: Did Israel have any effect on you?

MB: It *did* have an effect on me. I suddenly felt everything slipping away, when I was in Jerusalem. It was sort of like a road to Damascus in reverse, really. But it was an unwelcome road to Damascus, because I suddenly stopped believing in things, rather than actually believing in them, and I prefer to be positive.

GB: Do you mean suddenly?

MB: It was *really* suddenly. It was one day and it was the Room of the Last Supper that I was in. And the Room of the Last Supper was an old cave, and I said to an Israeli soldier, "Is this the Room of the Last Supper?" and he said, "Yeah, it is . . . What did you expect? A Renaissance table set for thirteen?" And I thought, "That's exactly what I expected. I expected a Leonardo da Vinci painting, that's what I expected. This is ridiculous. I have had a false view of it." And I wasn't cross with anybody except myself for having had an over-simplistic view of it.

And then a great period of loss came into my life, because all my certainties were gone. So, far from it being a great relief, I'd lost all these friends. I'd lost a lovely Irish God and the important person in Heaven, St Patrick, who is interceding for us all, and I was really disappointed to see them go.

GB: This sense of loss—how long did that last with you? And also tell me what was the reaction of your parents, when you told them . . . if you told them?

MB: Well, I told my father. I said, "I think we've been misinformed about these things." [Laughs.] And he said, "Oh, but you must do exactly as you like, as you're over twenty-one." I was twenty-three. "On the other hand, your mother has very simple faith and it would disturb her and she'd be having notions of Hell and everything; and you're such a kind person, I don't think you'd want to do that." And he said, "You could just leave the house—you don't have to go to Mass—on a Sunday." And I thought, "Well, that's reasonable enough. I wouldn't hurt my mother about that, I certainly wouldn't."

And so, when she died, I remember my father saying to me, "Maeve, you don't have to do that any more. You did it when it mattered." Which was very good of him, because he knew to let people be independent enough and he also knew where a great hurt would be caused.

GB: What a lovely way for him to handle it!

MB: It was beautifully done, and I've always been very grateful for it. But the thought is there and I see people who are very devout—and many of my friends, you know, quite a considerable number of them— having, if not exactly the certainty, they do have a belief. And I remember a friend of mine, who was a nun, when she was dying, all the other sisters in the convent were just regarding it as her lovely happy release. They were thinking that she was going to go to a much better place, and they *really* meant it. And I thought, "How wonderful for them *really* to mean it like that! And who wouldn't envy that? What's not to like about that?"

GB: When you told me on *The Late Late Show* that you no longer believed, what reaction did you get from people?

MB: I got hundreds and hundreds—and that's not an exaggeration— hundreds of letters. Now, they contained everything: some of them were sort of fundamentalist statements about the Lord not being mocked; and some of them were novenas; and some of them were Mass bouquets; and some of them were slight accusations—you know, "Your parents did so well to bring you up, what a terrible way to repay them, by saying that you don't believe!" And I wrote back to everybody.

GB: Everybody?

MB: Well, everybody who wrote to me. I got a little card made and I put "Thank you very much for your kind words," even if the words were sometimes *not* too kind. "I will indeed think about what you say." Now, that *was* true. I *did* think about what they said. I didn't promise to change and to be a sinner returned, repentant, to the fold. But at least it was truthful.

GB: You said you missed it and you felt like you lost an old friend. Did you find anything to fill this hole in your existence?

MB: Well, the first thing I could tell you that I found was I found no resentment of the Church. Which was good. I never became anti-Catholic or anti-clerical. I would think that the Church was a lovely consolation for people who believed. If it keeps people on the straight and narrow, that's good.

What did I find instead of it? I've always been very strong about family and friends and I think, in a way, I valued friendship even more, because I thought, maybe, these are the only friends I'm going to have. I didn't think there was going to be a cast of thousands waiting for me at the pearly gates once I got in—because it never crossed my mind that I'd be going anywhere else. And the very interesting thing is, if you don't have a real, defined faith and if you don't believe in the Sermon on the Mount, say, and "Blessed are the poor and blessed are the meek . . ." If you don't believe that any more, then you've got to do something about it. If you see somebody who is terribly poor, there is no point in saying to yourself, "Well, that will be all right in the next world, because it'll all be evened out." And so it did make me more socially aware and more caring, I think, than when I thought that God was going to look after us and our friend, St Patrick.

GB: You never pray, obviously, do you?

MB: No, no. I wish and I hope for things, but I don't pray. And I'm not what Brendan Behan used to call "a daylight atheist." I don't remember God when the plane is doing somersaults in the air. I don't suddenly say, "Please, God, if you get me out of here, I'll be good. I'll go back to you and I'll take a crash course in it again and I'll catch up." I don't do that, because that would be silly and that would be acting under duress and fear.

GB: Is there loneliness about that?

MB: Well, my life is so full of good people and friends and family, I haven't really time to be lonely. I'm not a thoughtful, reflectful person. I have a busy, shallow mind, which gets itself involved with things the whole time and I don't spend time being lonely.

I had a friend who was a priest. I did say to him once, "Must be very tiresome for you meeting so many people who don't believe in what you do and why you're doing it." And he said, "Well, I think, often, if people just sat down and thought about it for a little bit, they might come round to thinking there's a lot of sense in it. But you won't do that, Maeve. [Laughs.] You never sit down and think about *anything*." Which is quite true. I would accept that.

GB: And what do you now believe Genesis and the Old Testament is, and indeed the New Testament—Matthew, Mark, Luke and John . . . ?

MB: Well, the Old Testament I hardly read, 'cause, you remember, we didn't really! Might be too dangerous for us. But the New Testament is a story about a very good man, who lived two thousand years ago and who preached love rather than fear and who talked about equality of all people and who said, "Do as you would be done by," which nobody could argue with. Once, we were at a school retreat where the missioner told us to underline the words of Jesus and see was there anything you disagreed with. And there isn't.

GB: And when he is described as the Son of God, what is your image of that?

MB: Well, I just think that's a metaphor really.

GB: For?

MB: For . . . he was giving you a message from God. I don't think that he was *really* the Son of God.

GB: Do you believe in God, Maeve?

MB: No, not as such, but I think that there may be some greater purpose to the world than just us all coming into it and making a mess of it and then going out of it again. I mean, it's very sad to see so many of my friends dying now. I can barely look at my wedding photograph, 'cause so many people have disappeared from it. There has to perhaps be something a bit more, but I'm not going to sort out what it is and I just hope to live as good a life as I can, without doing any harm to anybody, and try to do a bit of good here and there. And that will keep me happy until I go.

GB: And why should we bother being nice to each other?

MB: Well, I don't think it's just the fear of God or the hope of recognition from God, or the love of God even, that makes us nice to each other. I mean, there's an innate decency in people. I've met more, much more, good people than bad people and if you assume that people are going to be decent and nice, then you're half way there. It's to do with optimism: thinking that the glass is not just half-full, it's *nearly* full. I think the glass is always right up to the top.

GB: All the time?

MB: It is, because I've been very lucky. I started off so well with a nice, loving family. And then I got a lovely job teaching and I was very happy teaching for seven years. And then I got a lovely job in the *Irish Times.* And then I fancied Gordon Snell and I got transferred to the London office of the *Irish Times.* That all worked out very nicely.

GB: Are you suggesting that you *tracked* Gordon Snell to London?

MB: I'm *admitting* it, but I wouldn't admit it if it hadn't worked. If he had escaped, I wouldn't have told you about it at all.

GB: And there was no feeling of gratitude, no sense of "Thank God for this"?

MB: Well, there is a lady in Dalkey, who runs a shop, and she said to me after she met Gordon, "You know that your mother must be praying for you in Heaven, that she found Gordon for you?" And she said, "You don't believe me?" And I said, "Well, I, erm . . ." And she said, "You don't mean to tell me that you think you got a man like that all on your own, do you?"

GB: [Laughs.]

MB: So, maybe somebody was helping from somewhere . . .

GB: So, what the woman in Dalkey was saying: your parents and your friends, who loved you, who died, they have still some sort of benign influence, at certain stages of your life . . . You don't . . . ?

MB: When my father died, one of his colleagues said something that was very, very useful: "You don't think that a great spirit like that could be just quenched, because he isn't around any more?" And I thought, "What a wonderful thing!" It's a great consolation. And my sister died last year, my youngest sister, and I've been trying to hold on to that: just because she's dead doesn't mean she's forgotten. She's thought of every day of my life and I feel, while people are remembered, they're not really dead, they're not really gone.

The most lovely thing of all would be to believe that you're going to see them again, but since I don't have that bit, at least I have the bit of keeping the memory alive.

GB: You made a great leap of faith going off to London to track Gordon. What made you so certain that he was the one for you? Do you believe there is only one person for a person?

MB: No, I don't think so at all. I think that that's been a great mistake for women, who have believed the novels and the dramas and all the rest of it, that there is one person, because that makes women often put up with behaviour on the grounds that "He is the one, he is the man for me." I mean, love has to do with being out for the other person's good more than your own. I mean, I would really prefer Gordon to be happy than myself to be happy. And I wasn't that way before I met him.

GB: That's a huge statement, Maeve.

MB: But it's the truth, because he's been nothing but generous and kind all through his life. And he believes the best of people. His face lights up when he meets people, all people, all the friends and children . . . We didn't have children, which was a pity, because he'd have been a wonderful father. I might have been the mother from Hell.

GB: Controlling?

MB: Controlling! I'm always trying to improve people and to change them. And one of my first editors in the book business said that I always have some self-righteous character in my novels—me!—who is telling other people how to behave and then saying in a smug, self-satisfied way, "It had been the right thing to do." She said it was quite nauseating, and every time she used to cross out "It had been the right thing to do," over and over. I used to write it about fourteen times in every book, and I find myself saying it still, because I could run anybody else's life for them—my own not quite so easily, but everybody else's is just child's play.

GB: In your books you've written about love and betrayal and romance and loyalty and disloyalty and treachery and all of those terms. Do you despair of human nature in any way?

MB: I don't despair of human nature at all, because, for every bad thing that you see or every act of cruelty, there are also enormous numbers of unsung heroes and heroines. There is great kindness and goodness and you only have to look around you to see how much of it there is.

I was in hospital recently during the flu epidemic back in January and I was in the big ward, and those day and night nurses were absolute saints. They were so patient.

GB: So, if you believe in that goodness, do you believe in badness? Do you believe in evil?

MB: I have met very few bad people. I've met very selfish people, but I've met very few really bad people. If people get side-tracked by greed and selfishness, if they somehow ride rough-shod over people and forget to divide equally the spoils of the nation, then that is a bad thing. And I think we were, with our Celtic Tiger, a little bit forgetful of all those who *didn't* have. The expression that used to kill me, and still does, when they'd be talking about some handbag in Grafton Street—you know, it would cost hundreds or thousands of pounds. They used to call them in newspapers a "must-have" handbag. That is such a silly phrase. I get into a temper thinking of it. *Who* must have it? That's nonsense.

GB: Okay, well, let me follow that on and ask you about the Hitlers and the Stalins of the world, the appalling, dreadful butchers of humanity. Do you think they get away with it?

MB: I think they have. I don't think that there is an International Heavenly Court that's going to punish them. It could be much simpler if there was. It would be so easy to think that Hitler, Stalin—hell; most of the rest of us—up there. [Points up.]

GB: Do you believe, then, that you arrive here with a hand of cards, whatever the cards are, you play them for the best you can, in all respects, and that's it?

MB: This is exactly my philosophy: that you've got to play the hand that you're dealt. People waste an awful lot of time wishing they'd been dealt a different hand. And there is no such thing as the cavalry coming in to rescue you or a man on a white horse. That's not going to happen. And you're not going to be happier if you're thin or rich or married, because I know a lot of thin, rich, married people who are miserable as hell. So, that's not the solution.

GB: Would you believe with Dawkins and his company that we arrive here as a random collection of genes and molecules and atoms and that's it? We do what we have to do and then we go, end of story, the light goes out?

MB: Yes, I think I would believe that, yeah. I don't think about it too much, because Dawkins is so articulate in what he writes, and so vehement that there shouldn't be a kind of escape into a dream world, that we must be practical and face it, we are a random collection of genes. And I do think that's probably, more or less, what it is.

GB: Is there a message of any kind in your books?

MB: I suppose the message is that we are in control of our own lives or that we have to shape our own lives and that it's up to us whether we are going to be happy or not; and that we shouldn't be blaming other people for the things that go wrong with our lives. We know we're here for a few decades and we've got to make the most of it.

GB: Suppose it's all true, Maeve. What will you do then?

MB: If I met God?

GB: If the whole thing is true?

MB: Well, I suppose I'd say, "Sorry, I got it wrong." [Laughs.] So, I suppose, I'd have to say "Goodbye" then, because I'd be down below, if that's the way it was.

But I'm not being flippant . . . If it was all true, I'd say, "Why did you make it so hard for us? Why did you make it so hard for us to believe in you, by asking us to deny our biggest gift, which is our reason? Why didn't you, if you wanted to have a test for us to get into Heaven, why didn't you have a test for us on how *good* we were to other people and how much we looked after other people in this world? Then you'd have had a happier world."

And maybe if there was a God, God would explain it to me, but it would be a most amazing conversation.